# A Diplomatic History of US Immigration during the 20th Century

**BENJAMIN C. MONTOYA**

# NEW APPROACHES TO INTERNATIONAL HISTORY

**Series Editor:**

Thomas Zeiler, Professor of American Diplomatic History, University of Colorado Boulder, USA

**Series Editorial Board:**

Anthony Adamthwaite, University of California at Berkeley (USA)
Kathleen Burk, University College London (UK)
Louis Clerc, University of Turku (Finland)
Cindy Ewing, University of Toronto (Canada)
Petra Goedde, Temple University (USA)
Francine McKenzie, University of Western Ontario (Canada)
Lien-Hang Nguyen, University of Kentucky (USA)
Jason Parker, Texas A&M University (USA)
Glenda Sluga, University of Sydney (Australia)

*New Approaches to International History* covers international history during the modern period and across the globe. The series incorporates new developments in the field, such as the cultural turn and transnationalism, as well as the classical high politics of state-centric policymaking and diplomatic relations. Written with upper level undergraduate and postgraduate students in mind, texts in the series provide an accessible overview of international diplomatic and transnational issues, events and actors.

**Published:**

*Decolonization and the Cold War*, edited by Leslie James and Elisabeth Leake (2015)
*Cold War Summits*, Chris Tudda (2015)
*The United Nations in International History*, Amy Sayward (2017)
*Latin American Nationalism*, James F. Siekmeier (2017)
*The History of United States Cultural Diplomacy*, Michael L. Krenn (2017)
*International Cooperation in the Early 20th Century*, Daniel Gorman (2017)
*Women and Gender in International History*, Karen Garner (2018)
*International Development*, Corinna Unger (2018)
*The Environment and International History*, Scott Kaufman (2018)
*Scandinavia and the Great Powers in the First World War*, Michael Jonas (2019)

*Canada and the World since 1867*, Asa McKercher (2019)
*The First Age of Industrial Globalization*, Maartje Abbenhuis and Gordon Morrell (2019)
*Europe's Cold War Relations,* Federico Romero, Kiran Klaus Patel, Ulrich Krotz (2019)
*United States Relations with China and Iran,* Osamah F. Khalil (2019)
*Public Opinion and Twentieth-Century Diplomacy,* Daniel Hucker (2020)
*Globalizing the US Presidency,* Cyrus Schayegh (2020)
*The International LGBT Rights Movement,* Laura Belmonte (2021)
*Global War, Global Catastrophe*, Maartje Abbenhuis and Ismee Tames (2021)
*America's Road to Empire: Foreign Policy from Independence to World War One,* Piero Gleijeses (2021)
*Militarization and the American Century,* David Fitzgerald *(2022)*
*American Sport in International History,* Daniel M. DuBois (2023)
*Rebuilding the Postwar Order*, Francine McKenzie (2023)
*Soldiers in Peacemaking*, Beatrice de Graaf, Frédéric Dessberg, Thomas Vaisset (2023)
*From World War to Postwar*, Andrew N. Buchanan (2023)
*The Fear of Chinese Power*, Jeffrey Crean (2024)

**Forthcoming:**

*China and the United States since 1949,* Elizabeth Ingleson

# A Diplomatic History of US Immigration during the 20th Century

Policy, Law, and National Identity

**BENJAMIN C. MONTOYA**

BLOOMSBURY ACADEMIC
LONDON • NEW YORK • OXFORD • NEW DELHI • SYDNEY

BLOOMSBURY ACADEMIC
Bloomsbury Publishing Plc
50 Bedford Square, London, WC1B 3DP, UK
1385 Broadway, New York, NY 10018, USA
29 Earlsfort Terrace, Dublin 2, Ireland

BLOOMSBURY, BLOOMSBURY ACADEMIC and the Diana logo are trademarks of Bloomsbury Publishing Plc

First published in Great Britain 2024

Copyright © Benjamin C. Montoya, 2024

Benjamin C. Montoya has asserted his right under the Copyright, Designs and Patents Act, 1988, to be identified as Author of this work.

For legal purposes the Acknowledgments on p. xi constitute an extension of this copyright page.

Series design by Catherine Wood
Cover image: Vietnamese refugees being towed behind a larger ship. Bettmann/Getty Images.

All rights reserved. No part of this publication may be reproduced or transmitted in any form or by any means, electronic or mechanical, including photocopying, recording, or any information storage or retrieval system, without prior permission in writing from the publishers.

Bloomsbury Publishing Plc does not have any control over, or responsibility for, any third-party websites referred to or in this book. All internet addresses given in this book were correct at the time of going to press. The author and publisher regret any inconvenience caused if addresses have changed or sites have ceased to exist, but can accept no responsibility for any such changes.

A catalogue record for this book is available from the British Library.

A catalog record for this book is available from the Library of Congress.

ISBN: HB: 978-1-3501-5824-5
PB: 978-1-3501-5823-8
ePDF: 978-1-3501-5826-9
eBook: 978-1-3501-5825-2

Series: New Approaches to International History

Typeset by Deanta Global Publishing Services, Chennai, India
Printed and bound in Great Britain

To find out more about our authors and books visit www.bloomsbury.com and sign up for our newsletters.

# Contents

List of Illustrations ix
Acknowledgments xi

Introduction 1

## PART I  Laws and Systems 25

1   A Synthesis of US Juridical Immigration Law, 1780s–2010s 27

2   A Synthesis of US Congressional Immigration Restriction, 1880s to 2000s 44

3   A Synthesis of the Parallel Developments of the International and the US Refugee Resettlement Regimes, 1921–80 67

## PART II  Case Studies 79

4   Japanese, 1910s–1920s 81

5   Mexicans, 1920s 91

6   Jews, 1930s–1940s 107

7   Chinese, 1930s–1950s 119

8   Vietnamese, 1970s 134

**9** Cubans, 1960s–1980 141

**10** Central Americans, 1980s–1990s 157

**11** Mexicans, 1980s–2000s 175

Conclusion 194

Selected Bibliography 201
Index 216

# Illustrations

## Figures

2.1  J.N. "Ding" Darling, "Some folks pick queer things to go crazy over," *Des Moines Register*, October 12, 1920  48
2.2  Herblock, "You can go back to wherever you came from," *Washington Post*, August 1, 1965  51
2.3  Protests against the Sensenbrenner Bill, Los Angeles, CA, May 1, 2006  61
3.1  Frank Miller, "A Little Higher, a Little Brighter" *Des Moines Register*, December 5, 1956  75
4.1  J.N. "Ding" Darling, "You can't blame Japan for feeling the insult," *Des Moines Register*, March 17, 1919  87
5.1  J.N. "Ding" Darling, "Register the aliens," October 12, 1926  93
6.1  Herblock, "Still no solution," January 25, 1939. Herbert L. Block collection  111
6.2  German Jewish refugees aboard the *U.S.S. St. Louis*, Havana harbor, Cuba, June 1, 1939  112
7.1  *The Wasp*, "The Chinese: Many Handed but Soulless," November 14, 1885  122
7.2  Madame Chiang visits President Franklin Roosevelt, February 17, 1943  125
8.1  Herblock, "US Policy," April 2, 1975. Herbert L. Block collection  135
9.1  Herblock, "Bay of People," May 7, 1980. Herbert L. Block collection  150
10.1  Eric J. García, "Hecho en Estados Unidos," 2017  171
11.1  "We do not blow up buildings we construct them," Las Vegas, NV, May 1, 2006  187
11.2  Eric J. García, "Illegal Love," 2013  189

## Tables

5.1 Number of Immigration Visas Issued to Mexicans between December 1926 and December 1929  102
5.2 Decrease in Number of Mexicans Applying for Visas, Month to Month Comparison from May 1928/1929 to December 1928/1929  103
5.3 Ratio of Refusals of Total Number of Mexican Visa Applicants, 1929, in Percentages  103
6.1 German Quota Immigration and the German Quota, 1933–40  113

# Acknowledgments

Many small victories were won to complete this book. Productive research and writing days amid a full teaching and service schedule over a span of three years. The small victories were also attributable to the help of others. The tracking down of sources and fending off of lending libraries for overdue books by Sarah Sides, Library Manager and Special Collections Coordinator at Schreiner University. The tedious and time-consuming work of formatting the book's bibliography by Zach Purcell, a busy-yet-still gracious History major at Schreiner University. The invitation from Thomas Zeiler, Professor of History and International Relations at the University of Colorado Boulder, to propose a volume for the NAIH series, and Bloomsbury's acceptance of my book proposal (okay, neither of those victories were small).

I am thankful for the various people who helped me get permissions for the images in the book: Sarah Alex at The Herb Block Foundation, Dan Lienau at The Annex Galleries, Bart Schmidt of the Drake University Digital Collections, Peter Balestrieri, Lindsay Moen, and Brad Ferrier at the University of Iowa special collections and archives, Carrie Harmon of "Ding" Darling cartoons, and Drew Cuthbertson for IMAGN. I am especially grateful to Eric J. García, a graphic artist who allowed me to display his work in my book.

The efforts of many made this book possible. Maddie Holder and her editorial staff, especially Megan Harris and Paige Harris, at Bloomsbury were gracious, responsive, and helpful throughout the project. Akshaya Ravi Pemmasani, Project Manager at Deanta, skillfully and efficiently steered the manuscript through its production phase. Joseph "Andy" Fry, Professor Emeritus at the University of Nevada, Las Vegas, a well-esteemed and well-liked senior scholar of US foreign relations, generously gave his time and energy to proofread the entire manuscript. I was highly fortunate to have completed an advanced degree under his guidance many years ago, and we continue to be friends. His skill in fixing and tightening the narrative is greatly appreciated. Eternal gratitude goes to my wife, Haley Dove Montoya, for endless stores of emotional support, for creating and protecting the time I needed to work, and for celebrating this project's many small victories along the way. Finally, thanks must go to my two children, Elias and Isla, and my mother, Susan, for keeping me grounded and reminding me that despite

Morrissey's lyric—"there's more to life than books, you know, but not much more"—there is indeed more to life than books.

I dedicate *A Diplomatic History of US Immigration during the 20th Century* to my History students at Schreiner University. I had you all in mind as I wrote these pages, and this work is meant for readers like you. Your passion and interest in History inspire me to teach well; your incisive discussion comments encourage me to reconsider well-worn interpretations of the past; your humor and levity remind me of the value of that most disarming of all qualities a faculty member can have: humility. I recognize, respect, and support your indomitable drive to pursue careers in History, teaching, research, archival work, and library science, for example, despite the much-discussed paucity of opportunities in the field. Rose-tinted glasses won't spare y'all from the rigors of professional development, but tenacity overcomes many obstacles.

# Introduction

Is the United States a nation of immigrants? What is the distinction between a citizen and a foreigner in a land predominantly populated by successive waves of immigrants? What ties the American nation-state together, a common ethnic-racial ancestry or a common commitment to civic principles? What role does the government play in creating, forging, preserving, and protecting American identity? What role does immigration law has in codifying who fits within the nation and who does not? If an American identity is inclusive, broadly open to anyone, where does the nation begin and end? If being American is exclusive, then what does that suggest about such founding principles as liberty and equality? How have the answers to these questions changed over time? How have they not? How are the questions and answers influenced by times of economic prosperity and depression, by times of peace and war? Most especially, how do the questions and answers change in relation to Americans' efforts to project their power abroad? In sum, how do US relations with foreign nations converge, conflict, or complement US responses to foreign peoples?

This book provides a synthetic discussion of the confluence of foreign policy and immigration policy throughout US history; it is not meant to offer a broad, overarching treatment of immigration in American history. While this work will definitely touch on some of those historical narratives, the overall story cannot be told here. Nor is this a grand treatment of the history of US diplomatic relations. A reader seeking such a work can easily find it in numerous other books.

Instead, this book offers case studies of eight different immigrant and refugee streams between the late nineteenth century and the early twenty-first century to demonstrate how US foreign policy interests shaped and were shaped by the arrival of foreigners to America's shores. As such, this book will discuss broad changes in US immigration and refugee policy, judicial immigration law, and the nature of US citizenship. The diplomatic historian Lars Schoultz has asserted that foreign policy considerations "intimately" influence US immigration policy, but he has found few examples of how such considerations *directly* shaped formal immigration policy.[1] This book aspires to show how both the imagination and the practice of foreign policy directly influenced US immigration policy. The dynamic of this analytical relationship is not always uni-directional. These case studies will show how the arrival of foreigners often shaped US diplomatic practices in ways Americans and their leaders did not anticipate or want.

No such historical relationship exists in a void. Therefore, this analysis must address the philosophical, legal, social, economic, and racial themes that influence the interplay of US foreign policy and US immigration policy. There are two purposes for taking these sideroads. One, to give readers a synthesized understanding of the often (very) dense scholarly conversations about the topics and, two, to show readers the various pressures, prejudices, and proclivities shaping the interaction between US foreign policy and US immigration policy.

The movement of people into the United States is classified in various ways: migration, immigration, and refugee flows. And the persons doing the moving are denoted in different legal ways—immigrants, nonquota immigrants, refugees—as well as many other unofficial ways—illegal immigrants, undocumented migrants, and economic migrants. These are not generic, interchangeable terms. A person's ability to legally immigrate to the United States often shields them from the legal penalties an "illegal" immigrant can face if apprehended. Legal status does not always result in social acceptance, however.[2] Americans have always been ambivalent about the presence of foreigners in US society. Yet those very terms—"American" and "U.S. society"—are fluid. Our early twenty-first-century understanding of who can be an American differs markedly from how Americans viewed the same issue in the early twentieth century. Immigration scholars have long discussed the processes of acculturation and this book can only cursorily touch on that. It is enough to say here, however, that perceptions and definitions matter: how persons are defined and viewed determines how they are received in US society. That reception can include political refuge, gainful employment, access to public services, and comity with native-born citizens and acculturated immigrant forebears. Conversely, those who surreptitiously cross the US border, those who overstay their visas, those who flood US ports of entry face much harsher responses from Americans and the US government. Workplace sweeps, border round-ups, home raids, familial separation, visa denials, withholding of permanent resident status, are common experiences for individuals who run afoul of US immigration law. Even if the United States' ability to regulate immigration is not always efficient and sometimes works at cross-purposes with national principles, the *perception* that it can and will regulate immigration has real consequences, not just for persons crossing the border but for their families who await their return and for persons who interact with immigrants within US borders.[3] Many years ago Joseph Carens, a political scientist, provocatively stated that citizenship in Western democracies like the United States was "the modern equivalent of feudal privilege."[4] By the end of this book, readers will understand what Carens meant.

A key objective of this book is to explain why some foreigners were accepted into US society and why some were not. To start to formulate an answer to this question we need to start by asking a set of questions. First, what is the difference between migration and immigration? A migrant is a person who intends to reside in a host country for a relatively short period of time. Migration is often spurred by the search for economic opportunities, and migration patterns are often frequent and *circular*. For example, an individual Mexican male migrant in his mid-forties who is the head of his household might spend six months working in the United States, return to Mexico for the remainder of the year, and then repeat the process in subsequent years.[5] By contrast, immigrants are those who seek to permanently settle in the United States. There is never one fixed reason why individuals decide to immigrate. Scholars argue that economic opportunity is a prime driver of immigration, but they also point to conditions in immigrants' home countries—civil wars, corrupt governments, and high rates of crime—as important factors behind immigration.

This explanation of immigration will serve as an early example of how formal definitions inadequately explain the complexities of the terms they define. Definitionally, immigration implies a degree of choice on the part of individuals to seek better lives. But the choice to immigrate becomes murky when factors such as violence, corruption, and poverty are considered. *Coercion* can prompt choice. There are two different types of people movement: impermanent settlement (migration) and permanent settlement (immigration). The following case studies will demonstrate how the line between migrants and immigrants is not always clear, is subject to outside stimuli affecting transnational politics, and is definitively shaped by developments and changes in US immigration law.

A common perception of US immigration law is that it allows an open border. This book will show this notion to be fallacious. At present, the various borders to cross into the United States—physical, legal, conceptual, political—have never been so rigorously, militantly, and expensively administered. Nor have the means of apprehension and deportation been so legally and reflexively robust.[6] In short, it has never been so difficult or dangerous to immigrate to the United States as it has been from the late twentieth century to the early twenty-first century.

Scholars disagree over what primarily drives this assiduous desire to regulate border spaces. Some argue that it is fear of foreigners, and that this fear has not only legitimized the political and marshal heft of immigration regulation bodies but that it has also criminalized the act of immigration itself—a process some legal scholars term as "crimmigration."[7] Other scholars argue that trade drives heightened border regulation. Employing Mexico as an example, they assert that militarization of the US Border Patrol between the 1970s and the early 1990s worked in tandem with US efforts to expand investment into Mexico. Hardening the border served to reinforce the perception of Mexico as a hapless nation and Mexicans as pliable migrant laborers.[8] As with most dilemmas, both arguments contain elements of truth.

Not that it was easy to immigrate to the United States before the 1980s. Restrictive quotas kept immigration from southern and eastern Europe to a trickle for much of the mid-twentieth century. Asian immigration to the United States was almost completely banned from the 1880s to the 1940s. Even before the famous Chinese Exclusion Act of 1882, during the antebellum period and through Reconstruction, state governments took actions to prevent the entry of persons who seemed "likely to become a public charge." Such legal actions had precedents dating back to the colonial era. This book will discuss the long historical debate over which government entity had the absolute right to regulate immigration: the federal government or state governments.

Yet institutional effectiveness should not be overstated. For much of US history immigration regulation resembled more of a jalopy than a juggernaut. The comprehensive, coordinated, and militarized nature of immigration restriction is a recent construct, dating back—really—to the 1990s and, spurred in no small part by innovations in communication and surveillance, for example, the drone. By contrast, for much of the history discussed in this book, immigration policies passed by Congress in Washington, DC, were difficult to enforce at multiple ports of entry and along thousands of miles of land borders between the United States, Canada, and Mexico. This "pronounced gap" between intention and result constantly bedeviled immigration restriction efforts.[9] It was not until the last years of the nineteenth century that a formal administrative body dedicated to immigration regulation was established, and not until the mid-1920s was the Border Patrol founded to regulate cross-border traffic. The effort to regulate immigration was "characterized not by strength but by struggle" even after these institutional bodies were in place.[10] US lawmakers throughout American history have had to accept that the sheer length of America's land borders and the vast variety of the topographies therein made laughable the prospect of completely closing off immigration.[11] A perennial theme running throughout this book is the development of US immigration regulatory bodies and their problematic efforts to block waves of migrants crossing into the United States.

How does this legacy of immigration exclusion align with the history of American liberalism? Some scholars such as Joseph Carens (quoted earlier) and legal historian Kitty Calavita argue that there is an "inherent tension" between border control and the liberal democratic principles that undergird the United States.[12] Other scholars such as Saskia Sassen, David Fitzgerald, David Cook-Martín, Karen Manges-Douglas and Rogelio Sáenz, and Douglass Massey see no tension at all, arguing instead that liberalism itself is inherently exclusionary. The process by which citizenship is delineated necessitates an out-group as well as an in-group. In other words, you cannot know who is a citizen until you know who is not. Many scholars of US immigration history, including this one, argue that race was built and construed as a prime prerequisite for determining who was fit to be an American citizen. "The US may have been a leading proponent of liberal democratic systems of governance," immigration historians David Cook-Martín and David Fitzgerald argue, "[but it] has been a laggard in the international trend toward admission based on universal racial equality."[13]

The case for exclusionary liberalism seems credible when one considers the ultimate purpose of liberalism: to forge a nation of citizens with equal rights under the law.[14] Focused on delineating individual rights, liberalism is inherently focused on establishing—and maintaining—corporate rights, or the contours of a nation. Just as one has to know who constitutes a citizen and who does not, the philosophical, legal, political, religious, economic, and physical lines that demarcate a nation need to be clearly drawn. Otherwise, how does one know where the nation begins and ends? In this regard, US immigration policy is instrumental in sharpening the distinction between citizen and noncitizen (alien), as well as the nation(al) from the foreign(er). Strict immigration policies, legal scholar Gabriela Gallegos argues, are the means by which a "line of demarcation" is maintained between Americans and non-Americans.[15]

Positing the immigrant as the foil of the citizen must be supplemented with a discussion of how immigration serves as a foil to nationhood. Since the early modern period, mercantilist economic theory held that human capital was considered an inextricable part of a nation's wealth. Through such an analytical lens unauthorized migration was tantamount to treason. The departure of people was likened to a nation bleeding internally. Therefore, the earliest manifestations of international law promulgated the concept that a sovereign's security required the exercise of control over the internal movement of people. Migration regulation had two purposes: to preserve the human capital of the nation and to ensure that foreigners did not enter a sovereign nation's territory unchecked, lest they were potential invaders.[16] This twin legal codification of the nation-state and that nation-state's sovereign right to control the movement of people generated a "view that immigration is a zero-sum game among competitive nation-states."[17]

Paralleling the dual development of the nation-state and its ability to regulate immigration was the growth of an assumption that a person's human rights follow their nationality. A person did not have inherent ("inalienable") human rights; rather, rights were dependent upon belonging to a nation. Under the Westphalian order that created our modern-day notions of a nation-state during the seventeenth century, the legitimacy of a country derived from its representation of a preexisting community. This community, often knit together through historical, cultural, linguistic, and ethno-racial ties, in turn, achieved political agency by virtue of its state. Nation and state formation was a symbiotic process: as a group of people began to identify themselves as a distinct body of persons, so they created a state that protected their group interests; and the formation of that state, usually signified by the creation of government, legitimized the distinctiveness of that body of persons. The correlating political ideology that followed the formation of nation and state was *nationalism*. It should be noted that this process of nation-state consciousness was exclusive and exclusionary in nature. It could not be otherwise. For reasons stated earlier, a body politic cannot exist without a reference to or catalog of the component parts that *do not* make up the nation-state.[18]

The fiery trials of the American and French Revolutions of the late eighteenth century forged an alternative model to this mode of inherent, exclusive nation-state consciousness. The constitutional epistles of those two revolutions, the Constitution of the United States (1787–8) and the Declaration of the Rights of Man and of the Citizen (1791), codified a new, *liberal* criteria for what comprised the authority of the state: the consent of the governed. In contrast to the exclusive nature of nationalist state-making, liberalism invited an inclusive, non-fixed, principled instead of predetermined, set of criteria that underlined the formation of a body politic.[19]

Or so it seemed. These two, rivaling theories of state formation, nationalism versus liberalism, will be a prime tension described in this book. Historian Gary Gerstle boils down these two forms of state formation into racial nationalism and civic nationalism. The former conceived of the United States as an ethno-racial body, composed of people who are held together by common blood, skin color, and by an inherited fitness for self-government. By contrast, the latter believes that the search for life, liberty, and the pursuit of happiness are not principles inherent to only one ethno-racial group but are instead open to any person, regardless of his or her language and skin color.[20] The historical debate between advocates of one over the other directly influenced how immigrants in US society and immigration to the United States were viewed.

The real complication to this philosophical contest over time in US history is not so much determining which side was winning, but realizing that they often coexisted, sometimes opposing, and at other times complementing one another. This harmonious contradiction is at the root of the ambivalent place immigration holds in US history. Otherwise, why did the United States, the biggest promoter of liberal democracy in world history, also have such a long history of immigration restriction? Why was this so? There are many reasons, some of which this book will detail. One of them is the ways in which immigration exacerbates the tensions between racial and civic nationalism:

while immigration appeals to the liberal, individualistic side of the modern liberal order, it also can be seen as threatening to the national, communitarian side of that same order.[21] Not only does immigration occupy a gray area between racial and civic nationalism but it also serves to inflame conflict between the two concepts. During times of rapid economic and social change in the United States, immigrants are often the "flashpoints" around which questions over the meaning of nationhood and nationalism, of inclusion and exclusion, are debated.[22]

The contest between racial and civic conceptions of nation was central to the extended arguments over whether or not immigrants can or should assimilate into their host country. This theme also produces the controversial and inflammatory category of "illegal" immigration. In a world composed of nation-states, where do individuals fit who are caught in the crosshairs of militarized border security and stringent immigration laws? How do the twin pressures of nationalism based on exclusion and liberalism based on choice make stateless individuals aberrant, legally invisible, and devoid of rights that host nations are bound to respect?[23]

To begin to answer these questions we need to unpack the complex term, "illegal immigration." First, civically, the term represents a "collision" between two processes by which citizenship is gained—either inherently or consensually. Can a sovereign nation impart citizenship—and all the privileges therein—upon persons who have entered the country surreptitiously? If it can, what does this suggest about the idea of earned membership? And regardless of whether a sovereign nation can do this or not, what does the presence of undocumented, aberrant persons within a polity suggest about the sovereign's (in)ability to control the movement of people within its borders? These dilemmas are complicated further when one considers the "dual identity" of undocumented immigrants who are at once both outsiders and contributors to a national community, primarily through their labor.[24]

Let's take a moment to excavate the origin of the term "illegal immigration." Chinese immigrants were called "illegals" and "sneaky Orientals" as early as the 1880s, around the time the Chinese Exclusion Act was passed by Congress.[25] The moniker *illegals* was extended to Mexican migrants during the Bracero program (1942–64). Scholars disagree on when the term "illegal immigration" became legally salient. Some, like this historian, say the 1920s was the period in which illegal immigration conceptually shaped US immigration policy, even if it was not codified into law.[26] Another argument holds that legislatively, the roots of illegal immigration can be attributed to the Immigration and Nationality Act of 1952, which divided the meaning of alien into two categories: immigrant and nonimmigrant. The former referred to a person who was lawfully present in the United States, a status known by its shorthand, "LPR" (lawful/legal permanent resident). The latter term, nonimmigrant, referred to a person who had been granted temporary entry under one of the more than twenty-five general categories of visas available through the US immigration system. The H-2A was the most commonly granted visa for temporary entry into the United States, often given to agricultural workers. "Illegal" has emerged as a term to describe persons who enter the United States without formal immigrant or nonimmigrant status.[27]

Regardless of when one believes the term originated in US immigration law and in the parlance of the US public, illegal immigration is a politically charged term that carries consequences for migrant-sending and migrant-receiving nations, for the governments that regulate the movements of people, and for the individuals who cross borders. Using the term "illegal immigration" often obscures the central role of the state in the process of immigration. The laws and policies formulated by the state, but also diplomatic alliances and antagonisms, and foreign aid disbursements by central governments all influence the movement of people. By boiling down immigration into two pseudo-legal categories—legal and illegal—commentators on immigration attribute the migration process to an individual's decision. Interestingly, both anti- and pro-migrant commentators contribute to the premise that individuals are the principal actors in migration. For critics of illegal immigration, migrants consciously break the law. Therefore, illegal immigrants are likened to criminals who deserve nothing short of apprehension and deportation. For defenders of undocumented migrants, migrants are victims of arbitrary and draconian legal requirements that do not take account for the conditions migrants face in their home countries, and minimize the manifold ways in which migrants contribute to the US economy.[28]

Instead, there is a broader, geopolitical context that spurs undocumented migration. A migrant's decision to enter the United States undocumented does rest on individual decision-making, to be sure, just as conditions in that person's home country can act as a push for that migrant to leave. Yet it is also important to recognize that states—both migrant-sending and migrant-receiving—are not passive observers to the movement of people. Instead, their legal, social and economic characteristics play a direct role in abetting immigration, sometimes intentionally and at other times unintentionally. Finally, the ways in which states interact with each other have a direct bearing on why people choose to cross borders and how they go about doing so.

Another problem with the term "illegal immigration" is that it simplistically cites economics as the prime driver of immigration. Unidimensional treatments of immigration as an economic phenomenon treat migrants as "autonomous economics units" who, depending on one's perspective, are either stealing jobs and have a net negative impact on the US economy or are filling jobs native workers do not want, thereby representing a net positive for the general economy. Instead, the causes of immigration are much more complicated. They include violence in home countries and a search for better wages in host countries, yet they also include factors that demonstrate the multi-variant characteristics of immigration. For example, the search for familial security is a prime driver of immigration: migrant laborers work to "self-insure" against diminishing wages and poverty in their home countries. Additionally, immigrants benefit from connections to migration networks, some of which exist for decades across generations of migrating persons and are tenaciously maintained despite the passage of restrictive immigration laws designed to close them. The pull of social migration networks is stronger than the fear of apprehension by immigration authorities. Almost half of all Mexican migrants, for example, have immediate family members with experience migrating to the United States, and a fifth of Mexican migrants have an immediate family member living in the United States. According to sociologists Douglas Massey and Fernando Riosmena, the durability of migration networks necessitates new thinking from lawmakers concerned with immigration policy. "Migration flows are much easier to turn on than to turn off," they state.[29] From these perspectives, immigration is a collective experience just as much as an individual decision. This is important to keep in mind when we consider why political and legal efforts to stop "illegal immigration," to close border crossings, fail to address the collective decision-making that underlies immigration.

A final problem with the term "illegal immigration" is its insinuation that immigration law is fixed, objective, and permanent. Instead, the law plays a huge role in perpetuating the problem of illegal immigration. First, it distinguishes between "good" and "bad" versions of migration. Second, in the process of determining bad immigration, immigration law does two things: it defines personhood by legitimizing state authority over immigration and it reifies the state's own reason to exist by legitimizing state control of the movement of people.[30] Justifying state power is no generic concept, for as will be shown, during the last decades of the twentieth century and into the early years of the twenty-first century, the powers of surveillance, apprehension, border patrol, and deportation have increased markedly. Immigration laws, anthropologist Nicholas Degenova argues, "serve as instruments to supply and refine the parameters of both discipline and coercion."[31] Even when state power is insufficient to completely block immigration, even when borders are too vast to completely close, the omnipotence of immigration restriction works to keep illegal immigrants as a marginalized group within US society. Ultimately, Degenova continues, the fight against illegal immigration rests "not to physically exclude [illegal immigrants] but instead, to socially include them under imposed conditions of enforced and protracted vulnerability."[32] Strangely, then, even when immigration restriction toward undocumented migrants is not completely successful in practical terms, it is still successful politically and even symbolically. "It is deportability, and not deportation per se," Degenova concludes, "that has historically rendered undocumented migrant labor a *distinctly disposable commodity.*"[33]

There are also important symbolic and economic incentives that revolve around the term "illegal immigration". Incomplete immigration enforcement is still immigration regulation. The political rhetoric of stemming illegal immigration gives the impression to frustrated US citizens that their elected officials are doing something about the immigration crisis. And the stigma of hiring "illegals" is hardly debilitating for US employers of migrant laborers; it actually incentivizes them to hire more undocumented laborers. Afforded fewer and fewer social protections and increasingly viewed as civic pariahs, marginalized migrants are easier to house poorly, easier to exploit, and easier to pay meagerly.[34]

The history of US immigration law is far from coherent but is instead characterized by a "constitutive restlessness and relative incoherence" as various generations of US leaders have attempted to codify and enforce the statutes.[35] In fact, illegal immigration is not a legal term at all, it is a political one. The reason the term is so complicated and controversial is that it involves the root problem described: the question of who and who does not belong to the nation.[36]

That question is easy to answer if there is no debate over who is fit to become a citizen. For much of American history, however, that concept has been debated heatedly. The controversy revolves around two broad questions. Is personhood *inherent* when being a person grants an individual—regardless of whether an immigrant or native, a citizen or noncitizen—constitutional protections? Or is one's personhood more *consensual* in that a person's status is abrogated by and reciprocated by the larger polity that grants legal standing and maybe even citizenship, and the constitutional protections that follow?[37]

The belief that a person is entitled to certain rights exclusively due to membership in the human race relies on philosophical concepts derived from Locke and Rousseau. They argued that each individual has worth and autonomy and that each person was born possessing rights. Additionally, they argued that persons have the ability to recast their nationality. In Locke's theory of recision, a person has the right to cancel their membership in a nation that violates their rights and can reformulate their "original liberty" to join a new nation. In short, if an individual has the right to freedom from abuse then they have the right to *escape* abuse.[38]

As often happens, however, reality diverges from philosophy. While the notion of who does and does not belong to a nation has been hotly debated, there is an internationally recognized right for any person to *emigrate* from their country if they are facing political oppression. The right to immigrate does not automatically follow from the right to emigrate, however. While there are international regimes that protect a person's desire to flee their home country, there is no analogous system of laws or agreements that guarantees that an emigrant refugee can be settled into a safe, host country.[39] The nation-state's sovereign right to set immigration policy precluding an individual person's right to immigrate is a predominant theme running through this book. This argument, definitively codified into US immigration law by the 1880s yet challenged repeatedly thereafter, rested on a simple assumption that the state's power to regulate the inflow of people followed from the sovereign state's right to secure its territory.[40] Therefore, the threat of foreign *invasion* was long associated with immigration. Additionally, the correlation between sovereignty and immigration restriction explains why generations of American lawmakers saw no irony in promoting liberalism while curbing the inflow of foreigners into the United States.

The conflict between the right to emigrate and the right to immigrate helps to explain why the United States has rarely brokered bilateral agreements on immigration, why the United States was a laggard in adopting international norms on refugee resettlement after the Second World War, why US economic aspirations are prioritized over the security of stateless emigrants, and, ultimately, why US immigration policy has hampered American diplomatic relations with many foreign countries. In short, for hundreds of thousands of migrants between the early twentieth century and the early twenty-first century, the right to migrate ended at US shores.[41] Interestingly, foreign policy considerations—not domestic pressures and less so economic concerns—frequently caused the United States to override its historical and customary aversion to the settlement of refugees on American soil.[42]

This relationship between liberalism and exclusion is evident when discussing globalization and immigration. Globalization rests on the free movement of goods, information, and people. This connection between the trade of commodities and the movement of people dates back centuries, to a time in which mercantilist economic theory likened the wealth of goods to the wealth of population. Much closer to the present, the history of the European Union and its installation of the Schengen Zone is an example of how these three facets of globalization interacted during the last decades of the twentieth century. By contrast, the United States attempted to formulate a type of globalization that liberalized the movement of goods and information but precluded the movement of people.[43]

There exists a scholarly assumption that liberal trade and liberal immigration policies tend to parallel each other; that the pursuit of free trade often coincides with a relatively unrestrictive immigration policy. There is a problem with this allegedly natural "affinity."[44] While there are similarities between trade and immigration that explain why they are often coupled together, there are also distinctions that explain why governments and the peoples they represent have markedly different reactions to the inflow of commodities and immigrants. Trade is about economics while immigration is not *just* about economics. In contrast to trade, immigration has political, cultural, and social ramifications beyond economic considerations. Trade liberalization focuses on expediting the free movement of goods and capital to strengthen the US economy. A different set of ideological concerns narrowly defines the nation and its citizenry. These concerns can lead to viewing immigration ambivalently.[45]

Another distinction between trade and immigration is that the wealth generated by the former does not obviously benefit the entire nation; the gains of immigration are not spread evenly across an economy, and instead benefit only certain industries. The wages earned by migrants are often sent to families in home countries (remittances) while the employers who benefit from hiring pliable workers benefit disproportionately from those who are not in the industries that rely on migrant laborers. Moreover, trade is reciprocal while immigration may predominantly flow in one direction. For example, the rate of American immigration to Mexico is much smaller than the rate of that parallels Mexican migration to the United States. This leads to still another difference between trade and immigration: the benefits that developed nations derive from immigration are almost always available through unilateral action rather than through negotiation with developing, migrant-sending countries. By contrast, the benefits of trade and foreign investment predominantly come through negotiated treaties, whether they be bilateral, regional, or multilateral. Developed nations can legislate whatever sort of immigration policies they want without having to engage with developing nations. By contrast, it is hard to imagine such a thing as a unilateral trade policy. Finally, in contrast to trade, for which there is a near consensus among economists that there is a strong positive fiscal impact associated with trade for nations, the debate over whether immigration represents a net loss or a net gain for a national economy is much more contentious and even acrimonious.[46]

These distinctions are important to enable readers to recognize to how moments of economic liberalization did not always coincide with moments of immigration liberalization in US history. In fact, in some ways, trade and immigration policies have a pendulum-like relationship: when one is up, the other is down. And like immigration policy, trade policy is predicated on how the United States interacts with the global community. In times of bilateral immigration policy (e.g., Burlingame Treaty of 1868 or Gentlemen's Agreement of 1907–8), the United States pursued a unilateral foreign policy (nineteenth century). In times of unilateral immigration policy (Hart-Celler of 1965), the United States pursued a multilateral foreign policy (twentieth century).[47]

There are exceptions to this pattern, notably the Bracero program, which was a temporary labor migration regime negotiated on a bilateral basis and initiated by a developed, migrant-receiving nation (the United States). The program temporarily allowed contracted Mexican laborers to work in US agriculture. Such schemes tend to be restrictive (the time duration Mexican workers were allowed to reside and work in the United States was limited to six months), reflect a low level of international coordination (the agreement was only between the United States and Mexico), and are contextually exceptional (the agreement was promoted by US entry into the Second World War, which saw the enlistment of millions of young American men into the military). The United States has set its immigration policy unilaterally since the end of the Bracero program in 1964.[48]

The distinction between trade and immigration cannot be so neatly drawn, however, for reasons of both economic prosperity and dependency. First, for reasons mentioned earlier, from the early modern period people were considered a part of a nation's wealth, and so to lose population was to lose national vitality. Much closer to the present, the establishment of trade agreements has created international linkages. With trade relationships comes economic dependence. In this interconnected world, the kind of world globalization theorists encourage when they appeal for free trade, a "disruption of supplies, a change in pricing or a shift in the global environment does not simply inconvenience one country or another," legal scholar Bayless Manning argued in 1977, "it can dislocate whole economies, ways of life, and worldwide systems of production, employment, sales distribution, finance, investment, and use."[49] The work people do and the products they produce are "inter-local": locally manufactured, grown, and processed commodities for customers of a global market. There are no *local* markets in an era of globalization. In this sense, the line between international and domestic concerns is transparent, it is "intermestic."[50]

This dependency, far from being alleviated by innovations in communication and transportation, is actually enhanced by improvements in economic production. Google an image of motor plants in Detroit, Michigan. Think about the last time you called a travel agent on the phone to book a flight ticket. Robots and computers do jobs that used to be occupied by human workers. As the US economy has moved away from its production base toward a services-based focus, the nature of work and the demand for laborers has changed, but in deceptive ways. To be sure, working on computers is a good idea right now but there are still houses to clean and lawns to mow. Who fills those menial jobs? Migrants. Ironically, then, as the US economy de-industrializes, it becomes more dependent on migrant laborers—what immigration scholar Kitty Calavita dubs a "Third World workforce"—to do the jobs native (and usually better educated) workers either avoid or cannot fill in adequate numbers in job sectors such as agriculture, the garment industry, construction, hotels, and restaurants.[51] In a spin on economist Joseph Schumpeter's theory of *creative destruction*—in which new industries "kill off" old ones in their relentless drive to expand markets—the deskilling of various industries that include construction, retail services, and produce picking makes it more likely that jobs in those sectors will be occupied by migrant laborers.[52]

Trade and immigration are not neatly separable for another reason. What happens, for example, when migrant workers are your most durable trade good? For countries such as Mexico and El Salvador, both of which have sent numerous migrants and immigrants to the United States, trade policy and immigration policy are equally important. They may even be indistinguishable (see Chapters 5, 10, and 11).[53] Remittances sent by migrant workers form a solid component of annual national earnings for countries like Mexico and El Salvador and often constitute a bedrock of migrant family incomes. But there are costs to the "necessary evil" of migration-trade policy: dangers of traversing international borders, vulnerability to human traffickers, exploitation by US employers, rough handling by border patrol authorities, and deportation.[54] For migrants and their families, there is a thin line between the hope of economic betterment and the dangers of migration. For governments of migrant-sending nations like Mexico, there is little difference between the products they export and the citizens who choose to migrate out of the country for work. And for migrant-receiving nations like the United States, there is a transparent demarcation between its liberalization of trade and its magnetic pull upon a host of migrant peoples.

This book will highlight many tragic moments, but in sum it will not relate to a tragedy. Instead, by the end of this discussion of immigration and US foreign policy, it is hoped that the reader will come to appreciate the indomitability of the human spirit, the ability to persevere in the face of almost insurmountable odds. This is not to view history through rose-tinted glasses, but rather to work against a pedagogical tendency that education scholar Peter Knight calls an endless series of "repetitive rehearsals of negative emotions."[55] The various migrant, immigrant, and refugee groups discussed in this book have experienced similar patterns of adjustment and adaptation to US society. Not all of them were accepted in similar fashions. Some were openly reviled and spurned by home and host countries. Some were embraced by the American people and the US government.

There are two objectives in offering a case-study approach to this subject. First, "lumping" all immigrant groups into one broad synthesis runs the risk of condensing a narrative treatment of immigration in US history. Race is the most common narrative arch offered by scholars of immigration, with class following close behind. Those scholars are not wrong: race and class were prime determinants to how Americans responded to immigration, how the US policymakers passed legislation restricting immigration, and how lawmakers handed down decisions that codified the contours of American identity and nationhood.[56]

For much of the time *preceding* this book's primary focus on the twentieth century, anti-Catholicism was a primary and durable lens through which Americans viewed immigration. As historian John Higham assiduously details in his landmark book on the history of American nativism, *Strangers in the Land*, anti-Catholic prejudice formed a solid foundation of nativist thinking in America from the colonial period to the Civil War. Historically, anti-Catholicism was rooted in the tensions and violence unleashed by the Protestant Reformation. During the sixteenth and seventeenth centuries, England warred continuously against Europe's Catholic powers, France and Spain. A "Protestant hatred of Rome" became an indelible part of English national consciousness.[57] Such religious hatred started to cross the Atlantic in the early 1600s as English settlers established colonies in North America. The pressure of being wedged between two hostile Catholic empires—the French in the north and west, the Spanish in the south and west—created a distinct, New World type of Anglo-American antipathy toward Catholics.[58] Anti-Catholic prejudice reached its apogee during the antebellum years, as hundreds of thousands of immigrants—especially Irish—arrived in the United States during the 1840s and 1850s. Charged with a "Protestant evangelical fervor," Higham states, American nativists "considered the immigrants minions of the [Pope] dispatched [to the United States] to subvert American institutions."[59] A new political party, the American (Know-Nothing) Party, was founded with the specific purpose of preventing the election of Catholic candidates to governing positions at the state and federal levels (see Chapter 1). Yet, anti-Catholicism waned in the post-Civil War decades and would not fundamentally shape the policy and public debates over immigration during the twentieth century. Despite a momentary flashpoint in the 1890s with the American Protective Association (see Chapter 2), American culture became more secular during the latter half of the nineteenth century, and the Protestant evangelicalism that had once underlined anti-Catholicism no longer animated American nationalism. Nevertheless, as late as the 1920s, with the resurgence of the Ku Klux Klan, anti-Catholic sentiment informed Americans' perceptions of immigrants. That prejudice, however, tended to predominate in rural areas far from the urban centers of a modernizing United States, among Americans who had no hands on the levers of power.[60]

In addition to racial and economic factors, foreign policy concerns also drove developments in US immigration policy. This is most obvious in the post-Second World War era, when foreign policy considerations, rather than domestic politics, precipitated a major revision of restrictive quota laws of the 1920s. The 1943 repeal of the Chinese Exclusion Act, for example, was a gesture toward a wartime ally rather than an attempt to right the wrongs done to Chinese Americans. The Bracero program was established in 1942 as a wartime expedient, not to serve as a bilateral attempt to resolve the immigration issue between the United States and Mexico. The Displaced Persons Acts of 1948 and 1950 were, at least in part, the result of "guilty consciences about the unconscionable refugee policy" of the United States during the Second World War. Subsequent pro-refugee actions during presidential administrations of the 1950s to the 1970s were driven by geopolitical priorities.[61] Hints of foreign policy shaping immigration policy came as early as 1907 and continued to be evident as recently as 2007. How the United States viewed foreign nations and the peoples of those nations played a significant role in how they reacted to the inflow of foreigners from the late nineteenth century to the early twenty-first century.

Second, by focusing on case studies, this book will not only demonstrate the commonalities of the immigrant experience but also the *differences*.[62] The geopolitical factors that precipitated Vietnamese refugee flows to the United States during the late 1970s were similar to those that caused the Mariel Boatlift crisis of 1980, in which hundreds of thousands of Cuban refugees swamped Florida ports. Yet exiles from South Vietnam faced a markedly different reception than the Marielitos from, what John F. Kennedy was wont to term, Castro's "imprisoned island." This book will explain why there was such a difference in this scenario and others. Hint, it has everything to do with foreign policy.

*A Diplomatic History of US Immigration during the 20th Century* is divided into two distinct sections. The first section, Laws and Systems, discusses the formulation and nature of US juridical and legislative immigration law as well as the development of the international and American refugee resettlement regimes. The book's first chapter will synthesize over 200 years of US jurisprudence in immigration law. The dilemmas at the center of immigration law pertained to not just who should be allowed to immigrate into a community but what political entity—federal or state governments—should hold the ultimate power over immigration policy. These debates cropped up in the first years of the American republic and continue into the 2010s.

Chapter 2 offers a concise treatment of major US immigration legislation during the twentieth century: the Johnson-Reed Act of 1924, which placed comprehensive quotas on European immigration streams and outright barred immigration from many parts of Asia; the Hart-Celler Act of 1965, which attempted to instill a dose of liberalism into US immigration legislation by replacing the quota system with hemispheric numerical ceilings on immigration; the Immigration Reform and Control Act of 1986, which attached criminal penalties to undocumented migration to the United States and the hiring of "illegal" migrants, even as it granted amnesty for thousands of erstwhile undocumented immigrants in the United States; and multiple laws from 1996, which collectively facilitated the US government's ability to deport undocumented immigrants and made it difficult for foreigners to receive amnesty in the United States.

Chapter 3 consists of two parts, the first of which summarizes the founding of the international refugee resettlement regime. Placing its origins in the interwar period under the powers of the League of Nations, the initial focus was to repatriate persons displaced by war. This continued to be the focus even after the end of the Second World War, as responsibility for refugees was transferred to the United Nations. The UN had a big task on its hands. Amid the Cold War, with all of its ideological tensions, a wave of decolonization throughout the "Third World" produced massive numbers of refugees. Local civil war, geopolitical conflict, and structural disparities in nations that expelled refugees made the idea of repatriation anathema. Instead, resettlement seemed the more humanitarian and lasting solution to refugee problems. But which nations of the global community would accept refugees? And in what numbers?

The second part of Chapter 3 discusses how the United States participated in the development of an international refugee resettlement regime. Using multilateral, UN-sponsored tools to satisfy unilateral foreign policy objectives, the United States largely underwrote the UN's efforts to resettle displaced people. It was not until the mid-1950s, however, that the United States itself became an asylum country for Cold War refugees. Subsequent decades witnessed a watershed of refugee crises from around the "Third World," calling into question the efficaciousness of American resettlement schemes and exposing the consequences of US diplomatic and military interventions into Asian and Latin American nations.

The book's second section will offer eight case studies of how US foreign policy interests sometimes complemented and at other times clashed with immigration and refugee flows to the United States from the late nineteenth century to the early twenty-first century. Chapter 4 details how the Japanese immigration experience to the United States was dramatically altered from the time of the Gentlemen's Agreement (1907–8), when Japan agreed to self-restrict the immigration of Japanese laborers to the United States, to the Johnson-Reed Act (1924), when the US government reneged on the Gentlemen's Agreement by adding Japan to the new quota laws of the 1920s. During the late nineteenth century, Japanese immigrants were welcomed into US society; however, by the early twentieth century, many Americans wanted to see a sharp curtailment of Japanese immigration to the United States. This shift in US immigration policy toward Japan was preceded by American racism toward Japanese immigrants and American discomfort with the presence of Japanese "picture brides" in the United States. The chapter will conclude by addressing the diplomatic fallout in US-Japan relations after Japanese immigration was included in the Immigration Act of 1924.

In contrast to Japanese immigration, Mexican immigration was not added to the quota of 1924. This was not for lack of trying. Chapter 5 discusses how, during the late 1920s and early 1930s, immigration restrictionists worked tenaciously to block Mexican immigration. Yet these efforts eventually failed for fear that immigration restriction would undermine US-Mexican relations. The exceptional nature of US-Mexican relations during the 1920s explains why the quota was not extended to Mexico's immigration to the United States. Yet, Mexico was not completely spared from immigration restriction during the interwar years. The political rhetoric and racist language that undergirded the quota effort highlighted a growing racial prejudice toward Mexican immigrants in the United States that inaugurated a non-legislative, consular-led form of exclusion—administrative restriction.

Chapter 6 discusses how the convergence of economic depression, an intractable American isolationism, a commitment to restrictive immigration quota laws from the 1920s, and latent anti-semitism in American society stymied the US government's ability to respond to the European Jewish refugee crisis during the 1930s and 1940s. Scholars debate whether the administration of Franklin D. Roosevelt could have done more to provide safe haven for Europe's Jews. That debate will be touched on here. Such a discussion demonstrates how US immigration restriction had diplomatic and humanitarian consequences. For European Jewish refugees, the strictness of US immigration law and the recalcitrance of US diplomatic insularity made the escape from Nazism problematic.

The Second World War seemingly revised one of the original totems of US immigration restriction law, Chinese exclusion, which dated back to the early 1880s. Chapter 7 discusses how the military and diplomatic contexts of the Second World War led to the repeal of Chinese immigration restriction. This easing of exclusion was quickly undermined when China fell to communism in 1949. Suddenly, all immigration from mainland China was diplomatically and politically impossible. Xenophobic reflexes toward the Chinese combined with Cold War fears motivated the US government to stop illegal Chinese immigration. What came under particular scrutiny was Chinese immigrants' use—often over many generations—of falsified documents that seemingly authenticated a Chinese person's legal ability to enter the United States ("paper sons"). Part of the US government's effort to stem illegal Chinese immigration was by instituting the Chinese Confession Program which, during the mid to late 1950s, incentivized Chinese immigrants to expose members of their community—often members of their families—who had entered the United States illegally to US immigration authorities. In the early years of the Cold War, traditional racism and budding anticommunism in US society combined to marginalize Chinese immigrants in ways that resembled the erstwhile exclusion era.

## INTRODUCTION

Chapter 8 details how the fall of South Vietnam in April 1975 confronted the United States with the prospect of resettling tens of thousands of Vietnamese on US soil. The US government quickly rose to the challenge and became a place of safe haven for those fleeing war zones in Southeast Asia. The initial wave of Vietnamese boatpeople welcomed to the United States included persons who tended to be the wealthier, better educated, and politically connected members of South Vietnam. For the US government, the resettling of Vietnamese boatpeople had the advantage of looking like a humanitarian response to Vietnamese fleeing socialism while it was also a convenient Cold War strategy to embarrass fledgling socialist states, as their citizens fled to the United States. This diplomatic snub to communist Vietnam became more complicated as more Vietnamese attempted to enter the United States during the late 1970s. Poorer, less educated, and less connected to the United States, these subsequent waves of boatpeople faced harrowing journeys as they attempted to flee Southeast Asia. Also, they received ambivalent, and at times hostile, responses from Americans upon their arrival on US shores.

Chapter 9 shows how reforms to US refugee law in the context of the Vietnamese boatlift crisis were quickly tested, and shown ineffectual, by the Mariel Boatlift of 1980. Waves of Cuban emigrants made their way to the United States in the wake of the Cuban Revolution of 1959. Cubans were welcomed and the US government took great strides to resettle these emigrants throughout the 1960s and 1970s. American motives for resettling Cuban emigrants were not purely altruistic; instead, they were driven by Cold War foreign policy interests, specifically to embarrass the socialist regime of Fidel Castro in Havana. But a knife can cut both ways, such as in 1980, when Castro attempted to steer the Cuban emigration issue to his advantage. Not all of his objectives were met, and some of them backfired in his face, but the Mariel Boatlift—during which well over 120,000 Cubans arrived on US shores in the span of five months—exposed the contradictions at the heart of Cold War-inspired refugee policies of the United States.

Chapter 10 shows how US involvement in Central America directly instigated waves of refugees during the 1980s and 1990s. The administration of Ronald Reagan gave a great deal of support to right-wing military regimes in El Salvador and Guatemala and was obsessively focused on supporting an insurgent army (*contras*) in its effort to overthrow the Sandinista regime of Nicaragua. The violence and turmoil of these civil wars took on a pernicious quality as local conflicts were construed as part of larger geopolitical struggles between the United States, the Soviet Union, and Cuba. Benefitting from American backing and largesse, El Salvador's and Guatemala's right-wing governments, as well as the contras in Nicaragua, brutalized their populations. Many Central Americans, in turn, fled to the United States to escape violent civil wars. But their arrival revealed a blindspot between US Cold War national security policy and refugee policy. To actively resettle Salvadorans and Guatemalans fleeing their home countries would represent a tacit acknowledgment that the United States was supporting harmful regimes. Consequently, Salvadorans and Guatemalans were routinely denied asylum in the United States. They were instead classified as "economic migrants," and debate ensued within US immigration courts—and eventually among Americans themselves—about whether or not Salvadorans and Guatemalans should be granted asylum. For many of those refugees, their applications for permanent residence would languish for years. By contrast, the great majority of Nicaraguan refugees—who Reagan officials could argue were fleeing the socialist Sandinista regime—were welcomed and resettled in the United States. For the Reagan administration, rolling out the welcome mat for Nicaraguan refugees reinforced the US government's official critique of the Sandinistas. Questions of entry and asylum were complicated further by the early 1990s, as spikes in gang violence in cities such as Los Angeles were connected to the children of Central American refugees. By the mid-1990s, a new fear of Central American gangs coalesced with a recurring American ambivalence toward immigrants that resulted in the creation of new laws strengthening the US government's deportation abilities.

America's post-Second World War economic predominance was supposed to be the bedrock upon which "Third World" nations developed to such a degree that the spread of communism would be abated. Additionally, such development would prevent the inundation of immigration to the United States. It was not to be. Chapter 11 shows how protracted economic recession during the 1970s and a comprehensive turn to neoliberal economic reform between the 1980s and 1990s actually created the forces that led to ever-increasing rates of immigration to the United States, specifically from Mexico. There was plenty of contradiction here, for the same macroeconomic forces that increased US economic penetration into Mexico, for example, NAFTA of 1994, also spurred Mexican immigration. US officials at the federal and state levels responded to sharply increasing flow of undocumented immigration with border sweeps, legislation that made life for undocumented immigrants legally and socially difficult, and the construction of physical barriers along the US-Mexico border. After 9/11, the fear of "illegal immigration" became synonymous with terrorist threats to the United States, as immigration became a national security issue. Far from resolving transnational problems associated with immigration, globalization has made immigration an intractable issue in US-Mexican relations.

This book will conclude by arguing that the United States is going through a new type of Cold War. In contrast to the ideological struggle against socialist nations that characterized the Cold War from 1947 to 1991, Americans are presently embroiled in an existential crisis among themselves over what immigration represents for the nation. When the United States refers to itself as a "nation of immigrants," is that a positive or negative appellation? Past political figures like John F. Kennedy used the phrase to extol the long history of immigration to the United States. More recently, in the 1990s and early 2000s, a "nation of immigrants" is a phrase of derision for the birthright movement, advocates of which have attempted (and thus far failed) to change US naturalization laws to make it more difficult for foreign-born persons to gain citizenship in the United States. Such efforts are not new. They fundamentally challenge the constitutional definitions of personhood, and they speak to the discomfort many Americans feel in regard to immigration in the present day. The Conclusion ends with a suggestion of how historical empathy may provide a route through the rhetoric and bombast over immigration and refugee politics. At the center of immigration and refugee flows are humans who are driven to cross borders for a whole range of reasons. Keeping humans as the focus of the study of immigration reminds us that any lasting resolution to the problems associated with the transnational movement of people must spurn simplistic, reactive prescriptions and instead utilize humanitarian and empathetic solutions.

# Notes

1 Lars Schoultz, "Central America and the Politicization of U.S. Immigration Policy," in *Western Hemisphere Immigration and United States Foreign Policy*, ed. Christopher Mitchell (University Park, PA: The Pennsylvania State University Press, 1992), 217–18. The author did state the refugee policy, by contrast, was directly shaped by foreign policy concerns.

2 Elliott Robert Barkan, Jon Gjerde, and Erika Lee, "Comment: Searching for Perspectives: Race, Law, and the Immigrant Experience [with Responses]," *Journal of American Ethnic History* 18, no. 4 (1999): 160.

3 Erika Lee, "The 'Yellow Peril' and Asian Exclusion in the Americas," *Pacific Historical Review* 76, no. 4 (2007): 540.

4 Joseph H. Carens, "Aliens and Citizens: The Case for Open Borders," *The Review of Politics* 49, no. 251 (1987): 252.

5 Fernando Riosmena and Douglas S. Massey, "Pathways to El Norte: Origins, Destinations, and Characteristics of Mexican Migrants to the United States," *International Migration Review* 46, no. 1 (2012): 21.

6 Mathew Coleman and Austin Kocher, "Detention, Deportation, Devolution and Immigrant Incapacitation in the US, Post 9/11," *The Geographical Journal* 177, no. 3 (2011): 229.

7 Ian Davies, "Latino Immigration and Social Change in the United States: Toward an Ethical Immigration Policy," *Journal of Business Ethics* 88 (2009): 379; Karen Manges-Douglas and Rogelio Sáenz, "The Criminalization of

Immigrants & the Immigration-Industrial Complex," *Daedalus* 142, no. 3, Immigration & the Future of America (Summer 2013): 200.

8. Davies, "Latino Immigration and Social Change in the United States," 379; Timothy Dunn, *The Militarization of the US-Mexico Border, 1978–1992: Low Intensity conflict Doctrine Comes Home* (Austin, TX: University of Texas Press, 1996), 158–60, 164.

9. Kitty Calavita, "U.S. Immigration Policy: Contradictions and Projections for the Future," *Indiana Journal of Global Legal Studies* 2, no. 1 (1994): 143.

10. S. Deborah Kang, *The INS on the Line: Making Immigration Law on the US-Mexico Border, 1917–1954* (Oxford: Oxford University Press, 2017), 5.

11. Ibid.

12. Calavita, "U.S. Immigration Policy," 146.

13. David Cook-Martín and David Fitzgerald, "Liberalism and the Limits of Inclusion: Race and Immigration Law in the Americas, 1850–2000," *The Journal of Interdisciplinary History* 41, no. 1 (2010): 8.

14. Ibid., 8–9.

15. John A. Scanlan, "A View from the United States—Social, Economic, and Legal Change, the Persistence of the State, and Immigration Policy in the Coming Century," *Indiana Journal of Global Legal Studies* 2, no. 1 (1994): 81; Aristide Zolberg, "Changing Sovereignty Games and International Migration," *Indiana Journal of Global Legal Studies* 2, no. 1 (1994): 161; Gabriela A. Gallegos, "Border Matters: Redefining the National Interest in U.S.-Mexico Immigration and Trade Policy," *California Law Review* 92, no. 6 (2004): 1742; Eileen P. Scully, "The United States and International Affairs 1789–1919," in *The Cambridge History of Law in America*, 3 vols, ed. Michael Grossberg and Christopher Tomlins (Cambridge: Cambridge University Press, 2008), 608; Cristina Rodriguez, "Immigration, Civil Rights & the Evolution of the People," *Daedalus* 142, no. 3 (Summer 2013): 230; Juliet Stumpf, "The Crimmigration Crisis: Immigrants, Crime, and Sovereign Power," *American University Law Review* 56, no. 2 (2006): 377, 413.

16. Zolberg, "Changing Sovereignty Games," 155–6.

17. Mae M. Ngai, "No Human Being Is Illegal," *Women's Studies Quarterly* 34, no. 3/4 (2006): 293.

18. Scanlan, "A View from the United States," 81; Zolberg, "Changing Sovereignty Games," 161; Scully, "The United States and International Affairs," 630.

19. Hugh Liebert and Lee Robinson, "Disorder at the Border? Immigration and Homeland Security," in *Thinking beyond boundaries: Transnational Challenges to U.S. Foreign Policy*, ed. Hugh Liebert, et al. (Baltimore, MD: Johns Hopkins University Press, 2015), 44–5.

20. Gary Gerstle, *American Crucible: Race and Nation in the Twentieth Century* (Princeton, NJ: Princeton University Press, 2001), 5, 8–9.

21. Liebert and Robinson, "Disorder at the Border?," 45.

22. Dorothee Schneider, "'I Know All about Emma Lazarus': Nationalism and Its Contradictions in Congressional Rhetoric of Immigration Restriction," *Cultural Anthropology* 13, no. 1 (1998): 85.

23  Mae M. Ngai, "The Civil Rights Origins of Illegal Immigration," *International Labor and Working-Class History*, no. 78 (2010): 95–6; also refer to Ngai, "No Human Being is Illegal."
24  Rodriguez, "Immigration, Civil Rights and the Evolution of the People," 234.
25  Yukari Takai, "Asian Migrants, Exclusionary Laws, and Transborder Migration in North America, 1880–1940," *OAH Magazine of History* 23, no. 4 (2009): 39; Patrick Ettinger, "'We Sometimes Wonder What They Will Spring on Us Next': Immigrants and Border Enforcement in the American West, 1882–1930," *Western Historical Quarterly* 37, no. 2 (2006): 161.
26  Cf., Ngai, "No Human Being is Illegal"; Benjamin C. Montoya, *Risking Immeasurable Harm: Immigration Restriction and U.S.-Mexican Diplomatic Relations, 1924–1932* (Lincoln, NE: University of Nebraska Press, 2020).
27  Luis F. B. Plascencia, "The 'Undocumented' Mexican Migrant Question: Re-Examining the Framing of Law and Illegalization in the United States," *Urban Anthropology and Studies of Cultural Systems and World Economic Development* 38, no. 2/3/4 (2009): 376, 380, 383–4, 391–3.
28  Ibid., 406–7; Michael Jones-Correa and Els De Graauw, "The Illegality Trap: The Politics of Immigration & the Lens of Illegality," *Daedalus* 142, no. 3 (2013): 186.
29  Plascencia, "The 'Undocumented' Mexican Migrant Question," 408; Douglas S. Massey and Fernando Riosmena, "Undocumented Migration from Latin America in an Era of Rising U.S. Enforcement," *The Annals of the American Academy of Political and Social Science* 630 (2010): 296–9, 319; Riosmena and Massey, "Pathways to El Norte," 18–19.
30  Nicholas Degenova, "Migrant Illegality and Deportability in Everyday Life," *Annual Review of Anthropology* 31, no. 1 (2002): 424–5 (437).
31  Degenova, "Migrant Illegality and Deportability in Everyday Life," 425; Coleman and Kocher, "Detention, Deportation, Devolution and Immigrant Incapacitation in the US," 229.
32  Degenova, "Migrant Illegality and Deportability in Everyday Life," 429.
33  Ibid., 438–40, emphasis mine.
34  Calavita, "U.S. Immigration Policy," 151; Scanlan, "A View from the United States," 107; Jones-Correa and De Graauw, "The Illegality Trap," 188, 191.
35  Degenova, "Migrant Illegality and Deportability in Everyday Life," 425.
36  Ibid., 422.
37  Rodriguez, "Immigration, Civil Rights and the Evolution of the People," 229.
38  Joy M. Purcell, "A Right to Leave, but Nowhere to Go: Reconciling an Emigrant's Right to Leave with the Sovereign's Right to Exclude," *The University of Miami Inter-American Law Review* 39, no. 1 (2007): 182, 184.
39  Ibid., 178.
40  Zolberg, "Changing Sovereignty Games," 157.
41  Calavita, "U.S. Immigration Policy," 147–8.
42  Purcell, "A Right to Leave, but Nowhere to Go," 189–92.
43  Charles Keely and Sharon S. Russell, "Responses of Industrial Countries to Asylum Seekers," *Journal of International Affairs* 47, no. 2 (1994): 406–7.

44  Eytan Meyers, "The Causes of Convergence in Western Immigration Control," *Review of International Studies* 28, no. 1 (2002): 138.
45  Jennifer Gordon, "People Are Not Bananas: How Immigration Differs from Trade," *Northwestern University Law Review* 104, no. 3 (2010): 1110–11; Gallegos, "Border Matters," 1732, 1735.
46  Gordon, "People Are Not Bananas," 1110–11, 1131–8.
47  Ibid., 1117n28.
48  Ibid., 1113, 1116–17; Manges-Douglas and Sáenz, "The Criminalization of Immigrants & the Immigration-Industrial Complex," 202.
49  Bayless Manning, "The Congress, The Executive and Intermestic Affairs: Three Proposals," *Foreign Affairs* 55, no. 309 (1977): 307–8.
50  Ibid., 309; Ryan J. Barilleaux, "The President, 'Intermestic' Issues, and the Risks of Policy Leadership," *Presidential Studies Quarterly* 15, no. 4, Perspectives on the Presidency (Fall, 1985): 754.
51  Calavita, "U.S. Immigration Policy," 145–6, 150; Scanlan, "A View from the United States," 87.
52  Niall Kishtainy, *A Little History of Economics* (New Haven, CT: Yale University Press, 2017), 111.
53  Marc R. Rosenblum, "Moving Beyond the Policy of No Policy: Emigration from Mexico and Central America," *Latin American Politics and Society* 46, no. 4 (2004): 98–9.
54  Ibid., 98–100, 104.
55  Peter Knight, "Empathy: Concept, Confusion and Consequences in a National Curriculum," *Oxford Review of Education* 15, no. 1 (1989): 41–53.
56  Barkan, et al., "Comment: Searching for Perspectives," 145.
57  John Higham, *Strangers in the Land: Patterns of American Nativism, 1860–1925* (New York: Atheneum, 1970 [1955]), 5.
58  Ibid., 5–6.
59  Ibid., 6.
60  Ibid., 85–6, 266, 291.
61  Roger Daniels, "Immigration since World War II: The Need for a New Paradigm," *Polish American Studies* 55, no. 1 (Spring, 1998): 41.
62  Barkan, et al., "Comment: Searching for Perspectives," 141–5.

# PART I

# Laws and Systems

# 1

# A Synthesis of US Juridical Immigration Law, 1780s–2010s

This book will give a great deal of attention to how the federal government has formulated past immigration policy. Chapter 2 will provide an analysis of the key acts of the legislative branch that shaped US immigration policy. Chapter 3, in part, will discuss how the executive branch expedited the resettlement of refugees on US soil through the use of parole authority between the 1950s and the 1970s. The current chapter will show how the third branch of government, the judiciary, played a key role in determining how immigrant noncitizens were subjected to American law. In some eras of American history, the Supreme Court of the United States (SCOTUS) afforded the protections of due process to noncitizens, while in other eras it eroded the same protections. Paralleling Foucauldian notions of how the state creates its own raison d'être by disciplining aberrant citizens, the "regulation imposed by power is at the same time the law of construction of operation," between the early nineteenth century and the early twenty-first century the SCOTUS participated in a simultaneous process of interpreting and reinterpreting, framing and re-framing, US power over immigrants.[1] Additionally, the SCOTUS played a central role in balancing the interests of the federal government and myriad state governments regarding immigration policy. This balancing act was strongly influenced by justices' perceptions of whether immigration laws complemented or undercut US foreign policy interests. In short, an understanding of how US foreign policy and US immigration policy are interlinked is not complete until we consider the history of the judiciary's role in the formulation of immigration law and the definition of immigrants.

Two essential questions are at the center of US juridical law on immigration. First, which political entities, the federal government or state governments, have the ultimate authority to regulate immigration? And second, even when that balance between the federal government and the states is established, what criteria determine whether that balance is appropriate? Asked another way, can states have a part in regulating the movement of people and the settling of noncitizens, or is immigration of such importance that it is placed on par with national security interests, thereby falling squarely under the jurisdiction of the federal government? Interestingly, foreign policy considerations often informed the debate over these questions, and the answers arrived at were often influenced by changing perceptions of immigrants over time.[2]

The prospect of managing the inflow of people predates the founding of the United States by more than a century. Far from being a place of refuge for the displaced, nearly from the beginning of the British North American colonies, immigration was restricted by colonial assemblies. Mercantilist thought determined how colonial assemblies regulated the inflow of people just as it shaped political and economic beliefs of the seventeenth century. Population equaled wealth for colonial leaders. As such, indigent arrivees were considered burdensome and undesirable. Not only did they not bring wealth, but they also represented a net loss for the community in the form of poor relief. The more capital that was expended paying for the poor, the prevailing thought went, left less capital for maintaining community security and prosperity. Additionally, colonial immigration laws restricted the entry of criminals. The distinction between the poor and the criminal was often quite thin for colonial leaders, who routinely referred to indigent and criminal persons as "internal foreigners." Religious prejudice, often in the form of curbs on emigration by Catholics, was a third type of prejudice that accompanied the class and civic prejudices at the very root of American immigration restriction throughout the colonial period.[3]

Ratification of the US Constitution in the late 1780s significantly shifted local communities' abilities to both define a person—poor, criminal, and foreign—and to regulate the movement of that person. Under this new social contract, the category of US citizenship would determine who belonged to the larger community. Additionally, the ways in which the framers of government redefined the acquisition of citizenship was significant for later immigration laws. Breaking with the prevailing English theory of perpetual citizenship in which a citizen was defined as a lifelong subject of the British crown, US Constitution writers formulated a new form of voluntary citizenship, which perfectly accorded with the casting off their Englishness.[4]

Even as the newly constituted states now subscribed to a federally constituted notion of citizenship, it was a debate over the constitutionality of the 1798 Alien Act that began a centuries-long contest between the states and the federal government over immigration policy. At the time, legal historian Patrick Charles shows, the root of the debate was not whether it was constitutional or not to exclude or deport foreigners; nor did the contention have to do with whether foreigners could be excluded from the privileges and immunities of federal or state citizenship. Instead, the fundamental question at the time was who had the right to expel foreigners, the states or the central government? A consensus emerged claiming *foreign policy preemption*, which meant that any state regulations on immigration that seemed to conflict with the federal government's foreign policy objectives could be overruled (preempted). Otherwise, the states could "undermine the Constitution itself" if they had the ability to regulate immigration on par with their customary practices.[5]

There was something audacious to these legal debates of the late 1790s. The new federal government was telling the states that their customary powers to regulate immigration were now largely circumscribed. If the goal of colonial and state immigration laws was to manage the inflow of undesirable foreigners into the community, the federal government's foray into immigration law was driven by its diplomatic relations with foreign nations. The federal government's show of political territorialism was less brazen, however, when it is considered that US officials still viewed immigration through a transactional, mercantilist lens. Control over immigration was considered analogous to the federal government's control over commerce with foreign nations. But foreign affairs preemption was not a complete loss for states. There was a "statutory void" in which states could still, if only to a certain degree, restrict the movement of people in their territorial jurisdictions.[6] Nor was foreign affairs preemption a complete and categorical victory for the federal government.

Principles are one thing; practical application is another. The federal government of the United States was a "small, unassuming" body for most of the first half of the nineteenth century; it had to rely on state lawmakers, officials, and courts to regulate immigration. The federal government passed no legislation during the antebellum years to comprehensively restrict immigration. There were several reasons why. First, the US Constitution did not explicitly grant the federal government the authority to regulate immigration. The only statement on immigration came from Article 1, Section 9, which stated that Congress could not stop the importation of slaves until 1808. Second, the matter of states' rights versus federal power had not been determined. Americans disagreed among themselves about which political entity was the final arbiter of American sovereignty vis-à-vis the inflow of immigrants—states or the federal government—as the issue of slavery in the western territories gained momentum between 1820 and 1860. Related to this growing conflict was the politics of the Jackson era, during which the regulatory power constituted by a system of checks and balances was being challenged by a wave of democratic populism that decried the flexing of the central government's power. Third, was the challenge of big business, which regularly used the courts to challenge immigration restriction laws. Combined with the statutory void mentioned earlier, the administrative void left by the federal government afforded state governments space to continue some version of their customary control over immigration policy.[7]

The states inherited the tradition of the English poor laws from the colonial period, which made the relief of the poor the responsibility of the local community where they were legally settled. These laws gave localities various powers to prevent the settlement of persons who might later require support and to remove them to a place where they were legally settled. After the turn of the nineteenth century, American officials were especially angered by the widely shared belief, itself based on credible evidence from American consuls in Europe, that European governments were responsible for "dumping" poorer citizens in the United States. Consequently, as the nineteenth century evolved there were growing efforts by local and state authorities to regulate immigration.[8]

It fell to the US Supreme Court to systemize immigration restriction during the antebellum era. In 1837, in *New York v. Miln*, the state of New York sought to recover debt accrued from settling immigrants. The debate languished for several years until 1837, by which time a new chief justice, Roger Taney (later of Dred Scott notoriety), presided over the Supreme Court. Taney's court ruled 6:1 in favor of the constitutionality of New York's ability to collect on debts, on the grounds that it was "not a regulation of commerce, but of police; and that being so considered, it was passed in the exercise of a power which rightfully belonged to the states." The *Miln* decision provided the most comprehensive statement of constitutional doctrine in immigration law up to that time, and determined the shape of immigration policy until after the Civil War. Taney's court endorsed the establishment of a policy of selective immigration restriction, a policy that could be facilitated at the state level. But by upholding state regulation and grounding it on the powers reserved to them under the Tenth Amendment, the Supreme Court "foreclosed" the implementation of a more effective solution to the major problem of immigration in the name of a higher political objective. In this sense we can see how the growing tension between state and federal power shaped the tension between selective and numerical immigration restriction. Consequently, state regulations enforcing selective immigration restriction abounded, belying the common historical belief that the United States was laissez-faire about immigration until the 1880s. States such as New Jersey, New York, Massachusetts, and Maine enacted head taxes (ranging from $1 to $10) and bonds on immigrants—lunatics, aged and infirm, paupers—who were likely to become public burdens.[9]

It was a strange irony during the antebellum era that just as US jurisprudence was circumscribing the federal government's effort to regulate immigration comprehensively, a massive influx of immigrants entered the United States. In 1846, for example, less than 155,000 immigrants entered the country; in 1854 the number soared to almost 415,000. The 1850 census showed that 15 percent of the US population was foreign-born; the next census in 1860 showed that the proportion had increased to 22 percent. Not by coincidence, a nativist movement emerged in the 1850s that tapped into a growing social prejudice toward newcomers. By the middle part of the decade, the Know-Nothings had won many victories in municipal, state, and federal elections. Amazingly, however, within this growing context of anti-immigrant sentiment no comprehensive immigration restriction regime was established. The question is, why? One part of the answer lay in the growing sectional debate over states' rights and federal power. The *Miln* decision represented a victory for states' rights in the realm of immigration policy. Another part of the answer lay in the maturation of US capitalism by the 1850s. Economic transformations that had been forming since the end of the War of 1812 "crystallized" into a more advanced form of American capitalism. What historian Alfred Chandler would call a "managerial revolution" was taking place in the United States, accelerated by the influx of cheap labor. Leading businesses in railroads, telegraphy, and shipping, not to mention the industrialization of factory work, demanded a constant supply of cheap labor to develop the nation's infrastructure. By the 1850s, lobbyists from all of these business interests were pressuring lawmakers to keep the gates open to immigrants. Western states also had a high demand for immigrants, and these governments established immigration recruiting boards along the eastern seaboard and abroad to entice immigrants to the West.[10]

Within this shifting context, the Supreme Court moved away from the established precedent of state-led selective immigration restriction. Considering the growing influence of business on debates over immigration, it made sense that two challenges to the *Miln* decision of 1837 came from the shipping industry. In the late 1840s business leaders challenged New York and Massachusetts state laws that required shippers to pay health fees and head taxes for disembarking immigrants. In February 1849, the Supreme Court ruled 5:4 on what became known as the "Passenger Cases." This decision stated that the state laws interfered with immigration and thereby infringed upon federal authority in the sphere of interstate and international commerce. The Passenger Cases decision was a clear move away from states' rights-led immigration regulation. But it was an incomplete shift. While declaring head taxes unconstitutional, the Supreme Court did sustain the exercise of police power to enact financial measures designed to alleviate burdens accompanying the entry of pauper immigrants. The only difference was that states were prohibited from excluding outright those who were considered undesirable immigrants or from doing so indirectly through taxation.[11]

US immigration restriction policy remained ambiguous for the remainder of the antebellum period. Despite nativist pressure during the 1850s, America's gates were kept open. This state of affairs was encouraged by two strange bedfellows: business-minded northerners, whose industry became increasingly dependent on constant flows of cheap labor, and states'-rights southerners who resisted any notion of federal encroachment upon states' rights.[12] Yet just as the Civil War settled the sectional debate over states' rights and federal power, it also resolved the ambiguity regarding state and federal power over immigration restriction.

The 1860s witnessed a highwater mark of federal government encouragement of immigration. The demand for immigration multiplied massively between 1861 and 1865, as the American Civil War drew thousands of immigrants and turned away many thousands more from America's shores. American industry, much of it in the north and most of it inclined toward the Republican Party, pressured the Lincoln administration to encourage the inflow of cheap, tractable labor that could meet the high demand of wartime manufacturing. The Homestead Act of 1862 and the Act to Encourage Immigration of 1864 were noteworthy wartime measures. The former promised 160 acres of land to any immigrants committed to working federal western lands for at least five years. The latter established that pre-migration contracts prevented immigrants from entering the army. This law created the Federal Bureau of Immigration (FBI), which established immigration-recruitment agencies throughout Europe. While the 1864 act was rescinded four years later, it led to a proliferation of private agencies for labor recruitment in foreign countries. Some of these private agencies had direct links to the FBI and even shared the same building in Washington, DC. The Lincoln administration's recruitment efforts were successful: immigration for 1861 to 1862 reached only 89,000; for 1863 to 1865 numbers increased to 200,000 per annum.[13]

A crucial turning point in immigration law occurred in 1875 when the Supreme Court handed down *Chy Lung v. Freeman* and *Henderson v. Mayor of City of New York*, both of which—decided by the court on the same day—established that immigration policy was the sole legal domain of the federal Congress and not state legislatures. *Chy Lung* struck down a California statute regulating Chinese immigration. *Henderson* cited legal precedents arguing that transatlantic transportation of travelers or immigrants was a question of commerce and therefore was within the province of the federal government. By granting the federal government primacy over state governments in immigration policy, both decisions not only *seemed* to resolve a fifty-year long legal debate over immigration jurisprudence, but they also laid the foundation for restrictive legislation passed during the next half-century.[14]

The shifting nature of citizenship and naturalization paralleled the contentious debate between federal power and states' rights over immigration regulation during the early years of the republic. While the US Constitution was largely silent on which political entity should regulate immigration—the federal government or the states—it was explicit about citizenship and naturalization requirements. According to the 1790 naturalization law, the nation's first, only a "free white person" who had resided in the nation for two years could become a citizen. The residency requirement was raised to five years in 1795. Three years later, the same series of laws that precipitated the idea of foreign affairs preemption regarding federal regulation of immigration also raised the residency requirement for citizenship to fourteen years (the late 1790s witnessed the first of many nativist outbursts toward immigrants throughout US history). That revised requirement was made less punitive when in 1801 it was returned to the five-year criterion.[15]

The association of whiteness and citizenship starkly clarified the distinction between insiders and outsiders in the American polity. Yet an "apprehension" developed between national citizenship and national territory: even if it was clear who could and could not become an American citizen, it was unclear which political entity could exclude persons unfit to become citizens.[16] This apprehensive dynamic was at the root of the *Miln* and *Passenger* cases. It was complicated further by the expansion of national citizenship after the Civil War when, in 1868, Congress included the principle of *jus soli* (birthright citizenship) into the Fourteenth Amendment. Thereafter, a person's citizenship was attributable to one's birth in the nation and not to their whiteness. Crucially, the same amendment granted due process protections to all "persons" regardless of citizenship status.[17] National citizenship and national territory were now intertwined. This intertwining gave greater impetus to regulate the borders of the nation. Foreigners were now more closely associated with foreign lands. Yet this new clarity also came with a new apprehension: the birth of a person on American soil made them a US citizen, meaning the children of noncitizens would have all the rights attributed to any other US citizen, even if their non-naturalized, foreign-born immigrant parents did not. And even for noncitizens, the Fourteenth Amendment theoretically offered them constitutional protections by the right of their personhood.

Raising a massive army, financing a war, putting down a rebellion, creating a national welfare educational agency (Freedman's Bureau), and passing sweeping legislation to constitute a new, post-slavery order in the United States, the federal government of the United States, for which such terms as "administration" and "bureaucracy" were once foreign words, vastly expanded its powers during the 1860s and 1870s. The national judiciary, in particular, would emerge from the post-Civil War era with an important position in determining the contours of America's "new birth of freedom." Within that role, the "elites of the bench and bar" would help define the federal government's preeminent power over immigration regulation (as discussed earlier) but would also clarify a new distinction between citizen and foreigner.[18]

In fact, Americans were uncomfortable with the constitutional right that anyone born on US soil was a citizen. As discussed in Chapter 7, anti-Chinese agitation, which became apparent in California as early as the 1850s, took on national proportions during the early 1870s, just a few years after the ratification of the Fourteenth Amendment. This nativist prejudice culminated with the passage of the Chinese Exclusion Act in 1882.

It fell to the SCOTUS to enforce the nativist action by the legislative branch. In the process, the SCOTUS would be both enforcer and capitulator. In 1889, in *Chae Chan Ping v. United States*, the SCOTUS argued that a prime feature of a nation's jurisdiction is control over its territory, and control of national territory is the sine qua non of a country's sovereignty. Therefore, the court concluded, the US government had the right to prevent Chinese from immigrating to the United States. Justice Stephen Field likened the ability to exclude immigrants to the need to maintain national security:

> To preserve its independence, and give security against foreign aggression and encroachment, is the highest duty of every nation, and to attain these ends nearly all other considerations are to be subordinated. It matters not in what form such aggression and encroachment come, whether from the foreign nation acting in its national character *or from the vast hordes of its people crowding in upon us.*[19]

A few years later, a Japanese immigrant appeared in front of the SCOTUS to appeal an immigration court's decision to bar her from entering the United States by alleging that she would become a public charge. The plaintiff argued that the due process clause of the Fourteenth Amendment allowed her to enter the United States. The SCOTUS countered by stating that the ability to regulate immigration was a right embedded in the national sovereignty of the United States; therefore, the immigrant's desire to appeal her exclusion was legally impossible.[20] A year later, the court ruled in *Fong Yue Ting v. United States* that the federal government's power to regulate immigration was "immune from judicial review."[21]

Between the late 1880s and the early 1890s, then, sovereignty replaced constitutionality as the legal foundation upon which immigration was regulated. The nation's inherent need to protect itself superseded any appeals to due process. These years also witnessed a transition from liberal universalism to nationalist particularism as demonstrated by the formulation of the *plenary power doctrine*, in which the SCOTUS handed all authority over immigration policy to the other two branches of the federal government. Executive and legislative decisions on immigration would now be free from judicial review, the due process protections offered by the Constitution were "all but void" regarding immigration law, and immigration policy was "put into the same box" as foreign affairs.[22] Under plenary power, constitutional law scholar William Forbath states, "individuals had no rights and governmental power no limits that the courts were bound to recognize and enforce."[23]

The wedding of foreign affairs preemption of the 1790s and plenary power doctrine of the 1890s still left some knotty questions, however. First, which of the two branches of the federal government—the executive or the legislative—had primary control over immigration policy? And second, where were the state governments in all of this?

Attempts to answer the first question led to more confusion than certainty. At times, such as in *Knauff v. Shaughnessy* (1950), the SCOTUS declared that the executive branch had "inherent" authority to regulate immigration as part of its larger control over foreign affairs. At other times, such as in *Kleindienst v. Mandel* (1972), the court declared that immigration regulation falls under the complete control of the legislative branch.[24] Much of this juridical vacillation had to do with larger contexts, such as the executive branch's use of parole authority to respond to the massive, post-Second World War need to resettle millions of displaced people. In the 1950s, the executive branch enjoyed untrammeled use of this power; by the 1970s, however, in the wake of the Hart-Celler Act, Congress was attempting to reclaim a degree of control over refugee and immigration policy (see Chapter 2 for a more extensive discussion of this dynamic).

The second question was even harder to answer. While it may have been clear that foreign affairs preemption disallowed states from blocking the entrance of immigrants into the national territory of the United States, what was less clear was what powers states had over immigrants residing within their jurisdictions. States had been able to reserve a degree of influence over national immigration policy through their use of police powers since the *Miln* decision of 1837. Police powers is a category of laws that pertains to the health and safety of citizens of a state. Additionally, states could wield "alienage" laws to deny public benefits to immigrants, usually under the guise of protecting the citizens and resources of the local polity. Described as an "untidy body of laws," alienage laws defined the rights and obligations of noncitizens within the United States. Yet the problem remained: to what degree could the states restrict and exclude immigrants without running afoul of federal foreign affairs preemption?[25]

In 1915, for example, the SCOTUS blocked a state employment law that required a majority of the jobs in most industries be given to native-born Americans. The SCOTUS ruled in *Truax v. Raich* that such a law denied noncitizens "the opportunity of earning a livelihood," which in the justices' eyes was "tantamount" to blocking the entrance of immigrants into US society. The state law seeped into the federal government's preemption ability over state laws because it seemed to encroach upon the former's conduct of foreign affairs.[26] By contrast, in 1948, the SCOTUS let stand a state law that disallowed noncitizens—primarily Japanese—from owning land. Since such a law was considered the exercise of a state's police power that did not interfere with the foreign affairs primacy of the federal government; therefore, preemption was not applied in *Oyama v. California*.[27]

The distinction between state police powers and foreign affairs preemption was not just subject to the scrutiny of justices on the bench but was also shaped by geopolitical contexts. In 1939, the state of Pennsylvania passed the Alien Registration Act. There was an anti-immigrant character to the state law that was disturbingly analogous to anti-Jewish actions conducted by the Nazis during the 1930s (see Chapter 6). Under the Pennsylvania law, noncitizens had to register once a year with state authorities; pay an annual registration fee, carry an alien identification card at all times, show that card to register a car or to obtain a driver's license, and produce the card whenever a police officer demanded it. The SCOTUS struck down the state law in *Hines v. Davidowitz* (1942), arguing that it represented an encroachment upon the federal government's power over immigration policy. Additionally, Justice Hugo Black spoke for the court when he emphasized the importance of a uniform foreign policy by stating that federal power over immigration required one voice "for national purposes, embracing our relations with foreign nations, we are but one people, one nation, one power."[28] The SCOTUS elaborated further by discussing the interplay between the federal government, foreign affairs, and state laws regulating immigration.

> Legal imposition of distinct, unusual and extraordinary burdens and obligations upon aliens—such as subjecting them alone, though perfectly law-abiding, to indiscriminate and repeated interception and interrogation by public officials—thus bears an inseparable relationship to the welfare and tranquility of all the states, and not merely to the welfare and tranquility of one. *Laws imposing such burdens . . . provoke questions in the field of international affairs.*[29]

The SCOTUS continued to boldly preserve the federal government's foreign affairs preemption against the states in the latter half of the twentieth century. In striking down state laws that denied welfare benefits to resident aliens, *Graham v. Richardson* (1971), the court argued that state governments were violating the Equal Protection Clause of the Fourteenth Amendment and were encroaching upon the federal government's control over immigration.[30] Five years later, the SCOTUS seemed to take a direct shot at the very principle of state alienage laws when it decided in *Mathews v. Diaz* (1976) that only the federal government, not the states, can deny welfare benefits to noncitizens. If benefits can be construed as magnets for immigrants to the United States, the court asked, then what kind of distinction is there between alienage laws (of the states) and immigration laws (of the federal government)? The justices concluded that there was no distinction. Interestingly, this case showed how foreign affairs preemption was used to justify the federal government's monopoly over the denial of public benefits to immigrants. The same power that gave Washington, DC, control over immigration policy gave it the exclusive ability to deny benefits to immigrants. The divergence between the liberal universalism of the nation's founding and the nationalist particularism of the late twentieth century was on brazen display when the court wrote in the *Mathews* decision that "Congress regularly makes rules that would be unacceptable if applied to citizens."[31]

Ironically, as the federal government was clamping down on state alienage laws, it was preserving space for state police powers. The same year the SCOTUS handed down the *Mathews* decision, it upheld states' use of police powers to regulate immigration in *DeCanas v. Bica* (1976). The case considered whether the state of California could prohibit and punish employers for hiring unlawfully present aliens. The court decided it could, arguing that far from conflicting with federal immigration policy, the state law actually complemented it. The court unanimously declared that the California statute reflected "Congress's intention to bar from employment all aliens except those possessing a grant of permission to work in this country."[32] Essentially, the court argued that states had the authority to exercise these powers, even if they touched on federal immigration policy.[33] The *DeCanas* decision served as a "cornerstone" for subsequent state efforts to amplify their ability to restrict immigration.[34]

Aside from laying the groundwork for the employer sanctions that were written into the IRCA of 1986 (see Chapter 2), the *DeCanas* ruling made a key distinction between the types of aliens states could legislate against. This distinction would simultaneously save states from running afoul of federal preemption power and also create a judicialized form of illegal immigration. First, the 1976 decision established that if aliens were lawfully present in a state then their presence fell under the foreign affairs preemption of the federal government, but if aliens were not lawfully present, then states could pass laws against them. In such a scenario state police powers paralleled federal immigration law, thereby precluding the need for foreign affairs preemption. *DeCanas* laid another foundation of sorts by not only reviving arguments for the participation of states in federal immigration restriction but also by criminalizing undocumented immigration to the United States. Before the 1970s, entering the United States unlawfully was considered a civil offense; during the last decades of the twentieth century and into the twenty-first century, such an action became a criminal offense.[35]

The coupling of state alienage laws with federal immigration law continued during the 1980s as local criminal, employment, and welfare law combined with federal powers to create a formidable barrier to immigrate to the United States. Once in conflict, foreign affairs preemption now seemed married to state regulations.[36] The nuptials were still awkward, however, as demonstrated by *Plyler v. Doe*. In this 1982 decision, the SCOTUS struck down a Texas law that would have banned undocumented children from attending public schools without their families (often undocumented immigrant parents) reimbursing the state for the expense of their children's education. The court's decision, which was decided along the thinnest of margins (five justices for and four against), argued that the state law undermined noncitizen children's chances of meaningfully contributing to US society and denied them equal opportunities even though they had not made the choice to enter the United States illegally. *Plyler* was not a complete loss for state alienage law, however, for the SCOTUS also argued that states did have some legitimate authority to restrict illegal aliens, as long as the use of that regulatory power did not deny equal protection to those aliens. Finally, *Plyler* left a backdoor open for state alienage laws when it asserted that unauthorized aliens, by voluntarily choosing to enter the United States illegally, put themselves into a class of persons for whom equal protections could not be guaranteed.[37]

The jealous guarding of equal protection jurisprudence of the SCOTUS during the 1970s gave way to an awkward aligning of federal plenary power and state alienage laws during the 1980s. By the mid-1990s, with the Personal Responsibility and Work Opportunity Reconciliation Act (PRWORA), states and the federal government had settled their differences and walked arm-in-arm to jointly restrict immigration and criminalize the noncitizen. Passed among a raft of other congressional measures that sought to criminalize the act of undocumented migration and make it easier for the federal government to deport undocumented immigrants (see Chapter 2), the PRWORA devolved to the states the ability to grant or deny benefits to immigrants. This 1996 law did not just overturn the juridical precedent established by *Graham v. Richardson* and *Mathews v. Diaz* during the 1970s, but it also demonstrated how the federal government now worried less about foreign affairs preemption and instead worked to incorporate state powers and alienage laws to restrict immigration to the United States.[38]

In a way, the states' rights versus federal power over immigration policy had gone full circle by the 1990s. An open-ended debate for much of the nineteenth century, the SCOTUS decided by 1875 that the federal government had absolute authority over immigration policy. That plenary power was reinforced during the remainder of the nineteenth century when the judicial branch buttressed immigration regulation with the rights of national sovereignty. The SCOTUS often utilized foreign affairs preemption to deflect oblique and indirect state challenges to plenary power during much of the twentieth century. By the 1980s, however, the court seemed to be surrendering a degree of federal power over immigration policy, or at the very least allowing space for the states to also regulate and enforce the movement of noncitizens in US society. During the 1990s, that juridical space coincided with frustration from leaders of immigrant-receiving states such as California and Florida, the former of which responded with Prop 187 (see Chapter 2). In sum, the renewed role of the states in immigration regulation was not only influenced by state demands for more robust federal action to stem immigration, but it was also attributable to an *invitation* from the federal government to the states to work together to block immigration and to make life as hard as possible for noncitizens in the United States. Long considered analogous to foreign policy, federal immigration law was now *reimagined* and *domesticated* to simultaneously focus on foreign peoples (noncitizens on US soil) and foreign nations (points of origins for immigrants).[39]

And yet, just as suddenly as this shotgun wedding took place, the honeymoon came to an end. In 2007, the SCOTUS "summoned up the traditional vision of immigration law as foreign policy" when it struck down a city ordinance from Hazleton, Pennsylvania, that sought to withhold business licenses from local employers who hired undocumented workers.[40] As often happens, however, the two lovers vacillated in their professed affection and indifference to one another. For just as the SCOTUS seemed to foreclose the space allowed to state policies regarding immigration, in 2008 it passed down two separate decisions that argued that the historical police powers of states should not be superseded by the federal government and that both entities could concurrently regulate immigration.[41]

A crescendo moment in this conflicted, juridical relationship occurred in 2010 when Arizona passed SB 1070, which sought to reduce immigration to and the presence of noncitizens in the state through enhanced policing measures—such as the warrantless arrest of those suspected of being noncitizens—and restrictions on the hiring of undocumented workers. It became immediately apparent that such state-level proposals could trod upon the federal government's plenary power over immigration policy.[42] Yet there was debate over whether the law simply represented an example of state police power. Could law enforcement check the immigration status of anyone suspected of unlawful presence in the state? The SCOTUS said yes, as long as the verification process was not abused. Could the state adopt discriminatory legislation as a way to deter undocumented immigration? Again, the court said yes, as long as such designs aligned with federal policies.[43]

In the end, however, Arizona lawmakers made a mistake that is common to many beleaguered relationships: they said too much. For it was the opening sections of SB 1070, the description of the law's intention, that ultimately triggered the SCOTUS's use of federal plenary power to strike down most of the state statute in *Arizona v. United States* (2012). The "intent of this act," lawmakers wrote in SB 1070, "is to make *attrition through enforcement* the public policy of all state and local government agencies in Arizona. . . . The provisions of this act are intended to work together to discourage and deter the unlawful entry and presence of aliens and economic activity by persons unlawfully present in the United States." Such language transformed SB 1070 from a case of state police power to a fundamental regulation of immigration, the latter was of course considered an exclusive right of the federal government.[44]

Two hundred years since the start of the federal-state debate over the authority to make immigration policy, "American immigration law is at war with itself." According to legal scholars, it has vacillated between catering to local and state efforts to regulate the inflow of noncitizens, and federal efforts to monopolize immigration policy and append it to Washington, DC's larger control over foreign affairs.[45] Yet there is more to this juridical confusion than constitutional interpretations and re-interpretations in American courtrooms. Rather, it belies the notion of the United States as a "nation of immigrants," and instead demonstrates how American law has consistently—if at times confusedly—qualified, differentiated, barred, and ignored the rights of personhood that are inalienable to each noncitizen inside and outside the United States.

# Notes

1  Michel Foucault, *Discipline and Punish: The Birth of the Prison*, Alan Sheridan, tr. (New York: Vintage Books, 1995), 153.
2  Juliet Stumpf, "States of Confusion: The Rise of State and Local Power Over Immigration," *North Carolina Law Review* 86, no. 6 (2008): 1564.
3  Kunal M. Parker, "Citizenship and Immigration Law, 1800–1924," in *The Cambridge history of law in America, Three Volumes*, ed. Michael Grossberg and Christopher Tomlins (Cambridge: Cambridge University Press, 2008), 172–5; Stumpf, "States of Confusion," 1566–7, 1569; Zolberg, "Changing Sovereignty Games," 155–6.
4  Parker, "Citizenship and Immigration Law," 171.
5  Patrick J. Charles, "Recentering Foreign Affairs Preemption in *Arizona v. United States*. Federal Plenary Power, the Spheres of Government, and the Constitutionality of SB 1070," *Cleveland State Law Review* 60, no. 1 (2012): 143–4.
6  Stumpf, "States of Confusion," 1569, 1571; Charles, "Recentering Foreign Affairs Preemption in *Arizona v. United States*," 144, 146; Scully, "The United States and International Affairs," 617.
7  Peter Skerry, "Many Borders to Cross: Is Immigration the Exclusive Responsibility of the Federal Government?," *Publius* 25, no. 3 (1995): 74;

Gerald L. Neuman, "Qualitative Migration Controls in the Antebellum United States," in *Migration Control in the North Atlantic World: The Evolution of State Practices in Europe and the United States from the French Revolution to the Inter-War Period*, ed. Andres Fahrmeir, Olivier Faron, and Patrick Weil (New York: Berghahn Books, 2003), 111; Aristide R. Zolberg, "The Archaeology of 'Remote Control'," in *Migration Control in the North Atlantic World: The Evolution of State Practices in Europe and the United States from the French Revolution to the Inter-War Period*, ed. Andres Fahrmeir, Olivier Faron, and Patrick Weil (New York: Berghahn Books, 2003), 198–202; William E. Forbath, "Politics, State-Building, and the Courts, 1870–1920," in *The Cambridge History of Law in America, Three Volumes*, ed. Michael Grossberg and Christopher Tomlins (Cambridge and New York: Cambridge University Press, 2008), 643–96; Parker, "Citizenship and Immigration Law," 176.

8  Neuman, "Qualitative Migration Controls in the Antebellum United States," 106–19, 110; Zolberg, "The Archaeology of 'Remote Control'," 195–202, 201; Skerry, "Many Borders to Cross," 74.

9  Zolberg, "The Archaeology of 'Remote Control'," 202–6; Stumpf, "States of Confusion," 1570.

10  Zolberg, "The Archaeology of 'Remote Control'," 202–6.

11  Ibid., 211–14.

12  Ibid., 220.

13  Kitty Calavita, *U.S. Immigration Law and Control of Labor, 1820–1924* (New York: Academic Press, 1984), 34–8.

14  Catherine Collomp, "Labour Unions and the Nationalisation of Immigration Restriction in the United States, 1880–1924," in *Migration Control in the North Atlantic World: The Evolution of State Practices in Europe and the United States from the French Revolution to the Inter-War Period*, ed. Andres Fahrmeir, Olivier Faron, and Patrick Weil (New York: Berghahn Books, 2003), 237–52, 248 and 251n24; Aristide Zolberg, *A Nation By Design: Immigration Policy in the Fashioning of America* (New York: Russell Sage Foundation, 2006), 189–90; Michael B. Katz, "Was Government the Solution or the Problem? The Role of the States in the History of American Social Policy," in "Cities, States, Trust, and Rule," ed. Michael Hanagan and Chris Tilly, Special Issue in Memory of Charles Tilly (1929–2008), *Theory and Society* 39, no. 3/4 (May 2010): 487–502, information comes from 494; Stumpf, "States of Confusion," 1558–9, 1571; Kerry Abrams, "Plenary Power Preemption," *Virginia Law Review* 99, no. 3 (2013): 611–15.

15  Skerry, "Many Borders to Cross," 76.

16  Parker, "Citizenship and Immigration Law," 177.

17  Ibid., 184.

18  Forbath, "State-Building, and the Courts," 643–4.

19  Gerald Neuman, *Strangers to the Constitution: Immigrants, Borders, and Fundamental Law* (Princeton, NJ: Princeton University Press, 1996), 120, emphasis mine; Hiroshi Motomura, "Immigration Law After a Century of Plenary Power: Phantom Constitutional Norms and Statutory Interpretation," *Yale Law Journal* 100, no. 3 (1990): 459; Hiroshi Motomura, "The Curious

Evolution of Immigration Law: Procedural Surrogates for Substantive Constitutional Rights," *Columbia Law Review* 92, no. 7 (1992): 1634.

20 *Nishimura Ekiu v. United States* (1892): "It is an accepted maxim of international law, that every sovereign nation has the power, as inherent in sovereignty, and essential to self-preservation, to forbid the entrance of foreigners within its dominions.... In the United States this power is vested in the national government." Huyen Pham, "When Immigration Borders Move," *Florida Law Review* 61, no. 5 (2009): 1142n143; Motomura, "Immigration Law after a Century of Plenary Power," 460.

21 Motomura, "Immigration Law after a Century of Plenary Power," 553; Motomura, "The Curious Evolution of Immigration Law," 1633.

22 Stumpf, "States of Confusion," 1572; Abrams, "Plenary Power Preemption," 615–16; Forbath, "State-Building, and the Courts," 683–4; Scully, "The United States and International Affairs," 619; Parker, "Citizenship and Immigration Law," 186; Adam B. Cox and Cristina M. Rodríguez, "The President and Immigration Law," *The Yale Law Journal* 119, no. 3 (2009): 460.

23 Forbath, "State-Building, and the Courts," 683.

24 Cox and Rodríguez, "The President and Immigration Law," 461, 461n4; "Developments in the Law: Immigrant Rights & Immigration Enforcement," *Harvard Law Review* 126, no. 6 (2013): 1585; Purcell, "A Right to Leave, but Nowhere to Go," 193.

25 Abrams, "Plenary Power Preemption," 604, 610, 618; Parker, "Citizenship and Immigration Law," 195; Stumpf, "States of Confusion," 1581. According to legal scholar Juliet Stumpf, the "distinction between pure immigration law and alienage law is *famously slippery*, because immigration laws often govern the rights and obligations of noncitizens inside the United States, and alienage laws may provide noncitizens incentives to enter or leave." Stumpf, "States of Confusion," 1581n114.

26 Abrams, "Plenary Power Preemption," 619.

27 Ibid., 620.

28 Stumpf, "States of Confusion," 1608; Charles, "Recentering Foreign Affairs Preemption in *Arizona v. United States*," 147–8; Abrams, "Plenary Power Preemption," 622.

29 This quote can be found in both Abrams, "Plenary Power Preemption," 623 and Charles, "Recentering Foreign Affairs Preemption in *Arizona v. United States*," 148, emphasis mine.

30 Stumpf, "States of Confusion," 1584; Pham, "When Immigration Borders Move," 1130n65.

31 Stumpf, "States of Confusion," 1584; Hiroshi Motomura, "Immigration Outside the Law," *Columbia Law Review* 108, no. 8 (2008): 2059n105; Abrams, "Plenary Power Preemption," 625–6, 616n63.

32 Motomura, "Immigration Outside the Law," 2059–60.

33 "Developments in the Law," 1611; Chris Nwachukwu Okeke and James A. R. Nafziger, "United States Migration Law: Essentials for Comparison," *The American Journal of Comparative Law* 54 (2006): 547–8.

34  Abrams, "Plenary Power Preemption," 620; Stumpf, "States of Confusion," 1590.
35  Charles, "Recentering Foreign Affairs Preemption in *Arizona v. United States*," 148–9; Jones-Correa and De Graauw, "The Illegality Trap," 187.
36  Stumpf, "States of Confusion," 1565.
37  Abrams, "Plenary Power Preemption," 624–5, 637; Charles, "Recentering Foreign Affairs Preemption in *Arizona v. United States*," 149; Motomura, "Immigration Outside the Law," 2043, 2054. This juridical backdoor was built upon an edifice of diminishing due process rights for noncitizen persons in the United States. For example, in *Harisiades v. Shaughnessy* (1952), the SCOTUS stated that aliens could only "enjoy the hospitality of a State" for as long as that country deems it necessary. A year later, in *Shaughnessy v. United States ex rel. Mezei* (1953), the SCOTUS held that the continued exclusion of an entrant noncitizen without hearing does not amount to unlawful detention, because a noncitizen seeking entry does not possess constitutional rights. The precedent would be continued in the years after *Plyler*, such as in *United States v Verdugo-Urquidez* (1990), which denied constitutional protection to a noncitizen because they had no voluntary connection to the United States. (Calavita, "U.S. Immigration Policy," 148; Pham, "Why Immigration Borders Move," 1142n143; Stumpf, "The Crimmigration Crisis," 398n178).
38  Stumpf, "States of Confusion," 1585–6, 1594, 1606.
39  Ibid., 1600, 1612–13.
40  *Lozano v. City of Hazleton* (2007), Stumpf, "States of Confusion," 1603.
41  *Arizona Contractors Assoc. Inc. v Candelaria* (2008) and *Gray v City of Valley Park* (2008). Ibid., 1604.
42  "Developments in the Law," 1573–5. It can be argued that the SCOTUS allowed some room for precedent for the infamous "show me your papers" sections of SB 1070. For example, in *United States v. Brignoni-Ponce* (1975), the court held that "Mexican in appearance is a relevant factor" that can be taken into considerations in law enforcement decisions regarding whom to stop and interrogate. Manges Douglas and Sáenz, "The Criminalization of Immigrants & the Immigration-Industrial Complex," 220; Gallegos, "Border Matters," 1744; Okeke and Nafziger, "United States Migration Law," 550.
43  "Developments in the Law," 1573–5; Charles, "Recentering Foreign Affairs Preemption in *Arizona v. United States*," 156–7.
44  Abrams, "Plenary Power Preemption," 632–3, emphasis original; Charles, "Recentering Foreign Affairs Preemption in *Arizona v. United States*," 134. Relying on a precedent of another kind, in *Toll v Moreno* (1982) the SCOTUS argued that the federal government was not obliged to demonstrate exactly how state laws conflicted with plenary power. It was enough to apply foreign affairs preemption if the federal government deemed it necessary. Charles, "Recentering Foreign Affairs Preemption in *Arizona v. United States*," 150.
45  "Developments in the Law," 1567.

# 2

# A Synthesis of US Congressional Immigration Restriction, 1880s to 2000s

As the previous chapter discussed, the legal phenomenon of restricting the movement of people not only predates the founding of the American Republic but goes back nearly to the very beginning of the British North American colonies. It was not until the 1880s, however, that a consistent and systematic process was recognizable in federal legislation restricting immigration.

Racism was central in shaping US congressional immigration law, but class considerations also played a role in determining US citizenship for immigrants. In fact, class considerations preceded racial preferences in the history of immigration restriction. Dating back to the colonial period of US history, towns and cities restricted the entry of indigent natives, for it was assumed that the burden of poor residents—"internal foreigners"—would be too great for public services to bear.[1] This initial reflex to restrict the movement of people based on class considerations gave way to racist considerations as different ethnic and racial groups immigrated to the United States during the middle part of the nineteenth century. Racism remained the predominant driver of US immigration policy for the next 100 years, until roughly the 1990s, when class reemerged as a prime prerequisite for gaining entry into the United States. Thereafter, race and class influenced US immigration law in a complementary fashion. The goal in this section is less to draw an exact taxonomy of when US immigration policy was more classist than racist, or vice versa, as it is to notice how race and class interact in the history of US immigration policy, "to draw lines connecting race and class."[2]

## Johnson-Reed Act, 1924

The conflation of race and class increasingly informed restrictionists' rationale for curbing immigration and eventually exposed a rift between US immigration policy and US foreign relations. This process culminated when Congress passed the Immigration Act of 1924 (Johnson-Reed Act), which restricted immigration along racist lines. The Johnson-Reed Act was the first piece of legislation to comprehensively restrict immigration to the United States. The law was decades in the making.

In the years after the Civil War skilled labor unions protested the importation of contracted, skilled foreign labor. This practice had been established by the 1864 immigration law, which allowed companies to contract foreign skilled workers to work in American industry. During a time of war such workers were valuable in a labor-dependent wartime economy. Twenty years later, this scenario was obsolete as factory work had become increasingly automated and the demand for foreign workers had shifted toward unskilled immigrants. Nevertheless, labor unions pressured Congress to limit immigration. The result was the Anti-Contract Labor Law, or the Foran Act, passed in 1885 and named for its sponsor, Congressman Martin Foran (R-OH).[3] The irony of this law was that the great majority of immigration labor was not under contract, and therefore was not barred from entering the country. Rather, the Foran Act was important as a "symbolic action," in which Congress responded to organized unions' demands for immigration restriction, even when this legislation proved ineffective in stopping mass immigration. The Foran Act marked a turning point in attitudes toward immigrants without inaugurating a marked change in immigration patterns. It was a law that was passed to placate organized labor but not at the expense of alienating big business, which was dependent on cheap (and uncontracted) labor.

In the 1880s Congress remained fundamentally opposed to any action that would cut off European streams of cheap immigration to the United States; capital was simply too dependent on it. Therefore, a comprehensive, numerical form of restriction was out of the question. At the same time, congressional debates over the Foran Act revealed a growing denigration of cheap foreign labor based on perceived racial inferiorities. The rhetoric in support of the act was distinctly discriminatory, deriding immigrants as paupers, slaves, serfs, and inferior to Americans. Even as the bill under consideration was not specifically directed toward stopping the flow of unskilled workers, those very immigrants were labeled as inferior. A significant consequence of the Foran Act was the way in which legislators began to reflect and deploy the racist rhetoric nativists increasingly relied on to bemoan the arrival of immigrants to the United States. Essentially, racism started to play a role in shaping immigration restriction policy.[4] And yet, the selective, "universalist" approach to immigration policy still characterized immigration law. From 1891 to 1907 Congress substantially expanded the statutory restrictions on immigration to the United States. In 1891, polygamists, persons convicted of crimes involving "moral turpitude," and those suffering from contagious diseases were barred from entering the United States. Epileptics, insane persons, professional beggars, and anarchists were added to that excluded list in 1903.[5]

Great economic growth in the decades after the American Civil War expanded industries that relied on cheap, migrant labor. The expanding economy brought social change. The United States was a focal point for global immigration. Waves of "new" migrants flocked to the United States beginning in the 1880s. Millions of immigrants entered the United States from Eastern and Southern Europe.

Americans had always been ambivalent about the presence of immigrants. Historically, a process of acculturation seemed to resolve many of the racial tensions that newly arrived immigrants to the United States encountered.[6] From the 1880s on the problem with the "second" great wave of immigrants to the United States was their seeming inability or, even worse, their lack of desire to assimilate into American society. It was the profound foreignness of eastern and southern European and Asian immigrants that concerned Americans, who were uncomfortable with immigrants' growing presence in the nation. Americans were also troubled with the fact that the nation's great economic success was bound to the foreign worker. Immigration was part and parcel of economic prosperity.[7] Many Americans worried about the effect on the United States of the teeming masses of immigrants entering the country.

Anti-immigrant organizations responded to what was increasingly viewed as the undesirability of this new strand of immigrants. The American Protective Association (APA), founded in 1887, advocated for the limitation of numbers and types of immigrants entering the United States. The APA had over 2 million active members by the 1890s. The growing anti-immigrant sentiment of the 1880s was partly fueled by a latent American anti-Catholicism that stretched back to the colonial era (see Introduction). Immigrants were not only an economic and racial threat to the nation but also a religious danger. Groups like the APA argued that immigrants were "tools of Rome" who were intent on taking American jobs and undermining American institutions. Additionally, the Immigration Restriction League (IRL), founded in 1893, tapped into the growing demand among Americans for immigration restrictions. They laid particular stress on the racial dimension of immigration instead of relying on the economic arguments that most immigration opponents, such as labor unions, utilized.[8]

From the late nineteenth century into the early twentieth, the IRL campaigned to require a literacy test for all applicants for American citizenship.

The first literacy bill was introduced in Congress in 1895, where both houses quickly passed it, but President Grover Cleveland vetoed it in 1897, arguing that immigrants were not a threat to US society.[9] Congress again passed a literacy test in 1912, and it was vetoed, this time by President William Taft. The literacy test was passed once more in 1915, and rejected yet again, this time by President Woodrow Wilson. Wilson justified his veto by arguing that a restriction like the literacy test, had it been adopted earlier in the nation's history, "would very materially have altered the course and cooled the humane ardors of our politics."[10] But with war looming, as German U-boats sank US merchant marine ships and as many Americans believed the proliferation of foreign-born peoples constituted a danger to the nation, support for immigration restriction enabled Congress to override Wilson's veto.[11] The new "Literacy Act" was passed on February 5, 1917.

The Immigration Act of 1917 barred from admission any illiterate alien and completely disallowed immigration from southern and East Asia, making the 1917 act the first action by the US Congress in almost forty years to place substantive restrictions on immigration into the United States.[12] The Literacy Act was a turning point in immigration law and in Americans' view of immigrants. By disallowing illiterate immigrants from entering the United States, the law selectively restricted who could enter the country. Moreover, by associating illiteracy with "undesirable" immigrants, the law codified a new "racialist" approach to immigration regulation. Finally, by blocking Asian immigration outright, the law relied on a new focus on numerical limitations.

During the postwar period, popular US opinion began to push for a more comprehensive form of immigration restriction. Many Americans had lost faith that immigrants could be remade into citizens. Immigration opponents asserted that inborn racial traits precluded an immigrant's ability to assimilate. This view, that immigrants were racially flawed and inferior, was powerful, widely held, and contributed to immigration restriction laws.[13] Not long after it was passed the 1917 Immigration Act was deemed a failure because it did not establish an upper limit on annual immigration. Also, the resumption of large-scale immigration after the First World War demonstrated the literacy test's inefficiency in restricting the entrance of supposedly undesirable aliens into the United States. Finally, nativists chafed at the exemptions to the law's enforcement which allowed thousands of Mexican migrants to cross into the United States, responding to intense labor demand.[14] As nativists lamented the failure of their much-sought-after effort to restrict immigration through a literacy act, they changed their focus from selective to numerical restriction—a quota scheme (Figure 2.1).[15]

The subsequent 1921 and 1924 immigration acts codified racial and ethnic background to determine an immigrant's ability to enter the United States. The chief purpose of this legislation was to shift the weight of immigration

**FIGURE 2.1** Some folks pick queer things to go crazy over, *October 12, 1920*. *Presumably an image contextualizing the extent of Japanese immigration to the United States, "Ding" Darling's illustration reflected a generally held belief among Americans after the First World War that existing US immigration laws, such as the Immigration Act of 1917, failed to stem the flow of foreigners into the United States. "Ding" Darling Wildlife Society owns the copyright of "Ding" Darling cartoons.*

to the United States from poorer nations of Southern and Eastern Europe in favor of immigration from Northwestern Europe. The laws marked a triumph of the "racialist"/numerical approach to US immigration restriction. They also, legal scholar Kunal Parker argues, shifted the basic, inclusive premise of US immigration law to an exclusive one: from a "presumption" that most persons could immigrate to the United States, to a "presumption" that most persons could not immigrate to the United States.[16] First, the 1917 Act equated illiteracy with undesirability. Second, the 1921 Act used race to decide which immigrants were acceptable. This was the first piece of immigration legislation to utilize a quota-based system for the number of entrance visas given to nations around the world. Finally, the Immigration Act of 1924 continued the quota-based system and made it even tighter. While the 1921 Act allowed a 3 percent annual quota for nations based on the total of each nation's immigrant population in the United States according to the 1910 census, the 1924 version set a 2 percent annual quota based on the 1890 census of the United States. The 1924 Act reduced the total number of immigrants from quota-based countries to 150,000.[17] The increased impetus to restrict immigration led to the creation of the US Border Patrol in 1924 to enforce US immigration laws.[18]

## The Hart-Celler Act, 1965

Much has been made of the liberal turn in US politics during the 1960s. Beginning with the Kennedy administration, but especially during the time of Lyndon Johnson's years in the White House, the executive and legislative branches—both controlled by Democrats—embarked on a sweeping reform program, the likes and size of which had not been seen since the New Deal reforms of the Roosevelt administration. Collectively known as the Great Society reforms, reformist policymakers focused on everything from environmental protection to traffic safety. Four particular spokes of reform comprised the bedrock of the Great Society: federal aid to elementary and secondary education, Medicare and Medicaid, a civil rights act to guarantee voting rights, and, finally, immigration reform.[19] There is scholarly debate about whether the resulting immigration reform produced in 1965 under the name of the Hart-Celler Act really represented a substantial liberal turn in US immigration policy. Some scholars say Hart-Celler simply changed which international peoples were restricted from the United States, while other critics charge that Hart-Celler is responsible for leading to migration crises during the last years of the twentieth century. So which is it?

Forty years beyond their founding, the restrictive and discriminatory quota laws were still the law of the land for US immigration policy in the early 1960s. By the turn of the 1960s, the United States was one of the few nations in the Western Hemisphere to still have exclusionary laws based on race and ethnicity defining its immigration policy.[20] Liberal policymakers such as Senator Philip Hart of Michigan and Representative Emmanuel Celler of New York, concerned with issues such as civil rights and poverty in America, viewed the 1920s laws as an embarrassment and had a "self-conscious strategy" to reform the statutes.[21] Oscar Handlin, historian of immigration and public intellectual whose scholarship played a large part in shaping what would later become the Hart-Celler Act, was sharply critical of the national origins system.

"A quota system," Handlin wrote in 1952, "that sets up a hierarchy of desirable and undesirable peoples is offensive to our allies and to our potential allies throughout the world, and is a slur upon millions of our own citizens."[22]

Yet this liberal turn did not match prevailing US public opinion on immigration. According to public polls from the mid-1960s, as the Johnson administration pushed for reform of the national origins system, a third of the country wanted no change to the nation's prevailing immigration laws, while an additional 17 percent of Americans were indifferent to the issue of US immigration reform. Essentially, nearly half of the US population in the mid-1960s either supported the quota laws or did not want to see them changed. Finally, public polling data from 1965 shows that a mere 8 percent of the American public endorsed an increase in legal immigration. In short, there was no major groundswell for reform of US immigration law during the mid-1960s.[23]

Nevertheless, after it was signed into law by LBJ at a public ceremony just steps from the Statue of Liberty in New York harbor, the Hart-Celler Act phased out the national origins system over a three-year period. An overall quota of 120,000 visas was set for immigrants outside the Western Hemisphere and 170,000 visas for immigrants of the Eastern Hemisphere. A 20,000 annual visa cap was placed on each nation. Not every visa applicant was to be given equal consideration. Instead, the 1965 law established a table of seven preference categories within which visa applicants could be granted a visa to enter the United States. The seven preferences were divided into two general categories: family preferences and skill-based preferences and refugees. Around 74 percent of total preferences for visa allotment were to be granted to family members of US citizens or permanent resident aliens: sons, daughters, spouses, brothers, sisters. The remaining 26 percent of total preferences for visa allotment went to applicants based on their professional background or needs of the US labor market, as well as to displaced persons.[24]

The drafters of the Hart-Celler Act believed principles of equality and fairness explained their formulation of the visa allocation system. Instead, immigration historian Mai Ngai argues, the "core paradox" of the law was that instead the new law created a "system [that] has generated an ever-larger caste-population of unauthorized immigrants."[25] It was hoped among policymakers that a consistent application of immigration laws that did not rest upon race and ancestry as criteria for selection would correct years of discriminatory US immigration law. In this sense, there was a symbolic nature to Hart-Celler that is important to note.[26] On a practical level, by basing the majority of visa allotments on family reunification, supporters of the bill assumed that the Hart-Celler Act would maintain a homogenous American national identity. It was believed that the unification of families—as opposed to the immigration of single men—would result in higher rates of immigrant assimilation as well as attract more desirable immigrants to the United States.

**FIGURE 2.2** You can go back to wherever you came from, *August 1, 1965. The Hart-Celler Act, publicly signed by President Lyndon Johnson (LBJ) at the foot of the Statue of Liberty eight weeks after the publication of this Herblock illustration, was meant to end the ethnic discrimination ("snobbery") that had characterized US immigration law since 1924. Yet the eighty-ninth Congress' effort to instill fairness into US immigration law actually laid the foundation for a more intractable problem during the latter decades of the twentieth century: undocumented immigration. A Herblock Cartoon, © The Herb Block Foundation.*

The 1965 act was meant to encourage immigration of family members of Euro-Americans (Figure 2.2).[27]

Symbolically, the Hart-Celler Act was passed to instill fairness into a system that was deemed discriminatory to European immigrants since the interwar years. This retroactive fairness did not equate to prospective equality to waves of Asian and Latin American immigration, however. The Hart-Celler Act was enacted for domestic political reasons and international perception; it was not rooted in a rational, evidence-based understanding of international migration.[28] It was an attempt to correct the disconnect between the public image of the United States as the "leading proponent of liberal democratic systems of governance," and the international perception of the United States as a "laggard" in formulating an immigration admission program "based on universal racial equality."[29]

But policymakers did not do their homework, and the unintended consequences of the law were manifold. Policymakers hoped their new law would encourage European immigration, perhaps slight upticks from Southern and Eastern Europe, the very regions most discriminated against by the 1920s quota laws.[30] Yet lawmakers did not anticipate the eventual dominance of Asian and Latin American immigration. Had they known this would have transpired, immigration historian Roger Daniels states, "it is hardly likely that the law would have been enacted in its present form."[31] Between 1968 and 1980, Latin American immigration to the United States increased by 61 percent; Asian immigration to the United States by 127 percent.[32] Additionally, the symbolic goal of fairness and consistency in immigration policy resulted in every immigrant-sending country being treated the same. The problem with this notion was that it did not take into account issues of substantial inequalities in the world's distribution and wealth and population. Why, for example, should New Zealand get the same visa limits as Mexico? Another problem with the 1965 law was that it assumed human rights follow statehood (a theme addressed in the Introduction), instead of declaring a universal recognition of inherent human rights. Importantly, then, the Hart-Celler Act formed the basis for the notion of "illegal" immigration: if an individual migrant lacked state membership they were essentially invisible, aberrant, and illegal.[33]

The legal precept and philosophical oversight that would prove so instrumental in creating the notion of illegal immigration was supplemented by two other holes in the Hart-Celler Act. One, because the law was primarily focused on family reunification, it inadequately met demands of the US labor market, thereby laying the groundwork for waves of undocumented immigration to the United States during the rest of the twentieth century and beyond.[34] Second, by placing hemispheric ceilings on immigration, the Hart-Celler Act formed the basis for the phenomenon known as *illegal* Mexican immigration (see Chapter 11). Mexican immigration to the United States averaged around 50,000 per year up to 1965. During the Bracero program (1942–64), some 450,000 Mexicans entered the United States each year as temporary laborers. So when an annual per-country limit of 20,000 visas was passed on Mexico by the 1965 act, the ideals of fairness and consistency that allegedly underscored the law went out the window. With almost half a million Mexican immigrants entering the United States up to the mid-1960s, US policymakers did not ask themselves what would happen when country quotas were placed on states like Mexico. What they gave even less consideration was the "obdurate momentum" that Mexican migration to the United States had attained by the time of the passage of the Hart-Celler Act: more than twenty years of temporary contracted labor under the Bracero program, which was itself built upon decades of Mexican immigration to the United States. Essentially, for the first time, restriction laws were placed on Latin American immigration, notably on Mexico.[35]

The unexpected rise of immigration from Latin America concerned US leaders. During the late 1970s, US policymakers mounted "a concerted effort" to curtail immigration from the Western Hemisphere by reducing the possibilities for legal entry of Latin American immigrants into the United States. In 1976, Congress ended an exemption for immigration from the Western Hemisphere. The Hart-Celler Act placed a 20,000 annual immigration cap on nations of the Eastern Hemisphere. Eleven years later, Congress extended the 20,000 cap on their neighboring nations to the South. In 1978, Congress combined what had formerly been separate hemispheric ceilings into a single worldwide quota of 290,000. And in 1980, Congress lowered the worldwide quota by 20,000, to 270,000.[36]

So, was the Hart-Celler Act of 1965 a significant liberalization of US immigration policy or not? Some immigration scholars such as Daniel Tichenor and Cristina Rodriguez say yes, with the former arguing that even considering the many shortcomings of the law, the 1965 act did establish the notion that US immigration law should be free from racial and ethnic bias, while the latter goes so far to say that Hart-Celler Act was a "significant civil rights achievement."[37] Other immigration scholars such as Douglass Massey, Catherine Lee, and Mai Ngai not only call Hart-Celler a failure but also the root cause of our modern-day notions of "illegal" immigration. Conservative critics in turn argue that Hart-Celler was responsible for opening the floodgates to "out of control immigration" by the 1980s.[38] James Patterson, a historian, offers perhaps the most-balanced statement on the law when he states that it reflected "the hopefully liberal temper" of the mid-1960s.[39]

Readers can establish their own verdict on the Hart-Celler Act. For this book, three things are notable about the 1965 reform of US immigration policy. It failed to account for broad demographic shifts in immigration to the United States; it formed the baseline for the notion of illegal immigration; and it placed a numerical restriction on Latin American immigration to the United States for the first time.

## The Immigration Reform and Control Act, 1986

Immigration to the United States was definitely changing between the late 1960s and late 1970s. As European immigration to the United States declined after 1968, the flow of immigrants from Latin America and Asia rose markedly. By 1976 more than half of the legal immigrants who were admitted into the United States came from seven, non-European countries: Mexico, the Philippines, Korea, Cuba, Taiwan, India, and the Dominican Republic. By the late 1970s, more than 450,000 legal immigrants were entering the United States each year; by the 1980s, that annual average went up to 730,000. In absolute population numbers for the United States, this inflow was "hardly revolutionary": the total US population stood at 194 million in 1965 and would top 205 million five years later. And yet, as James Patterson shows, because birth rates of non-immigrant Americans had stabilized by the 1960s and 1970s, immigrants came to compose a "steadily higher" percentage of the US population. From a historic low of 4.7 percent in 1970, the percentage of foreign-born within the US population increased to 6.2 percent in 1980 and reached 7.6 percent in 1990 (the historic high for the percentage of foreign-born in the United States population was 14.7 percent which was recorded in 1910).[40]

Labor groups pressured US policymakers to curb illegal immigration not long after passage of the Hart-Celler Act. The 1970s witnessed a sudden influx of illegal immigration to the United States, to the tune of 6.6 million. Most of the immigrants were Latinos; two-thirds of them from Mexico.[41] The causes of this influx were manifold. Cancellation of the Bracero program in 1964, a sudden legal stroke shifted the classification of hundreds of thousands of Mexican migrants from legal to illegal. Also, labor demand from the United States increased during the late 1960s.[42] Regardless of new policies and visa preferences established in the mid-1960s, the demand for migrant labor among US employers remained insatiable. Democrats, backed by organized labor as well as civil rights advocacy groups, called for sanctions on employers—primarily agriculture growers—who knowingly hired illegal aliens. Congressmen from regions along the US-Mexico border responded by arguing that stemming the flow of illegal aliens would hamper the businesses that depended on such migrant labor. Senator James Eastland of Mississippi, longtime chair of the Senate Judiciary Committee, blocked any legal proposals that suggested punishing employers of illegal migrants. His retirement in 1978 opened a path toward a new round of reform in US immigration policy.[43]

US public opinion also played a role. By the late 1970s there was widespread public and media dissatisfaction with what was being termed a lack of control of borders and inadequate immigration laws. Public polls of the 1970s seemed to show that most Americans wanted immigration to the United States reduced.[44] Partly in response to public dissatisfaction over US immigration policy, as well as divisions on the same issue on Capitol Hill, the Select Commission on Immigration and Refugee Policy (SCIRP) was established in 1979 to propose solutions to the immigration problem. The committee submitted a report in 1981. To placate organized labor groups who argued that the hiring of illegal aliens was unfairly competitive against them, SCIRP recommended sanctions on employers who hired illegal aliens (what would later become the I-9 system during the 1980s). And to respond to humanitarian groups and Hispanic lobby groups which argued that the legally precarious position of illegality left Mexican migrants prone to abuse and prejudice and disregarded their contribution to the US economy, SCIRP recommended an amnesty for aliens who had resided and worked in the United States for a certain period of time.[45]

During the 1980s, policymakers first addressed the new prevalence of Asians and Latin American immigration flows to the United States. As the domestic political landscape changed dramatically regarding immigration. Political conservatives favored relaxing restrictions on immigration to continue a relatively unencumbered access to cheap labor for American businesses—such as growers, textiles, hotels, and restaurants—which depended on migrants. Additionally, to offset African American support for the Democratic party, the administration of Ronald Reagan (1981–9) actively courted Hispanic voters in the elections of 1980 and 1984 by promoting a limited amnesty program for illegal immigrants. Also, amnesty offered the US government an "expedient way" out of the heavy cost of prosecuting systematic and widespread violation of its immigration laws.[46]

On the political left, organized labor endorsed the idea of employer sanctions, even while black and Hispanic advocacy groups were ambivalent about the proposed reforms, fearing amnesty would cause competition with immigrants over social services. As this hodgepodge of special interests combining advocacy of civil rights with a resurgence of free market ideologies coalesced in congressional immigration reform debates, public polls in the 1980s showed that most Americans, not just ethnic minorities, opposed an amnesty program for illegal aliens as well as increases in legal immigration.[47]

After years of debate, Congress developed, and President Reagan signed into law, the Immigration Reform and Control Act (IRCA) in November 1986. Its final version sought to penalize and fine employers who knowingly hired undocumented workers, which represented a novel entry of federal immigration enforcement into employment law, a legal field customarily left to state governments. The new law also stated that aliens who had resided in the United States since 1982 could apply for legal status ("amnesty"). Eventually 3 million unauthorized immigrants were granted permanent resident status under the IRCA.[48]

Despite all the arguing and debate that went into the new law's formulation, the IRCA did not solve the problem of undocumented migration. First, paradoxically, employers were shielded from legal consequences of hiring undocumented workers as long as they filled out and kept on file the routine I-9 employee verification form. The burden of proving the veracity of the information on the I-9 form did not fall upon the employer but was rather placed on the migrant workers themselves who faced greater risks such as INS workplace raids.[49] Related to this, the law stimulated the production of false identification documents for those who sought to meet the growing need within the US economy for migrant workers.[50] Ancillary to these design flaws was the lack of enthusiasm for enforcement by federal officials who found that the IRCA had transformed their primary job from immigration regulation to immigration reduction.[51] The new law seemed to work in the short term, as the rate of undocumented migration to the United States slowed during the late 1980s. By the early 1990s, however, these rates were back to levels witnessed *before* passage of the IRCA.[52]

The IRCA's ignominious legacy was to exacerbate the undocumented Mexican migration issue by ending the flexibility of circular migration that had served the interests of the US and Mexican governments and economies for decades. Historically, Mexican migrants (documented and undocumented) had worked seasonally in the United States and returned to Mexico. Consequently, the permanent Mexican immigrant population in the United States was relatively low compared to other immigrant groups. Much of this had to do with ease of return to Mexico for migrants. But the IRCA's criminalization of undocumented migration ended this mutually beneficial system of circular migration. In the years after passage of the 1986 law, legal entry into the United States became more difficult and the Border Patrol started to take on its present-day characteristics as an "immigration enforcement industry."[53] Not coincidentally, the permanent population of Mexican *immigrants* (no longer migrants) in the United States grew after passage of the IRCA. Before 1986 roughly 45 percent of Mexicans returned to Mexico; by the early 2000s that return rate was down to 25 percent. As a result, from 1980 to 1995, the population of Mexicans in the United States tripled. It increased by another 30 percent in just five years between 1997 and 2002, from 7 million to 10 million. The undocumented population stood at 11 million in 2006 and rose thereafter.[54]

Despite the retrospective recognition of the IRCA's inability to stem immigration, there was still a function in its failure in the sense that the law responded to the special interests that supported it, and even to the public fear that demanded it. First, the amnesty aspect of the law at least gave lip service to those who feared the abuse of illegals in US society. Second, the IRCA kept corridors of migration open to employers even if the new law seemed to burden them with new regulations. And third, the IRCA seemed to show the American public that the US government was *doing something* about the immigration problem.

# 1996 laws

Symbolically, even philosophically, beyond the obvious tension of distinguishing which immigrants to include and which to exclude, was the fundamental divide between how to determine who is part of a nation and who is not. The Johnson-Reed Act of 1924 took a nationalist approach, in which a foreign person's ability to assimilate was tied to their racial and ethnic background. The Hart-Celler Act of 1965 attempted a more liberal approach of inclusion based on (relatively) objective numerical caps instead of the subjective racial/ethnic requirements of the Johnson-Reed era. Drafted during the post-Civil Rights era, it would have been abominable for the IRCA of 1986 to rehash the exclusionary racist language that underlined the immigration restriction laws of the 1920s; nevertheless, the 1986 reform introduced the most-robust statutory and legal regulations into US immigration law in generations.

At the same time, the IRCA represented a choosing of sides in US regulatory approaches to immigrants. Hart-Celler was, at its root, an attempt to imbue a liberal, inclusionary vision in US immigration law. The 1986 reform, with its implementation of an amnesty for undocumented immigrants, was an effort to resuscitate that liberal vision, to a certain extent, at least. It tried to balance the exclusionary and the inclusionary natures of personhood: if immigrants could prove they had been in the United States for a certain period of time, if they could show that they had contributed to the polity, then their personhood—which had arguably been denied because of a persistent "illegal" status—would be granted permanent residence.

But this coupling turned out to be incompatible. By offering blanket legalization for undocumented immigrants who had been in the United States since 1982, the amnesty aspect of the IRCA essentially showed that the formal legal regime of US immigration law had failed.[55] An immigration policy could not be both carrot and stick; it could not be both exclusive and inclusive. So, as the 1965 act leaned more toward inclusion, the 1986 act tried to balance both inclusion and exclusion. Finally, a set of laws passed ten years after the IRCA demonstrated how, at the dawn of the twenty-first century, US immigration policy leaned decidedly toward exclusion and conceptualized personhood in exclusive and not inclusive terms.

The late 1980s was a time of crescendo and convergence. Successive waves of refugees had been both welcomed and grudgingly accepted from countries in Southeast Asia and the Caribbean. During the same years, undocumented immigration—despite the accommodations stipulated by the IRCA of 1986—reemerged as an issue for the United States. The nation's borders seemed dangerously porous to many Americans. In contrast to immigration and refugee waves of earlier decades, Asians and Latin Americans disproportionately represented the newcomers in US society after the late 1960s. And by the 1990s, seven out of ten Mexicans who crossed into the United States were undocumented. Several factors drove this massive movement of people: pervasive social and economic gaps between the countries of origin and the United States, political and military conflicts that generated large numbers of refugees, and transnational social networks that facilitated paths of migration from origin countries to the United States.[56]

As Americans lauded the largely peaceful end of the Cold War in distant countries, they felt the bite of economic recession closer to home. The US economy experienced no job growth outside of the public sector during the early 1990s. The thinner Americans' wallets became the louder their leaders argued that "something had to be done" to get a handle on "out of control immigration."[57] Public polls of the early 1990s showed that most Americans wanted to see an overall decrease in immigration to the United States. Not for the first time in US history, the virulence of American nativist tendencies tended to follow the state of the economy: when times were good, nativism was low; when times were bad, nativism was high.[58]

But bad economics is not enough to explain the nativist 1990s. The blatant racist rhetoric that characterized debates over immigration during the first half of the twentieth century, especially the 1920s, was politically and socially untenable after the Rights Revolution among Americans in the 1950s and 1960s who were black, feminist, gay, Native American, or Chicano. Instead, the "defensive nationalism" that drove nativism was more coded, even as it was just as pernicious. Immigrants were no longer described as foreign hordes invading the United States, rather, there was a concern to "enforce our immigration laws"; foreign peoples were not directly accused of being inherently inferior to Americans, rather, "immigrants [were] turning the United States into a third world country"; immigrants were no longer openly denigrated as unfit to be US citizens, rather, they "have too many children" or "refuse to learn English."[59] Newer immigrants were blamed for the ills of US society, such as rising crime rates and a disproportionate reliance on social services. In 1994, public polls of California voters showed that public support for Prop 187 (see Chapter 11) did not rest alone in fears of losing jobs to immigrants, but was also attributable to the belief among Americans that the US government failed to adequately regulate the international border with Mexico, that tax revenues were unfairly distributed to support immigrants, and that welfare benefits were abused by noncitizen residents of the United States. While such accusations did not rest upon empirical evidence, as so often happens in human relations, it was the perception that mattered more than the reality. US media outlets increased their focus on the immigration issue and US leaders filled the airwaves with their political rhetoric about immigrants, while anti-nativist responses were swamped by the xenophobic groundswell underlying fresh calls for immigration restriction. In sum, immigration historian George Sanchez argues, it was a "profound sense of the decline of the American nation" that bound together the various elements of nativism in the United States.[60]

Yet, American xenophobia is a smokescreen as much as it is a window into the soul of the United States, for it hides as much as it reveals. What it shows is a dislike for foreigners; what it hides is a reaction against deindustrialization. What it expresses is a concern for the sanctity of borders; what it hides is fear that globalization is innovating many Americans' jobs into obsolescence. What it defends is national security; what it hides is an insecurity over stagnant wages. Finally, what American xenophobia obscures most are understandings of the ultimate causes of immigration to the United States and discussions of the ultimate solutions to the problems attributed to the resettlement of foreign peoples on US soil. Despite the explicit insinuation of their rhetoric, nativists are focused on forging broad, centralized government power to crack down on immigration. Such a goal flies in the face of small-government conservative ideologies. Instead, opponents of immigration seek a defense against what they perceive as threats to an individual's right to pursue happiness, which is to say, livelihood and security. It is this "language of liberal individualism," Sanchez argues, "that keeps many [white Americans] from seeking structural explanations for racial inequality."[61]

This sense of defensive nationalism informed congressional debates that resulted in sweeping immigration reform during the mid-1990s. The grievances of regional and local immigration opponents coopted national politics. Restrictionists emphasized border control as the prime motive for barring immigration to avoid using rhetoric that could be construed as anti-immigrant. Border regulation was posited as a solution to many problems attributed to immigration: it would curb national overpopulation, it would reduce crime, and it would preserve American national sovereignty and identity. For restrictionists, reinforcing the physical border of the United States was a practical objective of reducing immigration. But this action also had philosophical and political ends, such as stemming the rapid change affecting US society and countering the globalization of the world. In short, building a stronger border was a nationalist technique to beat back the onrush of transnationalism and domestic, ethnic diversity. Considered personified agents of globalization, and the discomfort with change it brought, immigrants were easier subjects to regulate than the multinational corporations that at once attracted migrant labor while transferring jobs across international borders.[62]

Republicans, many of whom advocated for robust immigration restriction, stormed to victory in the midterm elections of 1994 and controlled Congress. By 1996, tenacious legislative efforts paid off with a slew of bills that fundamentally changed the US government's ability to regulate immigration. First, the Antiterrorism and Effective Death Penalty Act (AEDPA), passed in late April, expanded the definition of criminal grounds for removal from the United States to include crimes that could be classified as misdemeanors in state courts, and did away with judicial review for all categories of immigrants eligible for deportation. Second, the Personal Responsibility and Work Opportunity Reconciliation Act (called the "welfare reform bill"), passed in late August, dramatically scaled back legal immigrants' access to publicly funded social services, such as Medicaid and food stamps, and devolved authority over select welfare services to states by ending the Aid to Families with Dependent Children, which was a program founded in 1935 that offered cash assistance to low-income families.[63] Third, and most important, the Illegal Immigration Reform and Immigrant Responsibility Act (IIRIRA), passed at the end of September 1996, made it harder for undocumented immigrants to adjust their status to that of a legal immigrant while simultaneously making it much easier for these undocumented immigrants—including minors and children—to be apprehended and deported. Under section 287(g) of the new law, local and state police could be trained to enforce federal immigration law, more offenses were deemed deportable, it was easier to deport criminals ("expedited removal"), and deportation decisions were made by immigration courts with stricter judicial review procedures. The IIRIRA stipulated that twenty-eight distinct offenses including "crimes of violence" that carried a prison sentence of a year or more could result in deportation. Dramatically, the law also instituted retroactive punishment, in which pre-1996 crimes that were formerly not defined as aggravated felonies were now classified as such, providing the government grounds for deportation. Convicted residents could be deported even if they had completed their prison sentences. Not coincidentally, deportations of undocumented immigrants shot up between 1990 and 2010: from 30,000 to 400,000 by one estimate. Sociologist Jacqueline Hagan and other scholars provide more detail on the increase in deportations. For most of the twentieth century up to 1990, deportations "remained fairly flat" at about 20,000 per year. Between 1990 and 1995 they increased to 40,000 per year. During the late 1990s, after passage of the IIRIRA, deportations rose to nearly 200,000 per year. The great majority of deportees were poor Latin Americans, mostly Mexicans, who were removed from the United States for noncriminal reasons.[64]

While the Hart-Celler Act of 1965 rested on the concept of family reunification, the IIRIRA of 1996 seemed focused on family dissolution. Far from breaking up historical patterns of migration to the United States, the harsh laws of the mid-1990s only made the process of movement more dangerous. The pressure to provide for family—whether they be in the United States or in the home country or both—often convinces deportees to take the risk of migrating again to the United States in order to find jobs that provide needed earnings and remittances. Thus the "unintended consequence" of harsher deportation policies was to sustain a pattern of undocumented circular migration. The threat of deportation weighs relatively little in a migrant's choice to attempt another trip across the border. "In other words," Hagan notes, "the policy does not end the migration of unauthorized or criminal migrants; it simply raises the human costs for migrants and their families."[65]

In contrast to the IRCA of 1986, the IIRIRA of 1996 significantly increased criminal penalties on undocumented immigrants while it did nothing to penalize US employers of undocumented workers. Also, the 1996 law dramatically strengthened the US government's ability to apprehend and deport undocumented migrants at the border and from the nation's interior. In this sense, the IIRIRA deterritorialized the US-Mexican border: whether undocumented migrants tried to enter or remain in the United States, they were illegal in the eyes of the law and were subsequently liable to be deported.[66] Not coincidentally, since passage of the IIRIRA, the number of mass worksite raids—think of them as interior versions of border sweeps—expanded markedly as well as the number of nonviolent, noncriminal immigrants arrested (and families separated) for immigration violations. The persistent legacy of the IIRIRA has been "a series of ever-expanding efforts to deter illegal immigration through higher penalties and fewer options."[67]

Despite the harsher penalties for entering the United States without proper documentation, the problem of illegal immigration persisted into the early 2000s. A complete breakdown in the type of legislative consensus that underscored the reforms of the 1920s, 1960s, 1980s, and 1990s exacerbated the issue. At least six different immigration reform bills were presented in Congress between 2005 and 2007. All of them either failed to receive a vote or failed to pass both the Senate and the House of Representatives.[68] Most notable among these proposals was H.R. 4437, the "Sensenbrenner Bill." As can be gathered from its formal name, the Border Protection, Antiterrorism, and Illegal Immigration Control Act, the bill likened immigration control to national security. The proposed law planned to increase border security and interior enforcement of immigration laws, as well as criminalize undocumented immigrants (and those

**FIGURE 2.3** *Between 3.5 and 5.1 million people participated in peaceful rallies in more than 160 cities across the United States in May 2006 to protest the Sensenbrenner Bill. Getty Images: David S. Holloway.*

persons who aided them), and place further restrictions on due process rights for noncitizens. Widely viewed as draconian, H.R. 4437 incited the largest street protests in US history in the spring of 2006. It is estimated that 3.5 million to 5.1 million people participated in peaceful rallies in more than 160 cities across the United States to protest the bill. Subsequently, while the bill was passed by the House of Representatives in December 2005, it failed to pass the Senate. By the early 2000s, the consequence of the "legislative deadlock" in Washington, DC, regarding immigration reform has been to rely on executive action to regulate immigration, such as efforts to build a border wall (see Chapter 11), as well as renewed efforts by state governments to restrict the movement of noncitizens in their jurisdictions (see Chapter 1) (Figure 2.3).[69]

# Notes

1. Parker, "Citizenship and Immigration Law, 1800–1924," 173–5.
2. David R. Roediger, *The Wages of Whiteness: Race and the Making of the American Working Class*. Rev. edn. London: Verso, 2007), 11.
3. Collomp, "Labour Unions and the Nationalisation of Immigration Restriction in the United States, 1880–1924," 244–5.
4. Calavita, *U.S. Immigration Law and Control of Labor, 1820–1924*, 49–66; Collomp, "Labour Unions and the Nationalisation of Immigration Restriction in the United States," 244–5; Matthew Frye Jacobson, *Barbarian Virtues: The United States Encounters Foreign Peoples at Home and Abroad, 1876–1917* (New York: Hill and Wang, 2000), 67; Parker, "Citizenship and Immigration Law," 191.
5. Ettinger, "'We Sometimes Wonder What They Will Spring on Us Next'," 171; Patrick Weil, "Races at the Gate: A Century of Racial Distinctions in American Immigration Policy (1865–1965)," *Georgetown Immigration Law Journal* 15 (Summer 2001): 626.
6. See Noel Ignatiev, *How the Irish Became White* (New York: Routledge, 1995) and Rogers M. Smith, *Civic Ideals: Conflicting Visions of Citizenship in US History* (New Haven, CT: Yale University Press, 1997).
7. Jacobson, *Barbarian Virtues*, 97.
8. Desmond S. King, *Making Americans: Immigration, Race, and the Origins of a Diverse Democracy* (Cambridge, MA: Harvard University Press, 2000), 52–3; Alan Dawley, *Changing the World: American Progressives in War and Revolution* (Princeton, NJ: Princeton University Press, 2003), 114; Higham, *Strangers in the Land*, 77, 80–2.
9. Michael LeMay and Elliot Robert Barkan, eds., *U.S. Immigration and Naturalization Laws and Issues: A Documentary History* (Westport, CT: Greenwood Press, 1999), 80–1.
10. Ibid., xxxiii–xxxiv and 106–7.

11  Gerstle, *American Crucible*, 96.
12  LeMay and Barkan, *U.S. Immigration and Naturalization Laws and Issues*, 110.
13  Neil Foley, *The White Scourge: Mexicans, Blacks, and Poor Whites in Texas Cotton Culture* (Berkeley, CA: University of California Press, 1997), 58.
14  Katherine Benton-Cohen, "Other Immigrants: Mexicans and the Dillingham Commission of 1907–1911," *Journal of American Ethnic History* 30, no. 2 (Winter 2011): 44.
15  Gerstle, *American Crucible*, 97; Michael C. LeMay, *From Open Door to Dutch Door: An Analysis of US Immigration Policy Since 1820* (New York: Praeger Publishers, 1987), 71.
16  Weil, "Races at the Gate," 626; Parker, "Citizenship and Immigration Law," 168, 198.
17  King, *Making Americans*, 207.
18  See Kang, *The INS on the Line*, for a full description of the history of the Immigration and Naturalization Service.
19  James T. Patterson, *Grand Expectations: The United States, 1945–1974* (Oxford: Oxford University Press, 1996), 569; Douglas S. Massey, "America's Immigration Policy Fiasco: Learning from Past Mistakes," *Daedalus* 142, no. 3 (Summer 2013): 6.
20  Cook-Martín and Fitzgerald, "Liberalism and the Limits of Inclusion," 8.
21  Ngai, "The Civil Rights Origins of Illegal Immigration," 95.
22  Mae M. Ngai, "Oscar Handlin and Immigration Policy Reform in the 1950s and 1960s," *Journal of American Ethnic History* 32, no. 3 (2013): 63.
23  Robert Dallek, *Flawed Giant: Lyndon Johnson and His Times, 1961–1973.* (Oxford: Oxford University Press, 1999), 228; Elliott R. Barkan, "Return of the Nativists? California Public Opinion and Immigration in the 1980s and 1990s," *Social Science History* 27, no. 2 (2003): 239.
24  Catherine Lee, "Family Reunification and the Limits of Immigration Reform: Impact and Legacy of the 1965 Immigration Act," *Sociological Forum* 30, no. S1 (2015): 540–1; Thomas R. Maddux, "Ronald Reagan and the Task Force on Immigration, 11981," *Pacific Historical Review* 74, no. 2 (2005): 200n5.
25  Ngai, "The Civil Rights Origins of Illegal Immigration," 93.
26  Ngai, "Oscar Handlin and Immigration Policy Reform," 64; Ngai, "The Civil Rights Origins of Illegal Immigration," 95.
27  Lee, "Family Reunification and the Limits of Immigration Reform," 542; Louis DeSipio, "A Return to a National Origin Preference? Mexican Immigration and the Principles Guiding U.S. Immigration Policy," *Perspectives on Politics* 9, no. 3 (2011): 567–8.
28  Massey, "America's Immigration Policy Fiasco," 6.
29  Cook-Martín and Fitzgerald, "Liberalism and the Limits of Inclusion," 8.
30  Daniels, "Immigration since World War II," 42.
31  Lee, "Family Reunification and the Limits of Immigration Reform," 543; Daniels, "Immigration since World War II," 42.

32  Maddux, "Ronald Reagan and the Task Force on Immigration," 200.
33  Ngai, "The Civil Rights Origins of Illegal Immigration," 95–6.
34  Maddux, "Ronald Reagan and the Task Force on Immigration," 200.
35  Massey, "America's Immigration Policy Fiasco," 6–7; Ngai, "The Civil Rights Origins of Illegal Immigration," 97; Maddux, "Ronald Reagan and the Task Force on Immigration," 200.
36  Michael LeMay, *Anatomy of a Public Policy: The Reform of Contemporary American Immigration Law* (Westport: Praeger, 1994), 31; Massey and Riosmena, "Undocumented Migration from Latin America in an Era of Rising U.S. Enforcement," 294–5.
37  Daniel J. Tichenor, "The Politics of Immigration Reform in the United States, 1981–1990," *Polity* 26, no. 3 (1994): 341; Rodriguez, "Immigration, Civil Rights and the Evolution of the People," 232.
38  James Goldsborough, "Out-of-Control Immigration," *Foreign Affairs* 79, no. 5 (2000): 89, 92.
39  Patterson, *Grand Expectations*, 579.
40  Ibid., 578 and 578n47.
41  LeMay, *Anatomy of a Public Policy*, 21.
42  Massey, "America's Immigration Policy Fiasco," 8; LeMay, *Anatomy of a Public Policy*, 21–4.
43  Maddux, "Ronald Reagan and the Task Force on Immigration," 201.
44  LeMay, *Anatomy of a Public Policy*, 25; Tichenor, "The Politics of Immigration Reform in the United States," 336.
45  LeMay, *Anatomy of a Public Policy*, 36; DeSipio, "A Return to a National Origin Preference?," 568; "Developments in the Law," 1611–12.
46  Tichenor, "The Politics of Immigration Reform in the United States," 337, 342; Susan Gonzalez Baker, "The 'Amnesty' Aftermath: Current Policy Issues Stemming from the Legalization Programs of the 1986 Immigration Reform and Control Act," *The International Migration Review* 31, no. 1 (1997): 7.
47  Tichenor, "The Politics of Immigration Reform in the United States," 340, 344–5, 360.
48  Dunn, *The Militarization of the U.S.-Mexico Border*, 37 and 42; Aristide Zolberg, "Reforming the Back Door: The Immigration Reform and Control Act of 1986 in Historical Perspective," in *Immigration Reconsidered: History, Sociology, and Politics*, ed. Virginia Yans-McLaughlin (New York: Oxford University Press, 1990), 323, 334–5; Leo Chavez, *The Latino Threat: Constructing Immigrants, Citizens, and the Nation* (Stanford, CA: Stanford University Press, 2008), 8; Mary Giovagnoli, "Overhauling Immigration Law: A Brief History of Basic Principles of Reform" (Immigration Policy Center, February 14, 2013), 2; Stumpf, "States of Confusion," 1583.
49  Marc R. Rosenblum and Leo B. Gorman, "The Public Policy Implications of State-Level Worksite Migration Enforcement: The Experiences of Arizona, Mississippi, and Illinois," in *Taking Local Control: Immigration Policy Activism in U.S. Cities and States*, ed. Monica Varsanyi (Stanford, CA: Stanford

University Press, 2008), 115; Degenova, "Migrant Illegality and Deportability in Everyday Life," 437.

50  Giovagnoli, "Overhauling Immigration Law," 7; Daniel James, *Illegal Immigration: An Unfolding Crisis* (Lanham, MD: University Press of America, 1991), 7.

51  Rosenblum and Gorman, "The Public Policy Implications of State-Level Worksite Migration Enforcement," 115; Dunn, *The Militarization of the U.S.-Mexico Border*, 42; Patricia Fernández-Kelly and Douglas S. Massey, "Borders for Whom? The Role of NAFTA in Mexico-U.S. Migration," *The Annals of the American Academy of Political and Social Science* 610 (March 2007): 107; see Kang for an update on this theme.

52  Dorothee Schneider, *Crossing Borders: Migration and Citizenship in the Twentieth Century United States* (Cambridge, MA: Harvard University Press, 2011), 246–7.

53  Massey and Riosmena, "Undocumented Migration from Latin America in an Era of Rising U.S. Enforcement," 295–6; Massey, "America's Immigration Policy Fiasco," 5.

54  Fernández-Kelly and Massey, "Borders for Whom?," 110–13; "Developments in the Law," 1613–14.

55  Rodriguez, "Immigration, Civil Rights and the Evolution of the People," 237.

56  Tichenor, "The Politics of Immigration Reform in the United States," 333; Marta Tienda and Susana M. Sánchez, "Latin American Immigration to the United States," *Daedalus* 142, no. 3 (Summer 2013): 60; Margarita Cervantes-Rodríguez, *International Migration in Cuba: Accumulation, Imperial Designs, and Transnational Social Fields* (University Park, PA: Pennsylvania State University Press, 2010), 153.

57  Keely and Russell, "Responses of Industrial Countries to Asylum Seekers," 402.

58  David Simcox, "Major Predictors of Immigration Restrictionism: Operationalizing 'Nativism'," *Population and Environment* 19, no. 2 (1997): 129, 131; Barkan, "Return of the Nativists?," 239–40.

59  George J. Sanchez, "Face the Nation: Race, Immigration, and the Rise of Nativism in Late Twentieth Century America," *The International Migration Review* 31, no. 4 (1997): 1013, 1015; Simcox, "Major Predictors of Immigration Restrictionism," 131–2.

60  Simcox, "Major Predictors of Immigration Restrictionism," 133; Barkan, "Return of the Nativists?," 256, 258, 261; Ramiro Martinez and Jacob I. Stowell, "Extending Immigration and Crime Studies: National Implications and Local Settings," *The Annals of the American Academy of Political and Social Science* 641 (2012): 189–90; Sanchez, "Face the Nation," 1021.

61  Sanchez, "Face the Nation," 1021, 1024.

62  Schneider, "'I Know All about Emma Lazarus'," 84–7, 94; Sanchez, "Face the Nation," 1025.

63  Jacqueline Hagan, Karl Eschbach, and Nestor Rodriguez, "U.S. Deportation Policy, Family Separation, and Circular Migration," *The International Migration*

*Review* 42, no. 1 (2008): 65; Jenna M. Loyd and Alison Mountz, *Boats, Borders, and Bases: Race, the Cold War, and the Rise of Migration Detention in the United States* (Oakland, CA: University of California Press, 2018), 176; Manges Douglas and Sáenz, "The Criminalization of Immigrants & the Immigration-Industrial Complex," 205–6; Jones-Correa and De Graauw, "The Illegality Trap," 188; Lisa Marie Cacho, "The People of California are Suffering: The Ideology of White Injury in Discourses of Immigration," *Cultural Values* 4, no. 4 (2000): 408; James T. Patterson, *Restless Giant: The United States from Watergate to* Bush v. Gore (Oxford: Oxford University Press, 2005), 374.

64 Monica W. Varsanyi, "Immigration Policy Activism in U.S. States and Cities: Interdisciplinary Perspectives," in *Taking Local Control: Immigration Policy Activism in U.S. Cities and States*, ed. Monica Varsanyi (Stanford, CA: Stanford University Press, 2008), 1–2; Coleman and Kocher, "Detention, Deportation, Devolution and Immigrant Incapacitation in the US," 230–1; Motomura, "Immigration Outside the Law," 2057–8; Hagan, et al., "U.S. Deportation Policy, Family Separation, and Circular Migration," 65–6; Massey, "America's Immigration Policy Fiasco," 9; Adam Goodman, *The Deportation Machine: America's Long History of Expelling Immigrants.* (Princeton, NJ: Princeton University Press, 2020), 176–7.

65 Hagan, et al., "U.S. Deportation Policy, Family Separation, and Circular Migration," 67, 76, 83–5; Massey and Riosmena, "Undocumented Migration from Latin America in an Era of Rising U.S. Enforcement," 314, 316; Gallegos, "Border Matters," 1738.

66 Peter Andreas, "U.S.: Mexico: Open Markets, Closed Border," *Foreign Policy*, No. 103 (Summer, 1996): 62; Varsanyi, "Immigration Policy Activism in U.S. States and Cities: Interdisciplinary Perspectives," 1–2; Giovagnoli, "Overhauling Immigration Law," 2; Chavez, *The Latino Threat*, 8–9; Schneider, *Crossing Borders*, 246–7; Kevin Johnson, "Aliens and the U.S. Immigration Laws: The Social and Legal Construction of Nonpersons," *University of Miami Interamerican Law Review* 28 (Winter 1996): 281; Cacho, "The People of California are Suffering," 389; Ayelet Shachar, "Territory Without Boundaries: Immigration Beyond Territory: The Shifting Border of Immigration Regulation," *Michigan Journal of International Law* 30 (Spring 2009): 815–17; Gallegos, "Border Matters," 1751.

67 Giovagnoli, "Overhauling Immigration Law," 3.

68 Stumpf, "States of Confusion," 1561–62n17.

69 Jones-Correa and De Graauw, "The Illegality Trap," 185; Stumpf, "States of Confusion," 1561. In 2005, approximately 300 immigration-related bills were proposed to state governments. Thirty-nine of them passed. By 2011, 1,607 bills were presented at the state level; 306 passed across forty-two states. Jones-Correa and De Graauw, "The Illegality Trap," 190.

# 3

# A Synthesis of the Parallel Developments of the International and the US Refugee Resettlement Regimes, 1921–80

The origin of the international community's concern for refugees can be dated to the late 1910s and 1920s, during which time foreign governments cooperated to resettle millions of displaced persons in the wake of the First World War (1914–18). The High Commissioner for Refugees (HCR), the first multilateral coordinating mechanism for refugees, was created in 1921. It resettled Russian, Greek, Turkish, Bulgarian, and Armenian refugees. Yet the HCR's resettlement programs were limited in time duration and focused solely on European refugees. Far from being founded for altruistic reasons, the HCR was primarily focused on maintaining the internal stability of nations, something many international leaders believed could be undermined by huge inflows of displaced persons. Toward this end, European governments erected protective barriers, closed borders, and expelled thousands of individuals across national frontiers. Upon its founding, then, the international refugee resettlement regime prioritized the sovereignty of nations over the humanitarian needs of refugees.[1]

Under the leadership of the League of Nations, the international refugee regime continued to have a delimited purpose during the interwar years. Much of this limited remit was attributable to international disagreement among government leaders over how to define a refugee, the main concern being that any supragovernmental body founded to protect refugees might impinge upon the sovereign rights of foreign nations. Instead, Western governments addressed the refugee problem in a piecemeal fashion: only specific national groups were designated as refugees, these refugees were provided minimal protections, and the mandate of the HCR was purposely restrained. As troops once again began to march across the European continent in the late 1930s, the League of Nations' inability to handle the refugee problem paralleled its failure to maintain continental security.[2]

The ineffectiveness of the Western refugee resettlement regime was more than just an exercise in fear. Instead, especially during the years of economic depression, it was based on concrete concerns about an instability that might follow refugee resettlement. First, tight fiscal constraints and high unemployment rates across Western nations limited any humanitarian impulses that argued for refugee resettlement. Second, again in a time of economic depression, there was little inclination among Western states to pressure refugee-generating countries to change their behaviors toward their citizens. Third, for many governments, placing barriers on immigration was considered a prime method for protecting their countries.[3] Hindsight reveals the disastrous results to such parochial thinking: the Nazi Holocaust of European Jews (see Chapter 6)

The community of nations had a newfound concern for universal human rights in the wake of the horrors of the Second World War (1937–45). A new refugee resettlement regime was taking shape even before the war ended. In 1943, the Big Three (Franklin Roosevelt of the United States, Winston Churchill of Great Britain, and Josef Stalin of the Soviet Union) established the United Nations Relief and Rehabilitation Agency (UNRRA). Rather than resettling refugees into third countries, the new UNRRA focused on repatriating the millions of displaced persons under Allied control to their home countries. Such a policy was problematic, however, as repatriation placed many refugees back into the adverse conditions—economic want, political oppression—that had initially caused them to flee.[4]

The UNRRA was abolished in 1945 and was soon replaced by the International Refugee Organization (IRO) in 1947. Over objections from the Soviet Union, the IRO sought to resettle, not repatriate, the more than 1 million refugees remaining from the war, many of whom were from Eastern Europe. The IRO switched to a model of resettlement for two reasons: to mitigate the burden repatriated persons might place on war-weary nations and their economies and to "internationalize" the refugee problem by distributing refugees and the costs of resettling them among North and South American nations, Western European nations, and even countries in Africa and Australasia. Significantly, the IRO adopted a universal definition of refugees based on "persecution or fear of persecution" on the grounds of race, religion, nationality, or political opinion. Just as important, the United States emerged as the "principal architect" of this new postwar refugee resettlement regime and exercised exclusive control over the IRO's leadership.[5]

"The IRO," political scientist Gil Loescher states, "turned out to be an extremely expensive operation." Not long after its founding, the United States and its Western allies became nervous about making open-ended commitments to refugee resettlement, especially as the places of origin of those refugees moved beyond Europe to countries in the "Third World," such as India, Korea, China, and Palestine, experiencing internecine struggles and civil wars during the late 1940s.[6] Interestingly, it was conflict between "First World" governments and the United Nations, the replacement of the defunct League of Nations, that led to another overhaul of the refugee resettlement regime. Washington, London, and Paris were uncomfortable with Geneva making unspecified and potentially interminable commitments to refugee resettlement. To preserve unilateral interests within the multilateral organization of the UN, the Office of the United Nations High Commissioner for Refugees (UNHCR) replaced the IRO in 1950.[7] The founding of the UNHCR represented, just as with the HCR in the 1920s, national sovereignty interests over international mandates. The US government and its Western allies placed "severe limitations" on the UNHCR's functional scope and authority to ensure that any refugee resettlement program would not pose a threat to their national sovereignty nor impose new financial obligations on them.[8]

In contrast to its aloofness to multilateral relations during the interwar years, the United States was at the center of the creation of an international effort to resettle war refugees. Indeed, considering the extent of destruction and damage caused by the Second World War, the United States was the only major nation capable of providing political and financial support for refugee resettlement. At the same time, the issue of refugee resettlement took place amid the beginning of a new international crisis, the Cold War. Foreign policy concerns started to subsume refugee resettlement considerations, and it was not long until US policymakers used the latter to address the former. For US leaders, the "most important aspect of the newly-formed refugee regime" was to maintain international attention on the plight of refugees from communist countries.[9] From the US foreign policy perspective, refugees started to change from potential social and economic burdens into powerful political symbols of persons seeking freedom outside the Eastern bloc. Unfortunately, for the refugees themselves, the possibility of resettlement was only as germane as its political symbolism in the Cold War conflict was relevant.

Not from a lack of international refugees but rather from a lack of American financial and diplomatic support, the UNHCR muddled through its first years of existence. The agency was unable to define an independent role from its benefactor nations and failed to meet the needs of the large numbers of refugees that teemed across the world during the 1950s.[10] The failed

Hungarian Revolution of 1956, however, offered the UNHCR a chance to escape irrelevancy. In November 1956, the Soviet Union sent forces to crush a popular reformist regime that had emerged in Hungary.[11] The departure of 150,000 refugees from Hungary in the wake of the failed revolution sparked the first full-blown Cold War refugee crisis. The resettlement of Hungarian refugees allowed the UNHCR to demonstrate for the first time how it was the nexus agency between displaced persons in need and countries of resettlement. With the Hungarian refugee crisis, UNHCR became the "centerpiece" of the international refugee regime.[12]

New floodgates burst open between the late 1950s and the late 1970s to propel millions of refugees onto the world scene. The UNHCR's reach and mandate simultaneously expanded to meet the proliferation of demand. During these years the character of the international refugee situation changed, as Eastern European refugee traffic waned while refugee flows from the "Third World" increased dramatically. There were three other distinct features to this new phase in the international refugee issue, having to do with geopolitics and the demographics. First, many of the refugees emanated from former European colonies throughout Africa and Asia. Rapid decolonization in a multitude of new nations, and the colonial-civil wars that followed in its train, displaced millions of people. Second, many of these displaced persons came from the very colonies held by founding members of the international refugee resettlement regime. The departure of colonial subjects was at once embarrassing and counterproductive for nations like Britain and France: embarrassing because refugee crises showed their inability to maintain their colonies, and counterproductive because the outflow of so many colonial subjects undermined the stability of these colonies. Third, in contrast to European refugees of the 1930s and 1940s, who were politically marginalized for their ethnicity or creed, "Third World" refugees were predominantly displaced by the internecine violence of their home countries and were profoundly poor in economic terms.[13]

In the context of this international refugee crisis spawned by decolonization, the Western states turned to the UNHCR. No longer the humanitarian puppet of Western powers, the UNHCR was the implement nations like the United States, Britain, and France used to resolve refugee issues. Western states, particularly the former colonial powers, bent and altered rules of the resettlement regime to facilitate the UNHCR's work.[14]

Far from a sudden flush of humanitarianism, foreign policy interests underlined this about-face by Western states regarding the UNHCR. "Third World" countries were the principal battlegrounds of the Cold War between the United States and the Soviet Union, and their respective allies. As such, Western governments came to believe that refugee crises across the "Third World" could be used as pieces in their geopolitical chess match against the USSR. "In the face of an escalating Cold War struggle," Loescher states, "Western governments came to perceive assistance to refugees as a central part of their foreign policies towards newly independent states. . . . Governments made little distinction between military aid, development assistance and refugee relief aid."[15] Since the UNHCR was a donor-dependent organization and since all of the donor nations to the UNHCR were non-communist Western states, the refugee resettlement regime became a de facto, non-military, humanitarian weapon in the hands of the "First World," against the "Second World," for the sake of the "Third World."[16]

Western states' initial hesitancy about the remit of the UNHCR to its eventual embrace of refugee resettlement as a reliable foreign policy instrument was demonstrated by the fight to redefine the term "refugee" for a Cold War world. The foundation for a definition took shape during the immediate postwar years, first in 1947 with the IRO (see earlier) and then in 1948, when the UN General Assembly published the Universal Declaration of Human Rights (UDHR), which stated that every person had the right to seek and enjoy asylum from persecution in their home countries and that foreign nations had a duty to consider granting sanctuary to displaced persons. This document was a direct, international expression of the rights of persons to emigrate to escape oppression. Notably, the UNHR also argued that every person had a right to nationality, meaning that there could be no such thing as a stateless person.[17]

A few years after the promulgation of the UDHR, the UN General Assembly held the Convention Relating to the Status of Refugees which produced what can be considered the first fixed definition of a refugee.

> A person who owing to a well-founded fear of being persecuted for reasons of race, religion, nationality, membership of a particular social group or political opinion, is outside the country of his nationality and is unable or, owing to such fear, is unwilling to avail himself of the protection of that country; or who, not having a nationality and being outside the country of his former habitual residence as a result of such events, is unable or, owing to such fear, is unwilling to return to it.[18]

The definition was limited by time and geography: the 1951 Refugee Convention stated that a refugee is a person affected by "events occurring in Europe (or elsewhere) before 1 January 1951." Ironically, the definition stated that while refugees had a right to seek asylum or to emigrate, there was no obligation on the part of states to accept those refugees (see Introduction).[19]

Within that qualification was the seed of what would become a staple of international refugee policy: the policy of *non-refoulement*, which stated that refugees could not be forced to return to their home nation if their freedom and life could be threatened, even if countries were not obliged to accept refugees. Non-refoulement had actually existed in international law since prominent League of Nations' member states, for example, France and Britain, promulgated it after the Convention relating to the International Status of Refugees in October 1933. But in the new, post-Second World War context, the 1951 Convention reiterated the policy of non-refoulment and worked toward making it a staple of international asylum law. Additionally, the 1951 Convention established a principle of nondiscrimination against particular refugee groups.[20]

The creation of an international regime of refugee resettlement after the Second World War was not done for altruistic reasons. Refugee resettlement was just as much about promoting regional and international stability in postwar Europe as it was driven by humanitarian concerns. The mandate given to the UN to resettle refugees was always considered ancillary to the sovereign authority of the member states which contributed and administered the international refugee regime. Nevertheless, something dramatic happened during the two decades after the end of Second World War: even within the constraints of the sovereign rights of nations, a multilateral body was created to facilitate intergovernmental cooperation to resettle displaced persons, and the notion of assisting and protecting refugees was normalized in international law.[21]

As the European refugee crisis abated by 1960, the temporal definition of "events occurring in Europe (or elsewhere) before 1 January 1951" failed to correspond to the causes of refugee crises thereafter.[22] The UN General Assembly attempted to respond to this altering refugee crisis with its Protocol Relating to the Status of Refugees in January 1967. First, the protocol extended the application of refugee protection for after January 1, 1951. Second, it reaffirmed the 1951 Convention's definition of a refugee.[23]

For "First World" nations, the 1960s and most of the 1970s were halcyon days of refugee resettlement. The majority of the world's refugees were resettled in the "Third World," far away from the borders of Britain, France, and the United States. Essentially, the Western powers, during these years, enjoyed the benefit of decrying communist countries for the refugees they produced while not having the burden of resettling those refugees. This arrangement would not last forever and would change markedly when refugees started to arrive on US shores in sizable numbers by the late 1970s (see Chapters 8, 9, and 10).[24]

While the United States played a central role in the creation of an international refugee resettlement regime after the Second World War, it was a laggard in regard to resettling displaced persons on US soil. The US Congress did not ratify the 1951 Convention and did not amend its own immigration laws to align with the humanitarian provisions of international refugee policy.[25] While the United States was a signatory nation of the UN when it was founded in 1945, it was not until October 1968—after the Protocol Relating to the Status of Refugees of the previous year—that the United States accepted the notion of admitting refugees when their lives and freedom were threatened because of their political opinions. Finally, it was not until March 1980 that the United States formally accepted the UN 1967 Protocol's definition of a refugee, aligning US refugee policy with UN Convention norms.[26]

Nonetheless, the United States was a place of refuge during the early Cold War. Instead of abiding by the multilateral norms that took shape between the mid-1940s and mid-1960s, the United States implemented a unilateral refugee policy. Until the mid-1970s, the United States readily accepted refugees from communist countries—such as Hungary (discussed earlier) but also Cuba (see Chapter 9) and Vietnam (see Chapter 8)—as a way to discredit socialist regimes, drain them of their human resources, and promote opposition activities against those governments.[27]

America has been a place of refuge for all types of displaced persons throughout the centuries: Protestant religious dissenters and royalists from England during the seventeenth century, ousted slaveholders from Haiti in the eighteenth century, German republicans and Cuban nationalists during the nineteenth century, as well as Mexican revolutionaries during the twentieth century. In relative terms, however, the numbers involved in those refugee flows paled in comparison with the number of persons displaced by international conflicts after 1945.[28]

The discrepancy over whether the United States was or was not a place of refuge involved first, intra-branch disagreement over refugee resettlement and, second, foreign policy considerations. As discussed in Chapter 6, the US government refused any idea of amending immigration quota laws to facilitate the resettlement of Jewish refugees during the 1930s and early 1940s. The war brought a sea change in how the executive and legislative branches approached the problem of internationally displaced persons. Just months after the end of the Second World War the administration of Harry Truman (1945–53) passed an executive order that admitted 40,000 refugees.[29]

In 1946, Congress approved the War Brides Act that allowed 120,000 refugees—albeit all related to members of the US armed forces—to enter the United States. Two years later, in 1948, Congress passed the Displaced Persons Act, which allowed the admittance of 200,000 refugees within a limited two-year period. This law began a trend in which US policymakers started to see the political salience of resettling refugees from communist countries. Another 400,000 refugees were resettled in the United States after the Displaced Persons Act was extended for another two-year period in 1950.[30] The word "refugee" had not appeared in American law until 1934; up to that time, there was little distinction between refugees and other immigrants in US immigration law.[31] Years later, the Displaced Persons Acts of 1948 and 1950 formalized a US refugee policy. Not only were they the first pieces of legislation in US history to directly address refugee resettlement, they also established the process by which refugees were allowed to settle in the United States. Screening and selecting would be done on foreign soil far from the United States, and persons would not be authorized to leave for the United States until their petitions had been evaluated and approved.[32]

The 1950s witnessed new legislation passed for individuals fleeing communist nations, as well as for other displaced persons from war-ravaged Europe. The Refugee Relief Acts of 1953 and 1954 authorized the admission of more than 200,000 persons over a multiyear period. The Refugee-Escapee Act of 1957 admitted persons fleeing communist countries and from the Middle East. Three years later, in 1960, the US Congress passed the Fair Share Act, which authorized the resettlement of another 20,000 refugees and worked to ease the burden of displaced persons camps in second-destination countries throughout the world.[33]

But it was the Hungarian refugee crisis of 1956, the event that had spurred the UNHCR into a new, proactive role in resettling displaced persons worldwide, that caused a true watershed in US refugee policy. The United States accepted a fifth of the total refugees from Hungary. Most importantly, a novel legal approach was formulated to meet this refugee crisis: *parole authority*. Authorized by Section 212(d)(5) of the Immigration and Nationality Act of 1952, the US attorney general admitted refugees into the United States without congressional approval. According to legal scholar Michael Churgin, the Hungarian refugee crisis was the "first of many times that the parole authority was to be used by the executive branch when no other mechanism existed to admit individuals deemed appropriate for entry, usually for a combination of political and humanitarian reasons."[34] The Eisenhower administration (1953–61) was the first to use parole authority to respond to refugee crises. By the 1970s, parole authority was the "central tool" of US refugee policy (Figure 3.1).[35]

Despite the "ad hoc" commitment to refugee resettlement during the 1940s and 1950s, Congress consistently refused to pass comprehensive refugee legislation. Instead, it preferred to approach each situation on a case-by-case basis without giving the executive branch a clear directive on refugee resettlement.[36] Therefore, in 1956 the executive branch established its own power to resettle refugees by utilizing the parole authority under the office of the attorney general.

Congress did not acquiesce readily to the executive branch's use of parole authority. It made several attempts to "rein in" the executive's use of it until, in 1965, Congress—together with sweeping changes to immigration policy in general (see Chapter 2)—established a visa preference category for the

**FIGURE 3.1** A Little Higher, a Little Brighter, *December 5, 1956. Political cartoonist Frank Miller depicts a smiling Lady Liberty in response to the Eisenhower administration's decision to resettle Hungarian refugees on US soil in the fall of 1956 (though the actual number was closer to 15,000). This was the first instance of the US government using parole authority to resettle in the United States displaced persons from abroad. © Frank Miller—USA TODAY NETWORK.*

admission of overseas refugees as part of the Hart-Celler Act. The numbers allowed to enter were limited and restricted to persons fleeing communism or the Middle East. In fact, this visa preference category can be seen less as a congressional effort to provide a humanitarian response to international refugee issues and more of an attempt to claw back control over US refugee policy and resettlement from the executive branch.[37]

Despite congressional efforts to curb it, the executive branch continued to use parole power in the 1960s to respond to refugee crises emanating from Cuba (see Chapter 9) as well as to respond to a Vietnamese refugee crisis in the 1970s (see Chapter 8). Indeed, it was the executive branch's persistent use of parole authority that formed an impetus for passage of the Refugee Act of 1980. The new law required the president to engage in "appropriate consultation" with Cabinet officials and congressional committee members regarding refugee resettlement into the United States. The Refugee Act of 1980 sought to encourage executive accountability and to end the executive's customary unilateral use of parole authority. The act had more bark than bite. Congress left the allocation and the refugee quotas up to the discretion of the president. According to legal scholars, Adam Cox and Cristina Rodríguez, the ultimate goal of Congress was not to wrest control over refugee policy from the executive branch, but instead to restrict the president's unencumbered use of parole authority and to make refugee policy more "transparent and consultative" between the two branches of government.[38]

But there was also a dose of liberalism infused into US refugee policy. By requiring the president to consult with Congress, the 1980 act attempted to ensure a more equitable treatment of refugees. A principle of nondiscrimination had been a part of UN-mandated refugee policy since the 1950s. In 1980, some American policymakers attempted to instill a similar principle into US refugee policy. Since the end of the Second World War, the US government disproportionately granted asylum to persons fleeing from communist countries. In fact, this political preference was written into US refugee law: the Refugee-Escapee Act of 1957, which created a permanent refugee admission category, rejected the UN's humanitarian criteria of refugee resettlement in favor of a definition of a refugee as anyone who was fleeing a communist or a communist-dominated country, or any country within the Middle East. A dose of liberalism seemed apparent in 1968 when the United States formally aligned its definition of a refugee with international norms established by the UN. Congress failed to develop comprehensive refugee policy reform, however, and US policymakers continued to view (and resettle) refugees through an anticommunist lens. In this sense, almost from its inception, postwar US refugee policy was infused with foreign policy objectives.[39]

# Notes

1 Gil Loescher, "The International Refugee Regime: Stretched to the Limit?" *Journal of International Affairs* 47, no. 2 (1994): 352–4.

2 Ibid., 354.

3 Ibid., 354–5.

4 Marc R. Rosenblum and Idean Salehyan, "Norms and Interests in US Asylum Enforcement," *Journal of Peace Research* 41, no. 6 (2004): 679; Idean Salehyan and Marc R. Rosenblum. "International Relations, Domestic Politics, and Asylum Admissions in the United States," *Political Research Quarterly* 61, no. 1 (2008): 105; Purcell, "A Right to Leave, but Nowhere to Go," 185–6; Loescher, "The International Refugee Regime," 355–6.

5   Dennis Gallagher, "The Evolution of the International Refugee System," *International Migration Review* 23, no. 3 (1989): 579–80; Loescher, "The International Refugee Regime," 356.
6   Loescher, "The International Refugee Regime," 357.
7   Ibid.
8   Ibid.
9   Ibid.
10  Gallagher, "The Evolution of the International Refugee System," 582; Loescher, "The International Refugee Regime," 358.
11  S. J. Ball, *The Cold War: An International History, 1947–1994* (London: Arnold Publishers, 1998), 94.
12  Loescher, "The International Refugee Regime," 358–9.
13  Ibid., 359–60.
14  Ibid., 360–1.
15  Ibid., 361.
16  Ibid.
17  Zolberg, "Changing Sovereignty Games," 163; Thomas Kleven, "Why International Law Favors Emigration over Immigration," *The University of Miami Inter-American Law Review* 33, no. 1 (2002): 71, 82; Kendall Coffey, "The Due Process Right to Seek Asylum in the United States: The Immigration Dilemma and Constitutional Controversy," *Yale Law & Policy Review* 19, no. 2 (2001): 312.
18  LeMay, *Anatomy of a Public Policy*, 17.
19  Gallagher, "The Evolution of the International Refugee System," 580–1; Saskia Sassen, "Beyond Sovereignty: Immigration Policy Making Today," *Social Justice* 23, no. 3 (1996): 10.
20  Sassen, "Beyond Sovereignty," 10; Kleven, "Why International Law Favors Emigration over Immigration," 71; Rosenblum and Salehyan, "Norms and Interests in US Asylum Enforcement," 683–4.
21  Loescher, "The International Refugee Regime," 351–2.
22  Gallagher, "The Evolution of the International Refugee System," 583.
23  LeMay, *Anatomy of a Public Policy*, 17; Coffey, "The Due Process Right to Seek Asylum in the United States," 312.
24  Loescher, "The International Refugee Regime," 361–3.
25  Rosenblum and Salehyan, "Norms and Interests in US Asylum Enforcement," 683–4.
26  Michael J. Churgin, "Mass Exoduses: The Response of the United States," *The International Migration Review* 30, no. 1 (1996): 310; Coffey, "The Due Process Right to Seek Asylum in the United States," 312; Purcell, "A Right to Leave, but Nowhere to Go," 194–5.
27  Salehyan and Rosenblum, "International Relations, Domestic Politics, and Asylum Admissions in the United States," 105.
28  Roger Daniels, *Guarding the Golden Door: American Immigration Policy and Immigrants Since 1882* (New York: Hill and Wang, 2004), 72; David W.

Engstrom, *Presidential Decision Making Adrift: The Carter Administration and the Mariel Boatlift* (New York: Rowman & Littlefield, 1997), 4.

29 Churgin, "Mass Exoduses," 313.
30 Ibid.
31 Daniels, *Guarding the Golden Door*, 73.
32 Churgin, "Mass Exoduses," 313.
33 Ibid., 314.
34 Ibid., 314.
35 Cox and Rodríguez, "The President and Immigration Law," 502; Salehyan and Rosenblum, "International Relations, Domestic Politics, and Asylum Admissions in the United States," 107.
36 Churgin, "Mass Exoduses," 314.
37 Ibid., 315; Cox and Rodríguez, "The President and Immigration Law," 502 and 502n154.
38 Cox and Rodríguez, "The President and Immigration Law," 505n161, 506, 539.
39 Ibid., 506; Rosenblum and Salehyan, "Norms and Interests in US Asylum Enforcement," 684; Salehyan and Rosenblum, "International Relations, Domestic Politics, and Asylum Admissions in the United States," 107.

# PART II

# Case Studies

# 4

# Japanese, 1910s–1920s

Japanese immigrants started to arrive in the United States in noticeable numbers during the 1890s. By the turn of the century there were approximately 25,000 Japanese in the US population and were concentrated on the West Coast; by 1910, that number grew to 75,000.[1] Interestingly, and in contrast to the Chinese (see Chapter 7), Americans initially welcomed Japanese immigrants. Several factors explain this different reaction. First, the Japanese started to arrive as the US economy recovered from the 1893 depression. By contrast, Chinese immigration to the United States started much earlier, during the mid-nineteenth century, and anti-Chinese agitation paralleled economic downturns, such as the depression of 1873. Another explanation for the initial positive reception of Japanese immigrants in US society was that many Japanese worked in agriculture and resided in rural areas, where their population growth was not readily recognizable to most Americans. By contrast, Chinese immigrants resided in densely populated urban areas where their community growth was conspicuous, and they were drawn to work in heavy industries—mining, railroads, manufacturing—in which labor organization was predominant. Japanese immigrants were also welcomed, paradoxically, because they met the labor demands left vacant by the 1882 restriction on the entry of Chinese workers. Finally, Japanese immigrants were viewed differently from their Chinese predecessors because of the different public perceptions of China and Japan. Whereas China was viewed by Americans as poor and weak, Japan was seen as a powerful nation with rising aspirations in East Asia, as fact demonstrated by the Russo-Japanese War of 1905. This exceptional view of Japan was illustrated by the US government negotiating a bilateral treaty to accommodate Japanese immigration to the United States while it unilaterally banned Chinese immigration in 1882.[2]

Despite the initial dissimilarities in the US public's response to the Chinese and Japanese in their midst, Americans came to view the Japanese negatively. "[F]lurries" of anti-Japanese violence dated back to the 1890s, mostly in

California, but it was not until the turn of the century that a full-blown, anti-Japanese movement took shape along the Pacific Coast of the United States and Canada. San Francisco was the center of such agitation, but the corridor of prejudice stretched as far north as Vancouver, British Columbia, and as far south as San Diego. The first formal anti-Japanese meeting took place in San Francisco in May 1900. That same year, which was a presidential election year, the People's Party put an anti-Japanese plank in their campaign agenda and the American Federation of Labor pressured Congress to extend the legal restrictions on Chinese immigration to the Japanese.[3]

The agitation gained momentum during the early twentieth century. In February 1905, the *San Francisco Chronicle*, the most prestigious newspaper in California, began a campaign regularly denigrating Japanese immigrants. A month later, California's state legislature petitioned the US Congress to "limit and diminish" further Japanese immigration to the United States. Throughout the remainder of 1905 and early 1906, Japanese restaurants and other businesses in San Francisco were picketed, boycotted, and vandalized. Notably, in May 1905, delegates from over sixty organizations, most of them labor unions, formed the Asiatic Exclusion League (AEL).[4] The AEL led anti-Asian activities along the Pacific Coast. For example, in May 1907, a white mob attacked Japanese restaurants and bathhouses in San Francisco. Four months later, 150 white men attacked South Asian residents, primarily Punjabi Sikhs (who were erroneously referred to as "Hindoos"), in Bellingham, Washington.[5]

This sudden American antipathy toward Japanese immigrants was partly attributable to a long arch in shifting US opinion against "new" immigrants from Southern and Eastern Europe. As opposed to the "old" immigrants of Northern and Western Europe, between the late nineteenth and early twentieth century, Americans came to believe that immigrants from nations like Italy, Russia, and the Ottoman Empire were unassimilable. Americans were losing faith in the melting pot idea that all immigrants eventually assimilate into US society and do their part to contribute to the collective national whole. Similar negative beliefs were taking root regarding Japanese immigrants.[6]

Other diplomatic and geopolitical factors, some dating back decades, drove American opposition to Japanese immigration. Hawaii, long in the annexationist sights of US leaders, had for years up to the 1890s encouraged Japanese immigration to the island to meet labor demands. Fearing the rapid rise of the Japanese presence in the archipelago nation (from 116 Japanese in 1884 to 25,000 in 1897, or, one-quarter of the nation's entire population), the Hawaiian government abruptly attempted to stop the arrival of Japanese immigrants. Japan responded to what it viewed as a disgraceful treatment of its citizens by sending two warships. Suddenly confronted with the prospect of losing access to Hawaii, the administration of William McKinley (1897–1901), sent US naval vessels to meet the Japanese threat. Despite a brief war scare, however, peace was maintained and the United States formally annexed Hawaii in August 1898 in the immediate wake of the Spanish-American War.[7] Just a few years later, Americans were impressed by Imperial Japan's crushing defeat of the Russian Empire in the Russo-Japanese War of 1904–5. Yet this newfound US respect for Japan also caused fear among Americans. The confidence that came with great military victory emboldened Japanese officials to assert the rights of their nationals in the United States. This diplomatic confidence bred anxiety among Americans who feared that the eastern empire's rising power might threaten US territorial holdings across the Pacific, specifically the Philippines and the Hawaiian Islands. These geopolitical fears translated into xenophobic alarms, as some Americans believed Japanese immigrants were "fifth column" agents of the Japanese empire. Therefore, many nativist attacks against Japanese between 1905 and 1907 were justified as methods of maintaining national security.[8]

Anti-Japanese sentiment along the West Coast reached a flashpoint in early October 1906 when the San Francisco School Board ordered all Japanese students in its public schools to attend the segregated school for Chinese students. The school segregation order caused a full-blown diplomatic crisis between the United States and Japan and led to the boisterous intervention of President Theodore Roosevelt.[9]

While Roosevelt admired Japan's growing military might during his time in office (1901–9), he initially did little to protest rising anti-Japanese sentiment along the West Coast. Privately, in 1905, Roosevelt communicated to Japan that the US government and the American people at large had no sympathy for violence and prejudice against the Japanese. Publicly, in December of that same year, Roosevelt stated in his annual address to Congress that the United States should not discriminate against immigrants—regardless of race and religion—who wanted to become citizens.[10]

A year later, during his 1906 annual address to Congress, Roosevelt used his bully pulpit to roundly condemn the San Francisco School Board's action of the previous October. Far less vague than in his address the previous year, Roosevelt left listeners in no doubt about how he viewed anti-Japanese actions on the West Coast, stating that such activities was "most discreditable to us as a people, and it may be filled with the gravest consequences to the nation."[11] Roosevelt got even more pointed later in the same message.

> But here and there a most unworthy feeling has manifested itself toward the Japanese [such as] shutting them out of the common schools of San Francisco [and] mutterings against them in one or two other places, because of their efficiency as workers. To shut them out from the public schools is a wicked absurdity . . . I recommend to the Congress that an act

be [passed] specifically providing for the naturalization of Japanese who come here intending to become American citizens.[12]

Roosevelt's call for a congressional bill to facilitate the naturalization of a particular immigrant group was unprecedented. The president also described the problems anti-Japanese activities could cause in US-Japanese relations: "the mob of a single city may at any time perform acts of lawless violence which would plunge us into war . . . It is unthinkable that we should continue a policy under which a given locality may be allowed to commit a crime against a friendly nation."[13]

Congress responded to the pressure from the executive branch by passing a new immigration act in February 1907, which authorized the executive branch to negotiate an immigration agreement with the Empire of Japan. Despite the toughness of his public condemnation of the San Francisco School Board, Roosevelt was a consummate negotiator. He knew he had to give a little to get a little. So, when the San Francisco School Board rescinded the segregation order after a series of meetings between Roosevelt and California state officials, the president promised that the federal government would act to stem the flow of Japanese immigration to the United States. The subsequent Immigration Act of 1907 did just that by giving the executive branch the power to bar entry of any alien carrying a passport valid for any place other than the continental United States. While composed to apply to immigration in general, no one was under any allusions that the law was specifically meant to restrict Japanese immigrants from entering the continental United States.[14]

With the school segregation issue settled, the next step for Roosevelt and his secretary of state, Elihu Root, was to maintain the executive branch's promise to the state of California without offending Japan. The negotiations were complicated, but they resulted in the Gentlemen's Agreement, a series of six diplomatic notes exchanged between the two countries between late 1907 and early 1908. The agreement stated that Japan would not issue passports to laborers, either skilled or unskilled, for admission into the continental United States. In exchange for agreeing to self-restrict the immigration of workers to the United States, Japan was permitted to continue issuing passports to parents, wives, and children of laborers already in the United States. In essence, the Gentlemen's Agreement was a compromise: if Japan regulated its own immigration, then the San Francisco School Board would rescind its segregation order.[15]

The Gentlemen's Agreement of 1907–8 *seemed* to ease the tension over immigration between the United States and Japan, and anti-Japanese agitation along the West Coast *seemed* to wane. Eventually, however, xenophobic pressures against Japanese in the United States not only resulted in the abrogation of the Gentlemen's Agreement but also precipitated congressional legislation in the 1920s that comprehensively and permanently excluded Japanese immigration from the United States.

The first pressure that would eventually undermine the Gentlemen's Agreement was the issue of "picture brides," who were Japanese women, living in Japan, married by proxy to Japanese men, living on US soil, who they had never met in person. Neither American nor Japanese negotiators anticipated in 1907–8 that large numbers of single Japanese men resident in the United States and Hawaii would bring over wives. Uncoincidentally, the population of Japanese-derived US residents started to grow during the 1900s and 1910s. And, thanks to the Fourteenth Amendment to the Constitution, which in part stated that any person born on US soil automatically gained citizenship, the offspring of Japanese immigrant couples in the United States became US citizens. Consequently, the population of Japanese-derived residents in the United States grew, first, with the arrival of picture brides and, second, with the birth of Japanese Americans (Nisei). For many Americans, just a decade after it was brokered, the Gentlemen's Agreement seemed to have failed to limit the Japanese presence in US society.[16]

Immigration restrictionists came to resent the admission of picture brides into the United States and believed it eroded the fundamental purpose of the Gentlemen's Agreement. Anti-Japanese agitation reemerged during the 1910s. In 1913, the state of California passed the Alien Land Law, which denied Japanese immigrants (Issei) the right to own land in the state and limited land leases to three years. In 1915, media mogul William Randolph Hearst's newspapers began running lurid stories warning of the "yellow peril."[17] This animus toward Japanese immigrants and Japanese Americans was accelerated by the general antagonism Americans felt toward foreign nationals in the United States in the years after the First World War. By the turn of the 1920s, Japanese immigrants, once lauded as preferable immigrants to Chinese, were viewed as threats to US society who took too much land and produced too many children.[18]

The Japanese government, fearing the United States might abrogate the Gentlemen's Agreement, ceased issuing passports to picture brides in March 1920. Japan hoped such an action would tamp down growing anti-Japanese sentiment in the United States, but the xenophobic momentum was inexorable and calls proliferated for comprehensive immigration restriction. As Congress considered such proposals during the early 1920s, the question was no longer *if* Japanese immigration would be restricted but rather *how* severe those restrictions would be.[19]

Anti-Japanese measures began appearing at the congressional level by 1923. A clause barring all Japanese immigrants from entry into the United States was inserted into an immigration bill proposed in the sixty-eighth Congress, which convened in December 1923. Worried that the bill, if passed, would disturb US-Japanese relations, the State Department and the Japanese Foreign Ministry worked to abort the clause. The Japanese Foreign Ministry sent frequent letters of protest to the State Department, and the State Department pledged its full opposition to the bill. This protest culminated in April 1924 with a letter to Charles Evans Hughes, the US secretary of state, from Masanao Hanihara, the Japanese ambassador to the United States, appealing to the Senate not to include the clause, which would totally prohibit Japanese immigration.[20]

> The manifest object of the [exclusion clause] is to single out Japanese as a nation, stigmatizing them as unworthy and undesirable in the eyes of the American people . . . [the exclusion clause] in apparent disregard of the most sincere and friendly endeavors of the Japanese Government to meet the needs and wishes of the American Government and people, is mortifying enough to the Government and people of Japan. . . .
>
> Relying upon the confidence you have been good enough to show me at all times, I have stated or rather repeated all this to you very candidly and in a most friendly spirit, for I realize, as I believe you do, the grave consequences which the enactment of the measure retaining that particular provision would inevitably bring upon the otherwise happy and mutually advantageous relations between our two countries.[21]

The vehemence of Japan's opposition to the exclusion laws was based on the racial prejudice that underlined it and the betrayal of past US-Japanese agreements on immigration. Japan felt the immigration question had been settled by the Gentlemen's Agreement of 1907–8. More importantly, Japan chafed at the racial implications of the law. "In Japan," historian Izumi Hirobe argues,

> the total ban of Japanese immigrants to the United States in 1924 was interpreted as a rejection of Japan, made exclusively on the grounds of race, by the existing world order, controlled by the Western nations. The Japanese interpreted this to mean that no matter how hard Japan tried to cooperate with the United States, they would never be treated as America's equal (Figure 4.1).[22]

Japan did not challenge the United States' sovereign right to formulate immigration policy, though it did assert that such an exclusionary law threatened to undermine harmonious relations between the two countries.[23] Rather, the Japanese government protested "the fact that discriminatory immigration legislation on the part of the United States would naturally wound

**FIGURE 4.1** You can't blame Japan for feeling it an insult, *March 17, 1919*. Arguing that US immigration laws allowed the dumping of undesirable immigrants into the United States, notably political radicals of all kinds, political cartoonist J. N. "Ding" Darling insinuates in his illustration that Japan had a point when it decried American efforts to block Japanese immigration. "Ding" Darling Wildlife Society owns the copyright of "Ding" Darling cartoons.

the national susceptibilities of the Japanese people." A formal letter of protest from the Japanese government to the State Department less than a week after the 1924 Immigration Act was signed into law on May 26 explicated this argument.

> It is, perhaps, needless to state that international discriminations in any form and on any subject, even if based on purely economic reasons, are opposed to the principles of justice and fairness upon which the friendly intercourse between nations must, in its final analysis, depend. To these

very principles the doctrine of equal opportunity now widely recognized, with the unfailing support of the United States, owes its being. *Still more unwelcome are discriminations based on race.*[24]

According to the Japanese ambassador to the United States, the Gentlemen's Agreement was formulated "for the purpose of relieving the United States from the possible unfortunate necessity of offending the natural pride of a friendly nation." Nonetheless, the immigration law including the clause to bar Japanese immigration passed Congress in April 1924. President Calvin Coolidge signed the Johnson-Reed Act the following month, believing the need to protect the sovereignty of immigration policy overrode any concerns about international sentiment regarding the law.[25]

Japanese citizens boycotted American goods, American society, and Christian churches in reaction to the exclusion law; they mutilated the US embassy flag and glorified as a hero a student who committed suicide on the steps of the US embassy in Tokyo as an act of protest. Editorial invective against the United States continued for years after 1924. According to a contemporaneous account, the exclusion of Japanese immigration infected every aspect of US-Japan relations, and for the average Japanese citizen, the 1924 act soured relations with the United States.[26]

# Notes

1 Catherine Lee, "'Where the Danger Lies': Race, Gender, and Chinese and Japanese Exclusion in the United States, 1870–1924," *Sociological Forum* 25, no. 2 (2010): 261; Daniels, *Guarding the Golden Door*, 40.

2 Lee, "'Where the Danger Lies'," 252, 260; Daniels, *Guarding the Golden Door*, 40.

3 Daniels, *Guarding the Golden Door*, 40–1.

4 Ibid., 41.

5 Lee, "The 'Yellow Peril' and Asian Exclusion in the Americas," 550–1; Takai, "Asian Migrants, Exclusionary Laws, and Transborder Migration in North America," 36; Parker, "Citizenship and Immigration Law," 193.

6 Charles Jaret, "Troubled by Newcomers: Anti-Immigrant Attitudes and Action During Two Eras of Mass Immigration to the United States," *Journal of American Ethnic History* 18, no. 3 (1999): 13, 18.

7 Walter LaFeber, *The American Age: U.S. Foreign Policy at Home and Abroad, 1750 to Present*, 2nd ed. (New York: W.W. Norton & Company, 1994), 204; George C. Herring, *From Colony to Superpower: U.S. Foreign Relations since 1776* (Oxford: Oxford University Press, 2008), 317.

8 Jaret, "Troubled by Newcomers," 21; Carl R. Weinberg, "The Gentlemen's Agreement of 1907–8," in Yukari Takai, "Asian Migrants, Exclusionary Laws,

and Transborder Migration in North America, 1880–1940," *OAH Magazine of History* 23, no. 4 (2009): 36.
9 Daniels, *Guarding the Golden Door*, 41.
10 Weinberg, "The Gentlemen's Agreement," 36; Daniels, *Guarding the Golden Door*, 41–2.
11 Daniels, *Guarding the Golden Door*, 42.
12 Ibid., 42–3.
13 Ibid., 43.
14 Ettinger, "'We Sometimes Wonder What They Will Spring on Us Next'," 172; Daniels, *Guarding the Golden Door*, 43–4.
15 Daniels, *Guarding the Golden Door*, 44; Weinberg, "The Gentlemen's Agreement," 36; Lee, "'Where the Danger Lies'," 249.
16 Daniels, *Guarding the Golden Door*, 44–5; Lee, "'Where the Danger Lies'," 261.
17 Weinberg, "The Gentlemen's Agreement," 36.
18 Lee, "'Where the Danger Lies'," 249.
19 Ibid., 264.
20 Izumi Hirobi, *Japanese Pride, American Prejudice: Modifying the Exclusion Clause of the 1924 Immigration Act*. (Stanford, CA: Stanford University Press, 2001), 7–8.
21 Ibid., 8–9; *Foreign Relations of the United States* (hereafter FRUS), 1924, Vol II: The Japanese Ambassador (Hanihara) to the Secretary of State, April 10, 1924, 372–3. Izumi Hirobe argues that Hinohara's use of the phrase "grave consequences" had the unexpected result of convincing legislators that they should pass the bill to restrict Japanese immigration.
22 Hirobe, *Japanese Pride, American Prejudice*, 9–10.
23 A formal protest letter from the Japanese government to the United States stated that sovereign nations have sole power over their immigration policy, "but when, in the exercise of such right, an evident injustice is done to a foreign nation in disregard of its proper self-respect, of international understandings or of ordinary rules of comity, the question necessarily assumes as aspect which justifies diplomatic discussions and adjustment." FRUS, 1924, Vol II: The Japanese Ambassador (Hanihara) to the Secretary of State, May 31, 1924, 401; Council on Foreign Relations, *Survey of American Foreign Relations*, ed. Charles Howard (New Haven, CT: Yale University Press, 1929), 1929, 512.
24 FRUS, 1924, Vol II: The Japanese Ambassador (Hanihara) to the Secretary of State, May 31, 1924, 398; *Survey of American Foreign Relations*, 1929, 512 [Emphasis mine]. The same note also addressed restrictionists' argument that Japanese immigrants were a menace to US society because they did not assimilate. The Japanese response to this accusation offers interesting insight into reasons why Mexican immigrants did not assimilate into US society, a fact for which restrictionists believed a quota on Mexico's immigration was justified. "It has been repeatedly asserted in defense of these discriminatory measures in the United States that persons of the

Japanese race are not assimilable to American life and ideals. It will however be observed, in the first place, that few immigrants of a foreign stock may well be expected to assimilate themselves to their new surroundings within a single generation. The history of Japanese immigration to the United States in any appreciable number dated but from the last few years of the nineteenth century. The period of time is too short to permit of any conclusive judgment being passed upon the racial adaptabilities of those immigrants in the matter of assimilation, as compared with alien settlers of the races classed as eligible to American citizenship. ¶ *It should further be remarked that the process of assimilation can thrive only in a genial atmosphere of just and equitable treatment.* Its natural growth is bound to be hampered under such a pressure of invidious discriminations as that to which Japanese residents in [the United States] have been subjected, at law and in practice, for nearly twenty years. *It seems hardly fair to complain of the failure of foreign elements to merge in a community, while the community chooses to keep them apart from the rest of its membership* For these reasons the assertion of Japanese non-assimilability seems at least premature, if not fundamentally unjust." FRUS, 1924, Vol II: The Japanese Ambassador (Hanihara) to the Secretary of State, May 31, 1924, 399 [Emphasis mine].

**25** FRUS, 1928, Vol I: The Secretary of State to the American Delegation, January 5, 1928, 564; FRUS, 1924, Vol II: The Japanese Ambassador (Hanihara) to the Secretary of State, April 10, 1924, 370.

**26** Council on Foreign Relations, *Survey of American Foreign Relations,* 512–13.

# 5

# Mexicans, 1920s

Since the early twentieth century, Mexican immigration had been overwhelmingly a migration of labor. Some workers were documented but many others were not. During the First World War (which the United States entered in 1917), the United States allowed Mexican laborers into the country on a "temporary" basis only, to regulate their movement back into Mexico at the end of the work season. In this respect, the US Congress was trying to find a middle ground between labor needs of the American Southwest and social pressure to restrict Mexican immigration to the United States.[1] As the war ended in 1918 and US legislators began to debate immigration restriction, Mexican immigration to the United States was well established and had come to play an essential role in the development of the American Southwest.

Since the 1917 Immigration Act, restrictionists in the United States had chafed at the exceptions and loopholes allowed to Mexican migrant labor on behalf of industries in the American Southwest. After 1924, restrictionists stated southwestern businesses' arguments for the continued immigration of Mexicans to the US—that migrants were docile, apolitical, and likely to return to Mexico after temporary seasonal work periods or expired contracts—became the very points for excluding Mexican immigration to the United States. Restrictionists believed the Mexican migrant was unassimilable and a threat to the racial, cultural, and social integrity of the United States. They argued that continued leniency of US immigration policies toward Mexico would result in the creation of a new race problem in the United States.[2] The American Eugenics Society warned that "Our great Southwest is rapidly creating for itself a new racial problem, as our old South did when it imported slave labor from Africa." A report from the House Committee on Immigration and Naturalization warned against "the creation of a race problem that will dwarf the negro problem of the South; and the practical destruction, at least for centuries, of all that is worthwhile in our white civilization."[3]

Numerous bills and resolutions to amend US immigration laws were introduced to Congress during the late 1920s. The measures ranged from proposals to halt immigration for fixed periods of time (e.g., ten years), to proposals to stop all immigration. The House Committee on Immigration and Naturalization, chaired by Representative Albert Johnson (R-WA), who was a staunch advocate for immigration restriction and one of the co-sponsors of the 1924 Immigration Act, sifted through more than 100 such measures. Among the handful of proposals the committee considered most promising was the application of the quota laws to nations of the Western Hemisphere, particularly Mexico.[4] The proposed extension of a quota to the Western Hemisphere, debated during passage of the Johnson-Reed Act in 1923–4, was abandoned to preserve amicable diplomatic relations and profitable trade between the United States and other American nations. After 1924, however, the growing rate of Mexican immigration to the United States and the increasing presence of Mexicans within US society, both real and perceived, reinvigorated restrictionists' efforts to apply a quota to the Western Hemisphere, and at the very least to Mexico.

For twenty years, between 1913 and 1933, Albert Johnson was the congressional champion of the restrictionist cause. Before entering Congress, he made his reputation as a small-town newspaper editor who staunchly opposed organized labor, particularly the Industrial Workers of the World. Elected to Congress as an arch-restrictionist, Johnson chaired the House Committee on Immigration and Naturalization from May 1919 until he left office in March 1933. During that time, he mobilized the restrictionist lobby for the passage and enactment of the 1921 quota law, introduced nationality quotas and absolute limits for immigrants, and co-sponsored the 1924 Immigration Act. By that year, historian Desmond King states, Johnson had become the "éminence grise" of American immigration policy.[5]

Representative John Box (D-TX) was another vocal restrictionist who opposed Mexican immigration. From East Texas, Box represented constituents in cotton-growing districts who faced stiff competition from cotton growers in the Southwest who employed cheap Mexican migrant labor.[6] Box deemed Mexicans a hazard to US institutions and ideals. By the late 1920s, Box had been trying to stop Mexican immigration for a decade. As a member of the House Committee on Immigration and Naturalization, he had a ready forum for his views. Opponents of the restriction of immigration believed the temporary presence of Mexicans in US society would defuse the debate over restriction. For Box, however, it was the very temporariness of contract labor which was most dangerous. Between scarce institutional resources to administer the border (the US Border Patrol was not founded until 1924) and southwestern industries' insatiable need for cheap labor, there was a high probability of Mexicans "getting away" and surreptitiously staying in the United States.

Since the US Immigration Service did not have the means to enforce the return of temporary Mexican labor, Box argued, Mexican immigration should be barred completely (Figure 5.1).[7]

Box tirelessly continued his effort to restrict Mexican immigration, even though his proposals continually failed throughout the 1920s.[8] He saw himself as the "voice of the people," as a man of the common people who wished to defend the nation against wealthy capitalists and foreign hordes. He believed his arguments for a quota on Mexican immigration represented the views of Americans across all strata of US society.[9] By the late 1920s, however, after

**FIGURE 5.1** Register the aliens, *October 12, 1926. Not long after passage of the Johnson-Reed Act of 1924, which established a restrictive quota on European immigration and completely barred Asian immigration, "Ding" Darling's illustration reflected a belief among many US legislators that it had been a mistake to not also restrict immigration from the Western Hemisphere, especially from Mexico. "Ding" Darling Wildlife Society owns the copyright of "Ding" Darling cartoons.*

years of failure, Box and like-minded quota advocates had gained nationwide appeal as Americans turned their attention to Mexican immigration in the wake of the Johnson-Reed Act. Box and other restrictionists devoted little attention to the potential diplomatic consequences a quota on Mexico's immigration would have for US-Mexican relations. For them, immigration policy was purely a domestic matter. Foreign nations were expected to accept the United States' right to regulate immigration.[10]

Proponents of Mexican immigration relied on various arguments to oppose the quota drive: that Mexicans were docile and apolitical (not likely to organize, demand higher wages, or work limited hours), law-abiding, non-diseased, likely to return to Mexico once seasonal work was complete and willing to do the stoop labor even the most "down and out" Americans were unwilling to do. Points raised by Fred Bixby of the California Cattle Raisers' Association typify these arguments against a quota on Mexican immigration. First, Bixby argued that Mexican migrants supplied much-needed labor to southwestern industries. "We have no Chinamen, we have no Japs," Bixby stated. "The Hindu is worthless; the Filipino is nothing, and the white man will not do the work." Second, Bixby argued that despite propaganda to the contrary, Mexican laborers were not prone to crime, diseased, or troublesome. "The Mexican is not the kind of man who would indulge in the tactics practiced by the [Industrial Workers of the World] or any similar organization. The Mexican is quite unassuming and will work as hard as he can as long as he has to do so. He is extremely loyal; he is not dirty; he is not diseased; he is not any worse than half the white men." Third, Bixby believed Mexican migrants were preferable racially to other types of migratory labor, namely that of African Americans.

> We do not desire the colored people [in the Southwest]. We do not like the cotton-picking type of colored people in our part of the country. We shipped in a few years ago when we first began planting cotton at Bakersfield two and three trainloads of Southern cotton-picking type colored people. They were most unsatisfactory from the very start. We were not accustomed to that sort of labor and to a degree the production of cotton was given up because of the fact that the labor was unsatisfactory. A Mexican in our part of the country is a better citizen and a better employee than the colored man.[11]

While immigration restriction was good generally, Bixby added, it was a bad idea to place a quota on Mexico and would only harm relations with that nation. Besides, Bixby concluded, quota restrictions were unenforceable because of shortages in money and personnel to guard the border. Some opponents of the quota added that Mexicans were physically endowed to do the stoop labor in hot temperatures.[12]

Representative John Garner (D-TX) also criticized the idea of restricting Mexican immigration to the United States. One of John Box's staunchest opponents, Garner believed a quota would be "disastrous." Not only would it cut off a much-needed labor supply, but it would also harm relations with Mexico. He argued that applying a quota to Mexico alone among other states of the Western Hemisphere would cause resentment among Mexicans.

> You could not apply the quota to Mexico and leave it open to Central and South America and Canada without [offending Mexico], and you will not ameliorate anything of the kind by any diplomatic methods you might proceed upon. . . . If we undertake to apply a quota restriction to Mexico and we do not apply it to Canada also, I do not know what reason we can give that will be satisfactory to a proud people and a people who feel that their honor has been impinged by our legislation.[13]

Frank Kellogg, the US secretary of state also opposed the quota drive in the late 1920s. He asserted that the improvement of relations with Mexico was "a source of considerable satisfaction to [the U.S.] government. . . . The interests of the United States in Mexico are of such importance that no action prejudicial to their advantage should be undertaken without a most careful weighing of the possible consequences." A quota on Mexico, Kellogg argued, would "seriously injure" US relations with its southern neighbor. Immigration restriction was a matter of "great national importance as far as the foreign policy of the United States [was] concerned." Economic justifications for a quota, he concluded, should be considered secondary to the diplomatic consequences of immigration restriction.[14]

Mexico voiced their own opposition to the American effort to curb Mexican immigration. Its leaders rejected American insistence that immigration policy was a purely domestic matter, citing the discriminatory implications of a quota. From the Mexican perspective, US immigration policy was inextricably tied to US-Mexican foreign relations.[15] Historically, the Mexican government had been ambivalent about immigration. On the one hand, it viewed immigration as a national disgrace because it was a sign that Mexico could not meet the needs of its people. Mexico's inability to provide sufficient work for all its citizens was embarrassing, while accounts of migrant abuse by American employers and border officials were infuriating. Also, the Mexican government criticized migrants as traitors who sought work abroad instead of working to build the nation.[16] On the other hand, the Mexican government looked favorably upon the "safety valve" effect of immigration to the United States. The Mexican government could not provide enough work for all its citizens, so immigration relieved the glut of workers in Mexico's labor market. Every migrant who left Mexico was one less unemployed (and frustrated) citizen with whom Mexican leaders had to contend.[17] Despite this ambivalence, the Mexican government generally tried to restrict immigration north. Internal and external factors, however, hampered such efforts. Internally there was a disparity between the Mexican government's warnings against the travails of immigration and its ability to prevent the departure of its citizens north. Externally, the booming United States economy and the effects of the Johnson-Reed Act undermined Mexico's effort to stem the tide of its immigration.

Constitutional considerations complicated the Mexican government's response to immigration. Article 11 of the 1857 Constitution (in place until 1917) established the freedom of exit from and travel within Mexico. The Constitution of 1857 made it illegal for the federal government to curb the transnational immigration of its citizens (Mexico City's historically problematic administration of its northern border also precluded any efforts to stop immigration). Article 123 of the Constitution of 1917, in an effort to protect its workers abroad while acknowledging the prevalence of Mexican immigration, restricted the exit of migrants unless they possessed signed labor contracts detailing wage rates, hours of work, and provisions that (American) employers would pay repatriation costs. Article 123, historian David Fitzgerald notes, was contradicted by the US ban on entering the United States *with* a labor contract. After 1917, then, Mexican migrants were breaking the law of at least one country as they migrated. Leaving Mexico without a labor contract went against Mexican constitutional law; leaving Mexico with a labor contract broke US immigration law. Instead of offering a degree of protection over its citizens in the United States, Mexico's 1917 Constitution only made migrants more vulnerable by guaranteeing that some part of their immigration was illegal.[18]

During the mid-1920s, as American restrictionists began to agitate for an extension of the immigration quota to Mexico, the Mexican government renewed its efforts to stem the tide of Mexican immigration to the United States. Mexico's 1926 immigration law put into federal hands the enforcement of Article 123's clause requiring a labor contract for immigration. By placing the Ministry of Foreign Relations in charge of monitoring immigration, the government of Plutarco Elías Calles hoped Mexicans would be dissuaded from migrating north. Also, federal officials tried to curtail immigration by subjecting Mexican travelers on US-bound trains to document searches and by offering Mexicans material incentives (e.g., land and subsidized travel) to repatriate.[19]

Despite these efforts, Mexican immigration continued at an increasing rate during the mid-1920s. Internal unrest in Mexico (e.g., the de la Huerta rebellion and the Cristero Rebellion), Mexico's economic stagnation after 1926, and the draw of the booming US economy accelerated the process. These federal efforts were also undermined at the local level. County governments had incentives to keep migrants moving north. Local officials in Mexico's central states issued travel documents to political rivals, while their counterparts in the Mexican north encouraged immigration to the United States as a way to relieve the glut of labor symptomatic of that region.[20]

By 1927 officials in Mexico City were lamenting the loss of human capital to the United States. An *El Universal* editorial from May 1927 captured the sentiment of many Mexicans when it stated that Mexico's "greatest affliction is the outpouring of its greatest energy source, its people.... The Mexican government should not allow Americans to restrict Mexican citizens from entering the United States but should instead restrict its citizens from leaving for United States."[21] The Mexican government would continue efforts to curb Mexican immigration north, and the challenge would continue to be insurmountable.

During the early months of 1929, the Mexican government solicited regional and state-level reports analyzing immigration. Mexican officials wanted to understand why Mexicans migrated, from where they migrated and why, and how regions or states of high immigration were affected by the departure of workers. This information was meant to resolve the "national problem" of immigration. To promote successful internal economic development, the Mexican government deemed it essential that immigration "be reduced to such reasonable limits that the population and economic and social situation of the country not be impaired."[22]

In response to these government inquiries, Manuel Gamio, a well-respected Mexican anthropologist, sociologist, and former undersecretary of Education, produced the most-authoritative contemporary studies of Mexican immigration. Gamio believed the nature of Mexico's history, economy, and social relations had left Mexicans in a wretched condition. "As an applied anthropologist," historian Arthur Schmidt states, "Gamio regarded scientific research as the essential prerequisite to change the conditions that trapped [Mexicans] in their 'backwardness' and forced migrants to leave their homeland in search of earnings in the United States."[23] Gamio challenged prevalent thinking of the time which focused on the race of Mexicans, and he regarded racial discrimination as an insult that solidified the social castigation migrants faced in the United States. In the midst of a nationwide US fear of Mexican migrants invading US society and debasing the racial stock of the United States, Gamio "stood firm" against this tide by arguing that the "race problem" was of American rather than Mexican making. "There is," Gamio wrote, "no scientific basis for an innate inferiority of the Mexican, nothing beyond the dark pigmentation of the Mexican to account for the racial prejudice against him."[24]

In a newspaper editorial from December 1928, Gamio warned that a quota would damage the political stability of Mexico. According to Gamio, the "brusque stopping" of Mexican immigration northward would bring such harm to Mexico that it would negate any advantage either nation would derive from a quota. While other Mexican observers of immigration thought that the sudden halt to immigration could jeopardize national development by burdening Mexico with an oversupply of labor, Gamio took this argument a step further by stating that the restriction of Mexican immigration threatened the very stability of Mexico itself. Mexico, he stated, had no clear picture of how many citizens were unemployed in the nation. While some countries (e.g., England and Germany), had the ability to provide temporary unemployment insurance to workers, Mexico, Gamio wrote, had no such wherewithal. Consequently, unemployed Mexicans who could not rely on a social safety net had to resign themselves to starve, to emigrate, or to rebel against the state. Such socioeconomic problems were largely averted while the safety valve of immigration was open to Mexicans. If that safety valve should be closed abruptly, Gamio believed, 100,000 or more *repatriados* would swell the ranks of Mexico's unemployed, and they would be forced to take act to satisfy their most basic needs. Gamio wrote that a "revolution of starvation" would immediately follow the passage of a quota law by the US Congress.[25]

Gamio's opposition to the quota corresponded to the safety-valve theory of Mexican immigration, which held that immigration was a necessary evil for Mexico since it relieved the nation of unemployed and kept political agitation at bay. Gamio's contribution to the safety-valve theory was the belief that American restriction of Mexican immigration threatened Mexico's political stability. And while Gamio agreed with other Mexican observers of immigration who argued that the immigration problem was based on economics, what he articulated best among other observers of Mexican immigration was that the remedy to the problem—just like the phenomenon of immigration itself—necessitated a transnational, bilateral, and "transcendental" solution from both the United States and Mexico.[26] For Gamio, the United States-Mexico border was not just an international division but rather a great convergence zone between the two distinct people of the Western Hemisphere: the Anglo-Saxon and the Latin American peoples. Along the contact zones of Arizona, California, New Mexico, and Texas it was necessary to study the interracial, cultural, economic, and psychological contacts developing within this "gigantic sociological laboratory" for the purposes of establishing a more "humane [sic], comprehensive and mutually beneficial" political relations between the United States and Mexico.[27]

Gamio, by diagnosing the socioeconomic causes of immigration in Mexico, demonstrated that racial justifications for immigration restriction were fallacious. Instead, he sought to show how solutions to immigration had to take into consideration the social, demographic, economic, and political factors that caused immigration. By explaining the reasons why immigration happened and from where it originated, Gamio hoped to repudiate the American justification for a quota based on the specious racial statements that Mexicans were inferior. Analyzing the work habits and productivity of Mexican migrants compared to those of other immigrant groups, Gamio argued that there was no Mexican inferiority that could legitimize racial prejudice against them. In this sense, Gamio refuted eugenicists who held that science explained a racial hierarchy of peoples. Instead, Gamio showed that racial prejudice was a cultural phenomenon. Any disadvantages Mexicans suffered vis-à-vis Americans—poverty, illiteracy, slovenliness—were rooted in the distinct economic, social, and political situations from which migrants derived and in which they resided, and worked, both in Mexico and the United States.[28]

Gamio held that there would be several negative consequences to the extension of the quota to Mexico. First, the present permanent immigrant population in the United States would remain indefinitely for fear of not being able to re-enter the country at a later time. Second, while the transitory migrant would not—at least theoretically—be able to enter the United States, thereby helping to resolve the Mexican immigration problem for Americans, the oversupply of labor (or, the shutting off of the safety valve) could cause social disorder and conflict in Mexico as many Mexicans—many of whom would migrate for work and become accustomed to the better working and living conditions across the border—would be out of work and would hinder Mexico's economic progress. Third, American industries—mainly in agriculture—that depended on Mexican labor would suffer in direct proportion to how much Mexico's immigration was restricted. Last, the quota would not stop illegal immigration and would likely abet it unless the United States were willing to expand massively its border patrol. The quota, then, was bad for both the United States and Mexico. While the problem of immigration may have been economic in origin, it required a solution that was multi-dimensional in nature: social, cultural, and political.[29] In short, Gamio argued that the best remedy for the problem of Mexican immigration was Mexico's political stability and economic progress.

Gamio's research revealed the structural problems that underlay immigration. A quota to restrict immigration, he argued, would only worsen Mexico's economic underdevelopment and would likely threaten the political stability of Mexico itself. Also, Gamio believed the quota would hurt the US economy and exacerbate many of the social threats American restrictionists hoped to obviate by barring Mexican immigration.

During the same month that Gamio editorialized against the quota effort (December 1928), Senator William J. Harris (D-GA) presented a bill that would only restrict Mexican immigration among all the other migration streams from the Western Hemisphere. Like John Box of Texas, William Harris represented constituents who wanted to reduce or eliminate competition from cotton growers in the Southwest who were employing Mexican laborers. The "Harris bill" represented a shift in restrictionists' approach to the extension of the quota. Instead of trying to cover the entire hemisphere with the quota, restrictionists believed it was more feasible to extend it to Mexico only. For many quota advocates, Mexico was the main culprit in the immigration problem and it was the presence of Mexican migrants, above all other immigrant groups, that posed the biggest menace to US society after the restrictions of 1924. The Senate approved the Harris bill in May 1930.

This focus on Mexico did not go unnoticed, nor was it taken lightly by either the State Department or Mexico. Mexican journalists decried the hypocrisy of Americans who benefited from Mexican migrant labor while trying to block Mexican immigration. Mexican workers declared their solidarity with the Mexico City government as it protested this disgrace to the nation's pride. Most importantly, the US State Department took direct action to counter the drive to place a quota on Mexico, by implementing *administrative restriction* or stricter enforcement of existing immigration laws toward Mexican immigrants. The enforcement of present laws promised at least two benefits. First, quota opponents such as Secretary of State Kellogg believed the reduced volume of Mexican immigration to the United States would eliminate the need for Congress to extend a restrictive quota to Mexico. Second, enforcing existing laws could end the precedent of exemption that had been officially and unofficially granted to Mexican immigration since at least the end of the First World War. Many restrictionists, such as Senator David Reed, believed a quota was justified for no other reason than combating the favorable treatment of Mexicans compared to European immigrants. For Reed and other like-minded policymakers, the exemption given to Mexico's immigration represented a yawning gap in US immigration law and a disconcerting laxity of the American consular service in Mexico. *Proper* enforcement of existing immigration law, it was hoped, would counter this additional justification for a quota on Mexico.

The first aspect of administrative restriction was the enforcement of existing exclusionary provisions from the 1917 Immigration Act. These provisions prohibited the entry of any immigrant who was illiterate, likely to become a public charge (LPCs), insane or diseased. Up to the late 1920s, this was the primary form of exclusion faced by Mexican migrants. In reality, consular officials enforced these provisions lightly, and those Mexicans seeking to migrate temporarily were not usually barred from doing so. The second component of administrative restriction was the requirement of a valid passport to obtain the immigration visa necessary for permanent (or more appropriately, non-temporary) immigration to the United States. This was not a new law, but it had almost never been enforced on Mexican immigrants. This form of restriction was primarily directed at legal immigration and was considered the most-effective measure for reducing Mexican immigration.

Starting in early 1929, American consular officials throughout Mexico began implementing administrative restriction with the goal of gradually rolling back the tide of Mexicans to the United States. The new consular policy succeeded where the previous strategy of relying on repatriation figures had failed. By strictly enforcing US immigration law toward Mexico's migrants, the State Department removed the exemptions that had spared Mexican immigration from restriction during the past decades. Administrative restriction worked because of its neutral position within the quota debate. The State Department could be seen as simply enforcing existing US immigration law instead of discriminating against Mexican migrants, thereby preserving harmonious US-Mexican relations.

Administrative restriction worked because it offered something for everybody. For American restrictionists, administrative restriction would curtail the growth of the Mexican population within the United States. For Mexican leaders, administrative restriction aided their socioeconomic goals by curbing Mexico's immigration northward, but without the blatant, underlining racist rhetoric that suffused the quota effort. Administrative restriction benefited American employers but was much more problematic for Mexican immigrants. Consular enforcement of US immigration laws only affected those Mexicans who sought a visa to enter the United States legally; it did nothing to stem the tide of illegal immigration. Arguably, administrative restriction may have abetted illegal immigration since legal entry into the United States became more difficult. This helps explain why American employers also benefited from administrative restriction: their access to pliable Mexican labor was preserved. Conversely, while the demand for work across the border remained high for Mexicans, administrative restriction reinforced the illegality of surreptitious immigration. This enhanced illegality made migrants more susceptible to abuse by *coyotes* and *enganchadores*, to exploitation by American employers, and to the physical dangers of transnational immigration.

Administrative restriction, by relying on stricter enforcement of existing immigration laws to curb Mexican immigration, actually fostered the conditions for increased illegal immigration. Glowing consular reports of the reduction of Mexican immigration and the refusal of visas failed to account for what happened to those Mexicans denied legal entry into the United States. For example, the consular report from Ciudad Juárez that cited a 36 percent visa refusal rate in December 1929 (100:275), alongside a 23 percent visa issuance rate (62:275), neglected to mention what may have happened to the remaining Mexicans who applied for visas that month (113:275, or 41 percent of the total visa applicants at Ciudad Juárez during December 1929).[30]

As early as the summer of 1929, administrative restriction appeared to be curbing Mexican immigration. Senator David Reed, an arch-restrictionist for most of the 1920s, reversed his previous call for a quota on Mexico in light of administrative restriction's apparent success, although he still advocated for a strengthened Border Patrol. To single out Mexico for restrictive measures like a quota, Reed believed, "might have serious international implications and lead to diplomatic as well as legislative difficulties." Not only would a quota undermine amicable relations with "our sister republic," Reed continued, but it would also injure US relations with the rest of Latin America.[31]

In December 1929, John Farr Simmons, chief of the Visa Office in Washington, DC, reported to Congress that Mexican immigration was down by almost 70 percent. By mid-January 1930, William Dawson, general vice consul in Mexico City, reported reductions in the number of visas granted to Mexicans (Table 5.1), a decrease in the number of Mexicans applying for visas (Table 5.2), as well as a rise in refusal rates of visa applicants (Table 5.3).

Data from consular districts on the border reported lower rates of visa refusals. William Blocker, the American consul in Ciudad Juárez, reported a visa refusal rate of 36 percent for December 1929, while his counterpart in Nogales, Maurice Altaffer, recorded a refusal rate of 37 percent for all of 1929.[32] The American consul in Nuevo Laredo, Richard Boyce, reported a visa refusal rate of 90 percent. Also, Boyce stated that the overall number of Mexicans going to the border to migrate had decreased. Subsequently, despite a lack of data to prove his point, Boyce believed the rate of illegal immigration was also down.[33] Such reports seemed to show that administrative restriction was working; it not only reduced the official rate of (legal) immigration, it also seemed to have a related effect of reducing illegal immigration. By spring 1930, the State Department reported that Mexican immigration had been reduced to such an extent that it was "no longer a problem." On 14 May, the same day Undersecretary of State Cotton gave his testimony before the House Committee on Immigration and Naturalization opposing the Harris bill

Table 5.1 Number of Immigration Visas Issued to Mexicans between December 1926 and December 1929[a]

| year | immigration visas issued |
|---|---|
| 1926 | 3,323 |
| 1927 | 3,743 |
| 1928 | 2,587 |
| 1929 | 815 |

[a] NARA, RG 59, 811.111 Mexico/298, Simmons to Carr, December 12, 1929.

Table 5.2 Decrease in Number of Mexicans Applying for Visas, Month to Month Comparison from May 1928/1929 to December 1928/1929[a]

|  | 1928 | 1929 | % decrease |
|---|---|---|---|
| May | 5,096 | 4,357 | 15 |
| June | 4,460 | 3,820 | 14 |
| July | 4,930 | 3,538 | 28 |
| August | 6,019 | 3,102 | 48 |
| September | 4,795 | 2,882 | 40 |
| October | 4,114 | 2,452 | 40 |
| November | 3,127 | 1,937 | 38 |
| December | 2,715 | 1,755 | 35 |
| TOTAL | 32,256 | 23,843 | 32 |

[a] NARA, RG 59, 811.111 Mexico/309, Dawson to Stimson, January 14, 1930, 1–3.

Table 5.3 Ratio of Refusals of Total Number of Mexican Visa Applicants, 1929, in Percentages[a]

| Month | refusals (in percentage) | Month | refusals (in percentage) |
|---|---|---|---|
| May | 34.5 | September | 50.4 |
| June | 42.0 | October | 48.5 |
| July | 44.9 | November | 47.1 |
| August | 47.6 | December | 52.6 |

[a] NARA, RG 59, 811.111 Mexico/305.5, Simmons to Dawson, December 30, 1928, 1–3.

(which had been passed by the Senate the day before), the State Department reported that administrative restriction had reduced Mexican immigration by almost 77 percent from previous years, "without resort to a numerical immigration quota."[34]

Restrictionists relied on race as a prime justification for placing a quota on Mexico. These justifications upset the national pride of Mexicans and risked harming amicable relations between the United States and Mexico. By contrast, the stricter enforcement of US immigration laws by American consuls removed the prospect (and reality) of restriction from a national context and instead situated it at a regional and local level. Such restriction, while highly effective, was incremental and individual. Instead of facing restriction because of their nationality, Mexicans were restricted individually for not meeting the immigration requirements of the United States. Additionally, administrative restriction entailed the enforcement of *existing* immigration laws; it did not require the passage of new legislation. As such, Mexicans were spared the national embarrassment they feared if Congress were to amend the Immigration Act of 1924 to remove Mexico from the list of nonquota nations. Further, Mexicans could hardly criticize immigration laws that were applied broadly and across the world. Finally, administrative restriction gave the consular service flexibility in enforcing immigration laws. Just as easily as it ratcheted up its strict exclusion of Mexican immigrants, it could relax the strict exclusion of Mexicans if time and economic needs required it. In short, administrative restriction defused much of the immigration problem by the early 1930s and made the application of a quota unnecessary. America's national sovereign right over immigration policy was preserved by administrative restriction, as were workable diplomatic relations with Mexico. And far from closing off access to Mexican migrant labor, American employers' access to Mexican migrant labor was actually abetted by administrative restriction, as the factors that made legal immigration more difficult made illegal immigration more necessary. The only losers from the new consular policy were Mexican migrants themselves. As legal channels of migration dried up, they were forced to enter the United States surreptitiously. Their undocumented migration and extra-legal presence north of the border eliminated any legal and political protections they may have benefited from otherwise. In sum, the quota debate of the late 1920s and early 1930s illegalized Mexican migrants in the eyes of Americans.

# Notes

1 Gilbert G. Gonzalez, "Mexican Labor Immigration, 1876–1924," in *Beyond La Frontera: The History of Mexico-U.S. Immigration*, ed. Mark Overmyer-Velázquez (New York: Oxford University Press), 29; George Sanchez, *Becoming Mexican-American: Ethnicity, Culture, and Identity in Chicano Los Angeles* (New York: Oxford University Press, 1993), 41.
2 David G. Gutiérrez, *Walls and Mirrors: Mexican Americans, Mexican Immigrants, and the Politics of Ethnicity* (Berkeley, CA: University of California Press, 1995), 53–5.
3 Dawley, *Changing the World,* 100 and 367n38. Cf. Gutiérrez, *Walls and Mirrors,* 54–5.
4 Archivo Histórico de la Secretaría de Relaciones Exteriores (hereafter AHSRE): LEG, 782, exp 16: *Congressional Digest,* "Immigration Problem—1928," May 1928, 152.
5 King, *Making Americans,* 201.

6   Francisco E. Balderamma and Raymond Rodríguez, *Decade of Betrayal: Mexican Repatriation in the 1930s* (Albuquerque: University of New Mexico Press, 1995), 18.

7   "Such a system would break down because of its administrative impossibility," Box argued in the early 1920s, "and would be ruinous in its effects upon the country."

8   U.S. House of Representatives, Committee on Immigration and Naturalization, *Temporary Admission of Illiterate Mexican Laborers: Hearings*. 66th Congress, 2nd Session (Washington, DC: Government Printing Office, 1920), 302–3; U.S. House of Representatives, Committee on Immigration and Naturalization, *Imported Pauper Labor and Serfdom in America: Hearings*. 67th Congress, 1st Session (Washington, DC: Government Printing Office, 1921), 17.

9   "A few men can make more noise in Washington than a million men can make at home," he declared before the House Committee on Immigration and Naturalization in late February 1928.

10  National Archives and Records Administration (hereafter NARA), RG 59, 811.111 Quota, 10/102, Brandt to Carr, February 21, 1928, 4; AHSRE: LEG, 782, Exp 16: *Congressional Digest*, "Immigration Problem—1928," May 1928, 161.

11  AHSRE: LEG 782, Exp 16: *Congressional Digest*, "Immigration Problem—1928," May 1928, 161–4.

12  AHSRE: LEG 761, Exp 2, 1928–1930, "Statement of Fred H. Bixby . . . ," 26–7; AHSRE: LEG, 782, Exp 16: *Congressional Digest*, "Immigration Problem—1928," May 1928, 161–4; NARA, RG 59, 811.111 Quota, 10/104.5, Brandt to Carr, n.d.; *New York Times*, "Oppose Bill to Bar Mexican Immigrants," 33, February 25, 1928; Balderamma and Rodríguez, *Decade of Betrayal*, 17.

13  NARA, RG 59, 811.111 Quota, 10/103, Brandt to Carr, February 23, 1928; AHSRE: LEG 782, Exp 16: *Congressional Digest*, "Immigration Problem—1928," May 1928, 157.

14  AHSRE: LEG 761, Exp 2, 1928–1930, "Statement of Hon. Frank B. Kellogg, Secretary of State," 156–69; *New York Times*, "Kellogg Opposes Davis Quota Plan," 13, March 6, 1928. Cf. United States Senate, Committee on Immigration and Naturalization, *Restriction of Western Hemisphere Immigration: Hearings*. 70th Congress, 1st Session (Washington, DC: Government Printing Office, 1928), 155–72.

15  Dawley, *Changing the World*, 290.

16  David Fitzgerald, *A Nation of Emigrants: How Mexico Manages Its Migration* (Berkeley, CA: University of California Press, 2008), 3; Timothy J. Henderson, *Beyond Borders: A History of Mexican Migration to the United States* (Malden, MA: Wiley-Blackwell, 2011), 32.

17  Henderson, *Beyond Borders*, 32.

18  Fitzgerald, *A Nation of Emigrants*, 40–1; Michael P. Smith and Matt Bakker, *Citizenship Across Borders: The Political Transnationalism of El Migrante* (Ithaca, NY: Cornell University Press, 2008), 28.

19 Smith and Bakker, *Citizenship Across Borders*, 28; Fitzgerald, *A Nation of Emigrants*, 43.
20 Jaime Aguila, "Mexican/U.S. Immigration Policy prior to the Great Depression." *Diplomatic History* 31 (April 2007): 220 and 224; Fitzgerald, *A Nation of Emigrants*, 43.
21 Aguila, "Mexican/U.S. Immigration Policy prior to the Great Depression," 224.
22 NARA, RG 59, 811.111 Mexico/172, Morrow to Kellogg, February 25, 1929; NARA, RG 59, 812.5611/35.5, Dawson to State Department, March 25, 1929, 8. The Mexican states solicited for reports on immigration were Coahuila, Guanajuato, Jalisco, Michoacán, Nuevo Leon, San Luis Potosí, Tamaulipas, and Zacatecas. Most migrants derived from Guanajuato, Jalisco, and Michoacán.
23 Arthur Schmidt, "Mexicans, Migrants, and Indigenous Peoples: The Work of Manuel Gamio in the United States, 1925–1927," in *Strange Pilgrimages: Travel, Exile and Foreign Residency in the Creation of Latin American Identity, 1800–1990s*, ed. Ingrid E. Fey and Karine Racine (Wilmington, DL: Scholarly Resources, 2000), 167.
24 Ibid., 172.
25 NARA, RG 59, 812.5611/24, Dawson to Kellogg, 12/13/28, 1–2.
26 NARA, RG 59, 811.111 Mexico/166, Dawson to Kellogg, 02/09/29.
27 "Why the Social Science Research Council Favored the Study of Mexican Immigration into the United States and commended it to Dr. Manuel Gamio," in Dwight W. Morrow Papers, Bx 2, fldr. 63, Archives and Special Collections, Amherst College Library.
28 Ibid., 99.
29 AHSRE: LEG 761, Exp 1, Manuel Gamio, "Quantitative Estimate of Mexican Immigration to the United States," 103–4.
30 NARA, RG 59, 812.5611/40, Blocker to Stimson, January 7, 1930, 1–3.
31 *New York Times*, "Opposes Quota on Mexicans Now," July 3, 1929, 8; NARA, RG 59, 811.111 Mexico/291.5, Simmons to Reed, December 5, 1929.
32 NARA, RG 59, 812.5611/40, Blocker to Stimson, January 7, 1930, 1–3: of the 275 Mexicans who applied for visas in December 1929, 100 were refused. NARA, RG 59, 812.5611/41, Altaffer to Stimson, January 24, 1930, 1.3: of the 3,059 Mexicans who applied for visas, 1,117 were refused.
33 NARA, RG 59, 811.111 Mexico/328.5, Davis to Simmons, February 27, 1930.
34 *New York Times*, "Pass Bill to Apply Quota to Mexicans," 56, May 14, 1930; *New York Times*, "Fewer Mexicans Enter," 10, June 14, 1930.

# 6

# Jews, 1930s–1940s

The United States faced four distinct refugee crises during the twentieth century, pertaining to Cubans in the 1960s and 1970s, Vietnamese during the late 1970s and early 1980s, and Central Americans during the 1980s and 1990s. It was the Jewish refugee crisis of the 1930s and 1940s, however, that has led to years of scholarly debate over what the United States could and *should* have done differently. Scholars tend to agree that the United States was slow to respond to Nazi oppression of Jewish Germans, which started after the regime of Adolf Hitler took power in Germany in January 1933. The real root of scholarly disagreement is whether more European Jews could have been saved by changes in US immigration law and a more robust response from the Franklin D. Roosevelt administration (1933–45). "Seething with retrospective outrage," scholars critical of the US response to Jewish refugees offer a whole range of explanations as to why the United States was slow to act: bureaucratic short-sightedness among American diplomats regarding the brewing crisis in Germany as well as a fair dose of anti-Semitism among leaders of the State Department, President Roosevelt's indifference to the crisis and his prioritization of battling the economic depression (up to 1939) and then confronting the Axis powers (after 1941); and most especially, a deep-seated xenophobia within the US public that precluded any political will to embrace the idea of wholesale resettlement of Jewish refugees in the United States.[1] By contrast, more sympathetic assessments of the US response to the Jewish refugee crisis argue that there were limitations on the US government that constrained its freedom of movement: call it the weight of public opinion or anti-Semitism in Washington, DC. These scholars argue that contending that the United States could have *done more* to save European Jews is to rewrite the past by assuming the US government was capable of doing exactly what later critics of it assumed it could have done. It also assumes that Americans had a full sense of the extent of Nazi atrocities toward Jews. As one scholar states, by the time Americans had a concrete idea of the Holocaust, "the fate of most of the Jews in Europe was sealed." To think that timely reform of US immigration law would have changed the fate of millions is to rewrite the past and also to exaggerate the historical agency of the United States in global affairs.[2] To weigh in on this scholarly debate, let's first consider the factors that led to the Jewish refugee crisis, and then assess the US response to the Jewish refugee crisis of the 1930s and 1940s.

The self-identified or Jewish-derived population of Germany (Jewish Germans) at the time of the Nazi takeover made up a small percentage of the nation's total population: 1.5 percent, or approximately 917,000. Jewish Germans tended to live in the larger cities of Germany; a third of them resided in Berlin. By and large, Jewish Germans were middle class and worked in trade and commerce. The Nazi persecution of Jewish Germans came as a shock not only for its brutality but also because Jews in Germany were better integrated into that country than anywhere else in Europe. The Russian Empire, for example, had a long history of pogroms against Jews within its population. Even compared to the United States, where Jews were barely represented in elite culture, Jews in Germany worked in professional fields such as law, medicine, and the professoriate.[3]

The dangers to Jews living in Nazi Germany were not immediately obvious. Hitler's anti-Semitism was a secret to no one. Since the 1924 publication of his "manic tract," *Mein Kampf*, Hitler had decried an "international Jewry" that was conspiring against Germany. Even as Hitler took power in 1933, Jewish Germans adopted a "wait-and-see attitude" when it came to how the Nazis would run Germany. Like most of the Western world, Germany had been experiencing a sharp economic depression since the late 1920s. Many observers believed that the ideological militancy of Hitler's regime would burn in the crucible of state governance. And it was hoped by some that the weight of dealing with the Great Depression would eventually overwhelm the Nazi government and lead to its ouster. Some Jewish Germans did emigrate during the early years of Hitler's, approximately 60,000. Very few of them went overseas, instead they entered surrounding countries—Austria, Czechoslovakia, and France—not planning to immigrate away from Germany permanently. The relative affluence of these emigrants made their arrival in foreign countries uneventful.[4]

Even though there was no comprehensive provision for the resettlement of refugees in US immigration law—that would not come about for another thirty years—the quota system established by the Johnson-Reed Act of 1924 allowed a comparatively generous annual allotment of immigration visas to residents of Germany: 25,957. By comparison, France's annual allotment was 3,086, Czechoslovakia's was 2,874, and Austria's was 1,413. Germany had the second-largest annual allotment for immigration visas to the United States, behind only Great Britain. State Department officials saw little justification to rush to resettle Jewish refugees during the 1930s so long as the German immigration quota remained unfilled.[5]

Much of the answer as to why the United States was ineffectual in its response to the torrent of Jewish refugees trying to immigrate to US soil lay in its strict quota laws. By its very "pervasive anti-immigration" nature, the National Origins system of 1924 prevented any notion of a generous visa allotment and, in the words of historian David Kennedy, it "constrained [President] Roosevelt's refugee policy as tightly as the Neutrality Acts constrained his diplomacy." But the "trickle" of Jewish refugees who gained asylum in the United States was also attributable to the bizarre interconnection of those laws with Nazi emigration statutes, the latter of which severely restricted the sum of money that a departing Jew could take out of Germany. A 1934 law limited that amount to $4. US immigration law customarily disallowed the admission to persons "likely to become a public charge," and in 1930 the administration of Herbert Hoover (1929–33) ordered consular officials to apply that clause strictly. Under such legal conditions, few "systematically impoverished" Jewish Germans could qualify for visas to enter the United States.[6]

In the United States, between 1933 and 1935, it was only members of the Jewish community who expressed concern about antisemitic rhetoric coming out of Nazi Germany. For US government leaders, the more immediate concern was the economic depression. The Democratic Party, which controlled the legislative and executive branches through most of the 1930s, was thoroughly committed to maintaining the quota laws that had been passed a decade prior. President Roosevelt focused on forging and preserving a coalition of support for his massive legislative reform program—The New Deal—was keen to avoid any actions that would fray Democrats' intraparty harmony. Additionally, officials in the US State Department opposed any special treatment of refugees that might antagonize the German government.[7]

The biggest impediment to any sizable US response to the issue of Jewish refugees was US public opinion. For as hard as it may be to imagine now, public anti-Semitism greatly influenced government (in)action. "Anti-Semitism," immigration historian Aristide Zolberg argues, "formed a negative background that constrained decision-makers from making choices that appeared *philo-Semitic* [pro-Jewish], and it severely handicapped the efforts of American Jews on behalf of refugees for fear of confirming reigning stereotypes."[8] Public anti-Semitism was likened to a bomb by one Democratic representative in Congress who feared that the Jewish refugee problem could expose chinks in the party's hegemony. If debate were begun to amend US immigration law to accommodate the resettlement of Jewish refugees, it "could lead to an explosion against us." This prejudice was not rooted in ignorance; the press had long reported to American readers the Nazi mistreatment of Jews.

Politically left-leaning newspapers such as *The Nation* and *The New Republic* argued that the restrictionist response to the plight of Jews was driven by anti-Semitism.[9] Journalists such as Dorothy Thompson went to great lengths to detail the plight of Jews in two books, *Refugees: Anarchy or Organization* (1938) and *Let the Record Speak* (1940). Even if many Americans, both Jewish and gentile, cringed at the knowledge of the violence being meted out to Jews in Europe, "sympathy," historian David Kennedy states, "stopped short of concrete support." Public polls showed the persistence of anti-Semitism in US society. Even as far into the Jewish refugee crisis as the summer of 1938, one public poll showed that more than 67 percent of Americans opposed the resettlement of European Jews on US soil. Another public poll from mid-1939 asked Americans the following question: "if you were a member of Congress, would you vote yes or no on a bill to open the doors . . . to a larger number of European refugees?" The great majority of non-Jewish respondents, up to 85 percent, said no.[10]

The issue of Jewish German emigration started to turn into a Jewish German refugee crisis in September 1935, when the Nazi regime promulgated the Nuremberg Laws, which stated that Jewish Germans who had left Germany temporarily in recent years were now permanently barred from returning to the country. The law precipitated a larger departure of Jews from Germany, and for the first time put noticeable pressure on the United States' annual visa allotment for German immigration. In 1936, nearly 7,000 visas were granted to Jewish Germans; in 1937, that number doubled to 12,532. These growing refugee flows were increased by cases of state-sponsored violence, such as the "Night of Broken Glass," or *Kristallnacht*, on November 9–10, 1937, when Jewish German communities were systematically attacked. Jewish homes were looted, synagogues were burned, businesses were destroyed, dozens of Jews were killed, and 20,000 were arrested as "criminals." By the end of that year, 130,000 Jewish Germans had left Germany, with over a quarter of them (35,000) making their way to the United States.[11]

At the same time that domestic violence was being visited upon Jewish Germans, and as many Jewish German emigrants who had left Germany between 1933 and 1935 now found themselves barred from ever returning to their home country, the Jewish refugee problem started to take on continental proportions as the Nazi regime expanded Germany's territorial domain. In March 1938, Hitler's government absorbed Austria in the *Anchluss*, bringing 180,000 European Jews under German control. For many European Jews, especially the 5 to 6 million Jews who lived in central and Eastern Europe, flight seemed the only reliable option (Figure 6.1).[12]

By the late 1930s, then, it was clear to Western leaders that there was a full-blown European Jew refugee crisis. Starting with the Munich agreement in September 1938, in which Britain and France acceded to Hitler's desire

**FIGURE 6.1** Still no solution, *January 29, 1939*. Over his decades-long career as a political cartoonist, Herbert Block (Herblock) often imbued wry humor into his illustrations. There is no levity in this cartoon from early in his career, however. Published eight months before Nazi Germany invaded Poland, the event that touched off the Second World War in Europe, Herblock condemns deliberating world leaders who failed to form an adequate response to many endangered European Jewish refugees desperately awaiting asylum. A Herblock Cartoon, © The Herb Block Foundation.

to absorb the Sudetenland region of Czechoslovakia, but especially after the Nazi government annexed the rest of that country in March 1939, another 400,000 European Jews fell under the power of Germany. Shortly after the *Anchluss*, Roosevelt "stretched to the limits" his presidential authority by ordering the merging of the German and Austrian quotas as well as the special expediting of Jewish visa applications. These actions resulted in nearly 50,000 Jews entering the United States during the next two years. Yet his call in the spring 1938 for a multilateral conference to address the Jewish refugee crisis—the Intergovernmental Committee—was so hedged with deference to a nation's sovereign right to restrict the admission of displaced persons as to be ineffectual. Some US policymakers tried to respond to the Jewish refugee crisis without broaching the subject of reforming US immigration law when they proposed increasing visa allotments by "mortgaging" quotas for later years. Such measures were so vehemently opposed that they were debated neither in the Senate nor in the House of Representatives.[13]

The Orwellian tangle of US immigration law and US public opinion took on heart-wrenching proportions in late May and early June 1939 with the case of the SS *St. Louis*. Many of the Jewish refugees on the ship were on the American quota list but held numbers that had yet to come up. In anticipation, and in hopes, that their numbers would come up, they boarded ships to ports in the Western Hemisphere to wait. The 930 Jewish refugees on this boat were lured to Cuba by a diplomat who had promised them safe haven in Havana while they awaited admission into the United States. When they were denied entry visas, thereby blocking their entry into US waters, the US Coast Guard escorted *St. Louis* along the coast of Florida to prevent anyone from swimming ashore. Soon thereafter, the vessel was forced to return to Europe with its Jewish refugee passengers still aboard. By early June, *St Louis* landed and disembarked its passengers in Antwerp. While a fourth of the passengers were allowed asylum in Great Britain, France, Belgium, and the Netherlands, many of them fell into Nazi hands and were killed as the latter three of those four countries capitulated to the Germans during the Second World War (Figure 6.2).[14]

About 127,000 Jewish refugees were admitted to the United States between 1933 and 1940. They either came to US soil as immigrants or held

**FIGURE 6.2** *German Jewish refugees sit and wait on the decks of the* U.S.S. St. Louis *as it sits in the harbor at Havana, Cuba, June 1, 1939. The vessel would subsequently be forced to return to Europe, where many of its passengers would eventually fall victim to the Nazi regime. Getty Images: Bettmann.*

Table 6.1 German Quota Immigration and the German Quota, 1933–40[a]

| Year | German Quota Immigration | German Quota Spaces |
| --- | --- | --- |
| 1933 | 1,919 | 25,957 |
| 1934 | 4,392 | 25,957 |
| 1935 | 5,201 | 25,957 |
| 1936 | 6,346 | 25,957 |
| 1937 | 10,895 | 25,957 |
| 1938 | 17,199 | 27,370[b] |
| 1939 | 33,515 | 27,370 |
| 1940 | 21,520 | 27,370 |
| Total | 100,987 | 211,895 |

[a] Adapted from Daniels, *Guarding the Golden Door*, 78.
[b] For 1938–1940, Austrian quota of 1,413 added.

temporary visas and were allowed to stay once those visas expired. While the United States resettled more Jewish refugees than any other nations, scholars debate if the US government could have done more to respond to the refugee crisis of the 1930s. Zolberg argues that another 110,000 European refugees could have been admitted into the United States under the existing quota restraints if the allotments for the early 1930s were filled. He further asserts that the miniscule quota allotments for Eastern European countries such as Poland (6,524), Hungary (869), and Romania (295), were woefully inadequate to meet the needs of millions of European Jews (Table 6.1).[15]

The outbreak of the Second World War in Europe in 1939 effectively closed the exit door for European Jews. The Nazi invasion and capture of Poland between September and October left millions of Jews in the hands of German forces. While nearly three-fifths of Germany's Jews were able to escape Hitler's regime by the late 1930s, there were still 250,000 to 300,000 Jews who were essentially trapped in Nazi-controlled Europe up to the outbreak of the Second World War.[16]

Far from easing xenophobic sentiment in the United States, Europe's descent into war redoubled desires to preserve strict US immigration law. Before the war, European Jews were excluded for prejudicial reasons but also because of fears that their resettlement would overwhelm US social services in a time of economic depression. That initial prejudice and fear increased after 1939 with a not-so-new kind of trepidation: that among waves of refugees there was a risk of subversives slipping into the United States and undermining its national security. Since the late nineteenth century, Jewish Europeans had been feared to be agents of radical ideologies such as anarchism, communism, and socialism. As a stateless people, Americans feared that Jews had no real sense of patriotism and no natural affinity with any nation-state. It was no coincidence, then, that Jews of Eastern Europe were one of the immigrant groups targeted by the Johnson-Reed Act of 1924, a law that would play such a central role in US reaction to the Jewish refugee crisis of the 1930s and 1940s. Additionally, it was not too much of a leap for antisemites around the world to fear that Jews were at the center of various international conspiracies—whether they be usurious or communist—to overthrow the Western world. In short, the anti-Semitism running throughout Hitler's political ideology was firmly embedded in a deep European context of prejudice toward Jews. And it was a prejudice that many Americans openly adhered to.[17]

This not-so-new trepidation was most evident when the US government cancelled the merging of the German and Austrian immigration quotas. Additionally, in June 1940—the same month that France fell to the Nazis—the Immigration and Naturalization Service (INS) was transferred from the Department of Labor to the Department of Justice and a registration requirement was imposed on all aliens. The INS was shifted to the Department of Justice because of the supposed threat represented by immigrants from enemy countries. This transferal was meant to last for the duration of the war but not beyond, yet the INS was never returned to the Department of Labor. This transferal of immigration enforcement to the main institutional body for legal matters in the US government would have enormous consequences for later reforms to immigration policies.[18]

Between 1939 and 1941, the US State Department took the guiding role in handling the Jewish refugee crisis. President Roosevelt was notorious for his distrust of the State Department, and often bypassed that institution as he formulated his diplomatic responses to crises between 1939 and 1941. But in the case of Jewish refugees, FDR was content to leave the US response to bureaucrats at State, indicating that he did not want to deal with the issue.[19] While FDR's thinking and approaches to the Jewish refugee issue are opaque, what is irrefutably clear is that there was an institutional antagonism in the State Department toward Jewish immigrants that played a direct part in how the United States responded or did not respond, to the refugee crisis. Simply, various State officials "consistently made it difficult for most refugees in general and Jewish refugees in particular to gain asylum in the United States."[20] Since the early 1920s, American Jewish leaders had complained about the culture of anti-Semitism in the State Department. During the war they pointed out particular figures who seemed to be purposefully marginalizing Jewish refugees—officials such as Wilbur J. Carr, who was a key fixture in the consular service for years; Avra M. Warren, head of the Visa Division; and Breckinridge Long, assistant secretary of state from 1940 to 1944, who, in the same month that the blending of the German and Austrian quotas was ended (June 1940), sent an interdepartmental memo that included this statement:

> We can delay and effectively stop for a temporary period of indefinite length the number of immigrants into the United States. We could do this by simply advising our consuls to put every obstacle in the way and to require additional evidence and to resort to various administrative devices which would postpone and postpone and postpone the granting of the visas.[21]

Some scholars argue that prejudice against Jews among State Department bureaucrats was directly responsible for "reducing to a trickle" the number of visas granted to Jewish refugees.[22] Whether anti-Semitism or an "overzealous concern with security" drove their incredibly "rigid stance" on the granting of immigration visas has been debated among historians.[23] For our purposes, the basic conclusion is that the US State Department was no more welcoming to Jewish refugees as war raged throughout Europe than they were before the onset of the conflict. This mattered because, considering FDR's delegation of the refugee matter to the State Department, the American consular service had incredible discretion over who and who was not allowed asylum in the United States. This does not mean that all American consuls were immune to the human suffering they witnessed. One consul, Raymond Geist, went into concentration camps to help individuals. Yet this humane response was idiosyncratic and did not constitute an official, consular response of the United States to the Nazi Holocaust. Another American consul named John G. Erhardt, for example, issued as few visas to refugees as possible.[24]

Whether it was inherent anti-Semitism or a fear of national security, the qualification standards for asylum in the United States were augmented during the early years of the war. In late June 1941 the Visa Division centralized the granting of visas in Washington, DC, which prolonged the waiting period of desperate applicants and subjected their applications to elaborate security screening. Additionally, a new policy was instituted that rejected affidavits of support from anyone other than immediate relatives, which begged the question, if your relatives had been taken to a concentration camp, who was left to vouch for your character for asylum?[25] In early July 1941 all US consulates in Germany were closed, making it impossible for a Jewish refugee to obtain a visa without first fleeing to another country, in which US consulates were still open. In combination with the disruptions of war and prejudice faced in other European countries, it is estimated that dense visa requirements prevented anywhere from 62,000 to 75,000 Jewish refugees from leaving Europe. It should be noted, however, that according to INS numbers, more than 34,000

Jews were allowed into the United States under the quota system between 1940 and 1942.[26]

Americans had been aware of Nazi war crimes against Jews and other Europeans since at least the fall of 1942. And yet it was not until the Allies began to win the war that public pressure mounted on the Roosevelt administration to do more to rescue European Jews. Huge public rallies took place in New York City and congressional resolutions started to proliferate. In mid-January 1944, Roosevelt was forced to confront the issue he had long sloughed off to the State Department. In response to an eighteen-page memo passed along from his secretary of the treasury Hans Morgenthau that decried the State Department's poor handling of the Jewish refugee crisis, Roosevelt confronted the issue more directly by creating by executive order the War Refugee Board (WRB). The board forged greater Cabinet-level involvement in handling the refugee crisis and put visa allotments into the hands of an official who was more amenable to a liberal awarding process. During that same year, the Roosevelt administration took further action by participating in the safe departure of Jewish refugees from war-torn parts of Europe. Zolberg argues that these WRB actions in 1944 represented "a definite shift" in how the US government had heretofore addressed the Jewish refugee crisis and laid the groundwork for a fundamental overhaul in US refugee policy after 1945 (see Chapter 3).[27] Roger Daniels, another immigration historian, is not so sure. According to Daniels, the WRB was not authorized to resettle refugees in the United States, instead placing refugees in camps in neutral African and European countries, and was responsible for rescuing only a "token" (less than 1,000) of Jewish refugees from Nazi-controlled Europe.[28]

The ultimate question is this: could the United States have done more to alleviate the plight of Jewish refugees between the mid-1930s and mid-1940s? Some, like Daniels, say yes: the annual immigration quota was routinely underfilled, evidence that more could have been done. While the United States did indeed take in the most Jewish refugees of all other nations, so many more thousands could have been saved.[29] Other scholars like Zolberg are hesitant to give an answer, arguing that it is easy to look back and assess what historical actors *should* have done, but much more germane to acknowledge what *could* have been done. By the mid-1930s, as the Jewish refugee crisis began, Zolberg argues that the quota laws of the 1920s had been "etched in stone"; they had "taken on an aura of legitimacy seldom achieved by ordinary [which is to say non-Constitutional] legislation." The laws were sacrosanct for more reasons than maintaining national security or national sovereignty, Zolberg concludes; they represented the American people's "inviolable determination to no longer be a nation of immigrants."[30]

American anti-Semitism hindered the US response to the Jewish refugee crisis. Could the Roosevelt administration have done more to find an inventive way around such social prejudice? During the late 1930s and early 1940s, Roosevelt carefully steered the nation away from its isolationist reflex in foreign policy toward the idea of entering the war to fight the Axis powers. Could Roosevelt have orchestrated a similar change of perspective in the American public regarding European Jews? How did the economic depression act as a vacuum in which any bold presidential action was obviated?[31] Considering the racial prejudice prevalent in US society at the time, evidenced in part by its commitment to adhering to the quota laws of 1924, the Great Depression's devastation of the US economy and psyche, and American fears about getting drawn into another European war, it is amazing the United States had any sizable response to the Jewish refugee crisis. This is not an apologetic appraisal, but rather a disappointed assessment of the shortcomings of "the land of the free" as a place of refuge and security for non-Americans.

## Notes

1 Zolberg, *A Nation by Design*, 271–2.
2 Ibid., 271–2; Daniels, *Guarding the Golden Door*, 71–2.
3 Zolberg, *A Nation by Design*, 272–3.
4 David M. Kennedy, *Freedom from Fear: The American People in Depression and War, 1929–1945* (New York: Oxford University Press, 1999), 410; Zolberg, *A Nation by Design*, 273.
5 Zolberg, *A Nation by Design*, 273, 275; Mae M. Ngai, "The Architecture of Race in American Immigration Law: A Reexamination of the Immigration Act of 1924," *The Journal of American History* 86, no. 1 (June 1999): 74, Table 1.
6 Kennedy, *Freedom from Fear*, 413; Zolberg, *A Nation by Design*, 273.
7 Zolberg, *A Nation by Design*, 274.
8 Ibid., 275, emphasis original.
9 Kevin MacDonald, "Jewish Involvement in Shaping American Immigration Policy, 1881–1965: A Historical Review," *Population and Environment* 19, no. 4 (1998): 327.
10 Zolberg, *A Nation by Design*, 275, 280; Kennedy, *Freedom from Fear*, 1999, 410, 417; MacDonald, "Jewish Involvement in Shaping American Immigration Policy," 327.
11 Zolberg, *A Nation by Design*, 277, 278; Kennedy, *Freedom from Fear*, 1999, 415.
12 Zolberg, *A Nation by Design*, 278.
13 Ibid., 279, 284–5; Kennedy, *Freedom from Fear*, 1999, 414, 416.

14  Daniels, *Guarding the Golden Door*, 79–80; Zolberg, *A Nation by Design*, 285; Kennedy, *Freedom from Fear*, 417–18.
15  Zolberg, *A Nation by Design*, 285–6; Ngai, "The Architecture of Race in American Immigration Law," 74, Table 1.
16  Zolberg, *A Nation by Design*, 286.
17  Jaret, "Troubled by Newcomers," 21; MacDonald, "Jewish Involvement in Shaping American Immigration Policy," 326.
18  Zolberg, *A Nation by Design*, 286–7; Sassen, "Beyond Sovereignty," 17n10.
19  Daniels, *Guarding the Golden Door*, 73–4.
20  Ibid., 74.
21  Long quoted in *Treatment of Latin Americans of Japanese descent, European Americans, and Jewish Refugees during World War II*, Congressional hearing, 2009, 74–5; Daniels, *Guarding the Golden Door*, 75–6.
22  MacDonald, "Jewish Involvement in Shaping American Immigration Policy," 327.
23  Zolberg, *A Nation by Design*, 287.
24  Daniels, *Guarding the Golden Door*, 75.
25  Zolberg, *A Nation by Design*, 287.
26  Ibid., 287–8.
27  Ibid., 289–90; Roger Daniels, "Immigration Policy in a Time of War: The United States, 1939–1945," *Journal of American Ethnic History* 25, no. 2/3, *Immigration, Incorporation, Integration, and Transnationalism: Interdisciplinary and International Perspectives* (Winter-Spring, 2006): 111.
28  Daniels, "Immigration Policy in a Time of War," 111–12.
29  Daniels, *Guarding the Golden Door*, 78, 80.
30  Zolberg, *A Nation by Design*, 291.
31  Daniels, *Guarding the Golden Door*, 76, 79; Zolberg, *A Nation by Design*, 291–2; Erika Lee, "Immigrants and Immigration Law: A State of the Field Assessment," *Journal of American Ethnic History* 18, no. 4 (1999): 98–9.

# 7

# Chinese, 1930s–1950s

Chinese immigrants had the ignominious legacy of being the first group of foreign noncitizens excluded from entering the United States. It is necessary to elucidate the deeply embedded racism in US society that underscored such legislation for two reasons. First, to appreciate how distinct the turn away from exclusion was during the Second World War era. And, second, to understand the reflexive return to an analogous type of ideological racism during the 1950s.

Anti-Chinese agitation dated back to the 1850s along the West Coast of the United States, no doubt sped along after the Burlingame Treaty was brokered between the US and Chinese governments in 1868. This treaty allowed for the unrestricted immigration of Chinese laborers to the United States. The amount of Chinese in the United States rose markedly and quickly: from 63,000 in 1870 to 105,000 in 1880.[1] Anti-Chinese agitation took on national proportions during the early 1870s as an economic downturn hit the United States. Amid recession, Chinese immigrants were deemed a threat to the nation. By the mid to late 1870s, Western state delegations were pressuring Congress to block Chinese immigration to the United States. Their exclusion was based on racial and class considerations, but there was also "a gendered logic" to the restriction of Chinese immigration according to immigration historian Catherine Lee. With a low female-to-male ratio, a fair amount of female Chinese immigrants were prostitutes, providing US restrictionists—politicians, intellectuals, and moral reformers—the opportunity to argue that Chinese women brought contagious diseases into the United States, thereby threatening not just society but the nucleus of society, the family; as evidenced by the Page Act of 1875, which made the importation of any female prostitute from "China, Japan, or any Oriental country" without their consent a federal crime.[2] Class considerations paralleled gender concerns over Chinese immigration, such as when the US government renegotiated the Burlingame Treaty in 1880 to give itself the power to "regulate, limit or suspend" the immigration of Chinese laborers whenever their presence "affects or threatens" the United States. Soon thereafter, in 1882, Congress approved a bill to suspend Chinese immigration for ten years. Skilled and unskilled Chinese workers were barred from entering the United States. By the end of the 1880s, the official rate of Chinese immigration to the United States had slowed to a trickle: from nearly 40,000 at mid-decade to ten by the latter half of it.[3]

The Chinese Exclusion Act was at its core a law to *selectively* restrict a certain race of foreign labor. Key to its understanding is that racism played a crucial role in getting the legislation approved. It was a rhetorical tool that immigration restrictionists in Congress used "again and again" to make the case for exclusion.[4] Racist rhetoric played two functions in the passage of the 1882 law. First, it demonized Chinese laborers as racially inferior workers who threatened the "native" American laborer. Second, by clearly delineating which immigrants were not fit to enter the United States, the exclusion act broadened the definition of American whiteness. In short, Chinese workers were the foil by which German, Irish, English, and American workers aligned themselves along "Caucasian origin."[5] The Exclusion Act of 1882 set a precedent of selectively restricting foreign laborers who were believed to threaten the American worker. This anti-Chinese immigration legislation was cemented further in 1889 when Chae Chan-ping, a laborer who had returned to China in 1887 after twelve years in San Francisco, was denied re-entry under the terms of the Scott Act (1888). The Scott Act, passed in Chae's absence, reaffirmed the Chinese Exclusion Act and further banned the return of any Chinese laborer who had returned to China. Chae pursued his case all the way to the Supreme Court, where he was denied in *Chae Chan-ping v. United States* (1889).[6]

The 1882 law against Chinese immigration was not wholly successful, in part because it was a unilateral congressional policy that tried to stem a transnational flow of Asian immigration. Not only were Chinese crossing the Pacific Ocean east to get into the United States, but they also traveled along north-south corridors across the Americas: from California to British Columbia in Canada, from Arizona to Sonora in Mexico, and from Cuba to Louisiana. Chinese immigrants worked in fisheries, logging camps, coal mines, and agriculture. The result of the Chinese Exclusion Act was not to close corridors of surreptitious Chinese immigration but to redirect them across the contiguous borders of Canada, Mexico, and the United States. For example, after 1882, Chinese laborers surreptitiously entered the United States either through Mexico or Canada. Immigration historians estimate that more than 17,000 Chinese immigrants entered the United States illegally between the 1880s and the 1930s. They entered through various access points across the United States: Seattle, Buffalo, San Diego, San Antonio, and El Paso, but also through ports of entry in the Gulf of Mexico, Florida, Louisiana, and Mississippi. Chinese immigrants, once in the United States, ventured to places such as Baltimore, New York, Philadelphia, and Boston.[7]

Congress sought to shut down illegal Chinese immigration. First, in 1884, it passed another law to supplement the exclusion act focused on protecting the Western states, particularly California, from "surreptitious arrivals." Additionally, shipmasters of vessels originating in Singapore and Hong Kong risked imprisonment and fines if they were found to have landed or attempted to land Chinese immigrants at US port cities. Additionally, an 1888 amendment to the exclusion act barred Chinese men from re-entering the United States once they had left its territory. Finally, in 1904, the Chinese Exclusion Act was made permanent.[8]

All of this legislative activity did not stop illegal Chinese immigration to the United States. Much of this had to do with the ruggedness and the remoteness of border regions, such as the US-Canadian border regions in the Pacific Northwest. With its innumerable islands and water inlets, the Puget Sound offered ample opportunity for surreptitious entry into the United States. Chinese would cross the border on the eastern side of the Cascade Mountains.[9]

The route for illegal entry across the US-Mexico border was more indirect. Chinese immigrants could take a steamer from Hong Kong to San Francisco. Instead of getting off the boat upon arrival, an action that would likely result in apprehension by US immigration officials, Chinese immigrants transferred to a Mexican steamer (there were no direct steamer lines connecting China to Mexico in the late nineteenth century) and took that vessel to a Mexican port on the Pacific side of Mexico. They then disembarked in Mexico and proceeded northward, crossing into the United States through remote areas anywhere from southern California, to southern Arizona, to West Texas.[10]

It was not the numbers of Chinese immigrants who entered the United States illegally that "shook a sense of security and confidence" among US immigration officials. Compared to the less than 18,000 Chinese immigrants who entered the United States over a span of nearly fifty years, it is estimated that 50,000 European immigrants crossed illegally into the United States from Canada in 1890 alone.[11] Rather, it was the racism that underlined US immigration regulation that drove the panicked response of US immigration officials to illegal Chinese immigration. The increase of Chinese immigration to the United States during the late nineteenth century coincided with a rise in anti-Chinese prejudice during the same years. Chinese were viewed as unfair labor competition for American workers because of their ability to exist below the standard of living and wages—to *underlive*—the typical native-born American had come to expect. Also, the Chinese were accused of being racially inferior, politically unassimilable, and immoral (Figure 7.1).[12]

**FIGURE 7.1** *"The Chinese: Many Handed but Soulless," November 14, 1885. The cover of this San Francisco newspaper (*The Wasp*) represented a common view Americans held of Chinese immigrants during the latter half of the nineteenth century, that Chinese were a multi-handed threat to US society. The Chinese, the prejudice held, peddled drugs to the addict (top middle and bottom left), displaced American workers like the maid (middle left), the washer woman (top right), the common laborer (top left), and the miner (bottom right), and disrupted the family (baby at bottom). Getty Images: Pictures from History.*

The US government's inability to stem illegal immigration also resulted from the determination of immigrants. The fact that Chinese immigrants bore the dangers and the expense (immigrants had to pay exorbitant fees to people smugglers who led them along treacherous corridors of migration) of surreptitious immigration "spoke volumes" about their desire to enter the United States, as well as indicated a stubborn reality that has affected immigration enforcement for a century and a half: formidable terrain, large and remote distances, and dangerous physical conditions make it hard to effectively patrol the border.[13] In sum, while the Chinese Exclusion Act and its subsequent amendments failed to completely stop the flow of illegal Chinese immigrants to the United States, they succeeded in castigating Chinese in the eyes of the US public.

The horrors of Japanese militarism in China during the 1930s, but especially the US entry into the Second World War against Japan, led to a dramatic sea change in American public and official opinion about Chinese immigration. Concerns over national security and winning the war against the Axis powers eventually led to the repeal of the Chinese Exclusion Act of 1882. The liberal turn in US immigration policy toward the Chinese was relatively brief, however, as the onset of the Cold War but especially the "fall" of China to communism in 1949 reinvigorated customary American prejudices against Chinese.

Japan made forays into the northeasternmost Chinese province of Manchuria in the early 1930s, but it was a minor clash between Chinese and Japanese troops in July 1937 at the Marco Polo bridge, near modern-day Beijing, that ignited a full-scale war between the two nations and started the Second World War in Asia. Soon Japanese forces had the Chinese army on the run. Japanese forces captured the Chinese capital at Nanking (now Nanjing) in mid-December 1937. For the next several weeks, Japanese troops committed horrible war crimes of rape, bayoneting, beheading, and machine-gunning. It is estimated that over 200,000 Chinese were killed by the Japanese at Nanking.[14]

Americans were "agape" at the ferocity of Japan's occupation of China. A Gallup poll in late 1937 showed that 59 percent of respondents favored China, while only 1 percent supported Japan. Another public poll from 1939 showed that nearly three out of four Americans sympathized with the Chinese. American sympathy toward China derived from the brutality of the Sino-Japanese war, but it was also the result of a deeper cultural sympathy among Americans for the Chinese. Generations of American missionaries who had served in China held deep emotional connections to the Chinese. The son of missionary parents and publishing tycoon, Henry Luce, regularly lobbied for stronger US support of China. That emotional, cultural connection was deepened in the early 1930s with the massive popularity of Pearl Buck's sentimental novel, *The Good Earth*. Coincidentally published at the same time that Japanese forces were seizing Manchuria, the book was read by millions of Americans during the 1930s. Again by coincidence, a film version of the book was released during the same year as the Marco Polo bridge incident.[15] Historian Michael Hunt estimates that approximately 40 million Americans— or nearly one-third of the US population during the 1930s—were exposed to Buck's work in one form or fashion (the work also premiered as a play in 1933). According to Hunt, the book offered a "seductive combination" of entertainment and insight into China, a country that Americans had longed looked upon with fascination. For readers and viewers alike, *The Good Earth* was an escapist diversion from the travails of economic depression; it was also a "reaffirmation" of values Americans celebrated, such as hard work and thrift. Finally, *The Good Earth* lauded rural life and agricultural work as antidotes to the baneful consequences of industrialization and urbanization in the modern era.[16] While growing US public sympathy for China did not correlate with an official American military alliance with the Chinese, a case for repealing the Exclusion Act of 1882 was forming during the late 1930s.[17]

The Japanese attack of December 7, 1941, on Pearl Harbor not only brought the United States into Second World War but solidified the movement to end the exclusion of Chinese immigration. The nearly sixty-year-old law was embarrassing for a nation fighting to liberate global peoples from Axis domination, especially when one of those Axis powers—Japan—was using the exclusion act as a prime plank in its wartime propaganda against the United States. Also, the exclusion act was a hindrance to an effective wartime alliance between the United States and China.[18]

Japanese propagandists started to call the Second World War "the Greater East Asia War" with the aim of liberating Asians from "Anglo-Saxon [British and American] imperialists" in the weeks after Pearl Harbor. Additionally, they promoted racial harmony among Asian peoples and decried American values of liberty and equality as "hypocritical."[19] While the message of harmony did not correspond with Japanese troops' treatment of the various Asian peoples they colonized, US officials quickly realized that the Chinese Exclusion Act could impede their nation's attempt to build a common front against Japan.

Pearl Buck, America's first woman to win the Nobel Prize in literature, emerged as a staunch opponent of racial discrimination against the Chinese after the United States entered Second World War. She stated to the hundreds of guests at a literary luncheon in New York City in February 1942 that racial prejudice was "the most vulnerable term in our American democracy." Victory in the war would only come if peoples of all races, colors, and nations cooperated. "We cannot win this war," Buck argued, "without convincing our colored allies—who are most of our allies—that we are not fighting for ourselves as continuing superior over colored peoples."[20]

The same month that Pearl Buck publicly criticized American racism, Charles S. Spinks, a specialist in East Asian relations, published an article arguing that a US alliance with China was crucial for defeating the Axis powers and creating a new world order based on freedom, justice, and equality among nations. That alliance could be undermined, Spinks concluded, by US immigration laws that did not treat the Chinese "with the justice and equality they deserve."[21] A few months later, in May 1942, Sumner Welles, the US undersecretary of state, stated in a public address that "the discrimination between peoples because of their race, creed or color must be abolished." The United States was fighting a war to "assure the sovereign equality of peoples throughout the world as well as in the world of the Americas."[22] US foreign policy necessitated a change in US immigration policy.

There was significant racist baggage to the exclusion act, however. This original totem of comprehensive immigration restriction rested on the assumption that Chinese were weak, lazy, and inferior. How could such a legacy of American prejudice correspond with the immediate wartime exigency of forming alliances? The growing American sympathy for Chinese, present for decades but more visible with every passing year of the Sino-Japanese war, went some way toward allaying this racist legacy. But it was the need to hold the Japanese at bay that spurred a recasting of Chinese in the American imagination during the early 1940s. Between December 1941 and April 1942, such notable newspapers as the *New York Times* and the *New Republic* lauded the importance of the US alliance with China and commended the strong fighting spirit of the Chinese. China was a "loyal ally with . . . inexhaustible manpower." Its "dogged struggle for independence" could help the United States "immeasurably in winning the war quickly." The leader of the Chinese Nationalists (or the non-communist Chinese), Chiang Kai-shek, was celebrated as a welterweight war hero who would play an instrumental role in defeating the heavyweight Japanese juggernaut. When Chiang's American-educated wife, Soong Mayling (Madame Chiang), visited the United States between November 1942 and May 1943, she was praised as a "graceful, charming and intelligent" woman. She "captivated and amazed" senators and representatives when she addressed both houses of Congress on February 18, 1943 (Figure 7.2).[23]

There was also a geostrategic incentive to reevaluate US immigration policy toward Chinese. The Americans and their British allies had a clear, "Europe

**FIGURE 7.2** *Madame Chiang with President Franklin D. Roosevelt the day before her celebrated address to a joint session of Congress in mid-February 1943. Getty Images: Bettmann.*

first" strategy of defeating Nazi Germany. But the allies differed regarding to their objectives in Asia. Unlike the conflict in Europe, the war in Asia was about colonies. Britain and other Western European nations such as France and the Netherlands wanted to defend or regain territories lost to the Japanese. By contrast, the Americans were set to grant independence to their primary Asian colony—the Philippines—and pressured the British to do the same for their colonies of India, Burma, Malaya, and Hong Kong. For President Roosevelt, China would be the queen on the chessboard of East Asian affairs by, first, countering any European efforts to recast power in Asia and thereby securing decolonization; second, by protecting against a resurgent Japan, and, third, by blocking Soviet expansion in the region. The Roosevelt administration hoped a strong, democratic, and Western-friendly China would fill the power vacuum in Asia after the Second World War.[24]

Repeal of the Chinese Exclusion Act was essential to creating a common American-Chinese Nationalist alliance against Imperial Japan. US legislators introduced several bills for repeal in the months following Madame Chiang's address to Congress. Private citizens added momentum for repeal. In late May 1943, notable citizens such as Pearl Buck and Henry Luce founded "The Citizens Committee to Repeal Chinese Exclusion and Place Immigration on A Quota Basis." The organization's goal was to emphasize the importance of good US relations with China as well as to lobby Congress to repeal Chinese Exclusion. Repeal pressure also came from the American media as newspapers and radio ran many accounts of commentators, convention addresses, and other programs encouraging the end of exclusion.[25]

This drive for repeal of the ban on Chinese immigration culminated in a series of congressional hearings addressing the issue. Between May and June 1943, the House Committee on Immigration and Naturalization summoned fifty-one witnesses to weigh in on the debate over repeal. The nativism that underlined the exclusion law was present as representatives from labor and veterans' organizations (such as the American Federation of Labor and the Veterans of Foreign Wars) and patriotic societies argued that Chinese were the "most debased people on the face of the earth," and that changes to US immigration law would threaten the economic stability of the nation.[26] The overwhelming majority of witnesses called to testify, however, supported repeal. Composed of civic organizations, missionary groups, intellectuals, and businessmen, advocates of repeal argued that the exclusion law should be eliminated, that Chinese immigration should be placed on the quota system, and that Chinese immigrants should be made eligible to become US citizens. That China would help the United States win the war in Asia was the most persuasive argument for repeal at the hearings.[27]

And yet, repeal was not a foregone conclusion when general debate opened in the House of Representatives in mid-October 1943. Some representatives argued that loosening immigration laws would undermine national security and would threaten keeping "America for Americans." Supporters of repeal, such as Samuel Dickstein, chair of the House Committee on Immigration and Naturalization, continued to argue that ending exclusion was a matter of social justice as well as recognition of China's "heroic resistance . . . against our common enemy." But it was the direct appeal of President Roosevelt that tipped the scales toward the legislative repeal of Chinese Exclusion, when he encouraged Congress to "take the offensive in this propaganda war and repeal the laws that insult our only ally on the mainland of Asia." Less than two weeks later, the House voted to repeal Chinese exclusion; the Senate followed suit a month later. Roosevelt signed the bill to end Chinese Exclusion on December 17, 1943.[28]

Scholars are guarded in the symbolic importance they grant the repeal of Chinese exclusion. Xiaohua Ma states that while "the United States was still patently a white man's country . . . the notion was beginning to prevail that equal opportunity ought to be given at least lip service." For Mai Ngai, the repeal was "an important democratic reform that ended a sixty-year-long racist policy." Finally, Roger Daniels argues that the repeal was "a kind of good-behavior prize" for China joining the wartime alliance against the Japanese and demonstrated that "the days of 'racial' exclusion in naturalization and immigration were numbered."[29]

In some ways, this scholarly restraint is surprising. The legislative act ending exclusion, the Magnuson Bill, allowed Chinese to naturalize as citizens, and provided a path for nonquota family immigration. Little anticipated at the time of its passage, this feature to the repeal legislation caused a significant demographic shift in Chinese American communities throughout the United States. The new naturalization provisions allowed thousands of Chinese American men to become citizens. Most significantly, post-repeal legislation opened the way for nonquota family immigration from China. First with the War Brides Act of 1945 but supported by the Alien Fiancées and Fiancés Act of 1946 and the Refugee Relief Act of 1953, 40,000 Chinese arrived in the United States during the fifteen years after the Second World War, sixty-three of whom were females.[30] In other ways this scholarly caution is justifiable. According to Ngai, the repeal legislation denoted Congress' "continued antipathy" toward Chinese immigration by assigning an annual immigration quota of only 105 slots. Unlike other quotas that were specific to nation-based immigration, the Chinese quota was race-based: regardless of their country or birth or residence, only 105 Chinese were allowed into the United States annually under the post-exclusion immigration regime.[31]

If foreign affairs in 1941 spurred a liberal turn in US policy toward Chinese immigration, then foreign affairs in 1949 caused a reversion to the customarily illiberal attitudes and actions Americans took toward Chinese Americans and immigrants. No one could say they did not see it coming. Despite the wartime rhetoric of a common alliance, millions of American dollars supporting the Nationalist cause, and the political gesture of repealing the exclusion act, the immediate postwar years were not kind to relations between the Americans and the Chinese Nationalists. On the one hand, Chiang was always considered a junior partner in the Anglo-American-Soviet alliance. The Nationalist leader resented that he was not included in Big Three summit meetings. For him, it was quite transparent that the Western allies simply viewed the Nationalists as a convenient bulwark against Japan while the war in Europe was won. On the other hand, American General Joseph Stilwell, who was assigned as a US military adviser to the Nationalist government not long after the Pearl Harbor attack, decided that Chiang was anything but the heroic leader that China supporters like Henry Luce regularly lauded in his newspapers back in the United States. The Nationalist government was weak, internally divided, corrupt, and unpopular with regular Chinese. Its army was mostly composed of conscripts who were poorly led, poorly motivated, and dependent on American military aid.[32]

Things did not improve when Japan surrendered in early September 1945, formally ending the Second World War in Asia. Soon civil war ignited between Chiang's Nationalists and the Chinese Communist Party led by Mao Zedong. Fearful of Soviet encroachment into China, and of the prospect of Mao's forces winning the civil war, the United States saw little choice but to continue aid to Chiang. Yet, despite the financial and military assistance from the United States, Chiang's cause disintegrated with breathtaking speed between 1946 and 1949. Once enjoying a two-to-one advantage in manpower and a three-to-one advantage in firepower, the Nationalists were soon vulnerable, facing an enemy that had mobilized the peasants and taken the initiative in the war. Once publicly praised as an Asian equivalent to George Washington, reports to the Truman administration from US military advisers in China now referred to Chiang as the "world's worst" leader. Endemic corruption and incompetence in his government eroded any connection Chiang could have established with Chinese civilians. Morale hit rock bottom among the Nationalists by 1948 when their troops were surrendering en masse or fleeing the battlefield without their equipment. Over the span of four months, according to historian George Herring, Chiang lost nearly 50 percent of his manpower and 75 percent of his weapons. In October 1948 alone, 300,000 Nationalists surrendered.[33] When Chiang's Nationalist government was forced to flee the Chinese mainland the following year, the calculus of Cold War geopolitics changed forever with the founding of the People's Republic of China (PRC). The "fall" of China to communism also recast the question of Chinese immigration to the United States.

The defeat of the Chinese Nationalists and the creation of the PRC had a massive effect on Chinese immigration and the Chinese American community. Almost overnight, Chinese immigration from the mainland became legally and diplomatically impossible, as the United States refused to recognize Mao's government (which meant that no quota allotment would be considered for the PRC). After 1949, internal rivalries within Chinese American communities became apparent between supporters of Chiang's Nationalist government based on Taiwan and the communist PRC.[34]

The defeat of Chiang was no less shocking for US foreign policy in East Asia. China was supposed to be the bulwark of democracy and Western interests in a region where the Japanese were beaten into submission, the Soviets were desperate for border security, and European empires were pining for the return of their colonies. Now, after 1949, not only was China no longer a team player, it had become a prime enemy of the United States in the Cold War.[35]

These new Cold War exigencies for foreign policymakers in Washington, DC, combined with Americans' nativist reflex toward Chinese, to create a new Chinese immigration crisis during the 1950s. The flashpoint of this crisis was the issue of "paper sons." It is estimated that tens of thousands of Chinese illegally migrated to the United States during the exclusion era (1882–1943). The most common method of entering the United States was by posing as a person who was legally admissible. False applicants commonly used fraudulent certificates that identified them as either American citizens by birth or as China-born sons of US citizens (a status formally known as derivative citizens). The central problem of illegal Chinese immigration, Mai Ngai argues, was the inability of US authorities to authenticate the identity of Chinese entering the United States. When American customs and immigration inspectors denied Chinese entry into the United States because of lack of documentation, the Chinese turned to the courts to overturn these decisions. As early as the 1890s, US district and circuit courts along the West Coast were inundated with petitions from Chinese immigrants. Typically claiming they were born in the United States but then taken back to China as young children, claimants provided oral testimony that was hard to dispute, not because judges were disinclined to block Chinese immigration but rather because there was no paper trail that contravened the testimonies provided by claimants. Ngai shows that between 1891 and 1905 the US District and Circuit Courts in San Francisco, for example, heard over 2,500 cases from Chinese petitioners and ruled in favor of over 60 percent of them. Ironically, the petition process that came out of the void of documentation to block illegal Chinese entry into the United States produced documentation that facilitated Chinese immigration. "Chinese immigrants," Ngai states, "thus invented a system of illegal entry built entirely upon a paper trail derived from the state's efforts to enforce exclusion." Oftentimes the documentation produced by these petition hearings was used by generations of Chinese immigrants to (falsely) authenticate their entry into the United States.[36]

The start of the Cold War, but especially the fall of China to communism, gave the US government a "new urgency" to stop this habit of illegal Chinese immigration. The problem of fraudulent entry could not be detected through the paper trail. Confession seemed the only reliable method to find out who had immigrated to the United States illegally. But what set of circumstances, Ngai asks, would induce Chinese paper immigrants to confess?[37]

An additional problem from the American point of view was a "kind of political tolerance" in the Chinese American community for the PRC. While the Communist Party was never strong among Chinese Americans, support for the PRC grew steadily after 1949. Unlike exiles and refugees from other communist nations later in the twentieth century, such as Vietnamese (Chapter 8) and Cubans (Chapter 9), the Chinese in the United States were not harsh critics of Mao's regime. Many of them came to have "at least a grudging admiration" for the ways in which China modernized under the communist government and the international respect that was afforded to the new PRC and, more generally, for the Chinese.[38]

This kind of support emanating from the United States for a communist nation was anathema to US leaders and soon resulted in a multipronged government assault on Chinese immigrants and Chinese Americans. The FBI, for example, investigated, harassed, and at times raided the headquarters of left-wing Chinese organizations as well as conservative *family associations*, groups based on the fictive assumption that all persons with the same or similar last names were related. Much of the FBI's suspicion of these organizations lay in the fact that these associations communicated regularly with their counterparts in the PRC. In addition to the FBI, the State Department and the INS regularly harassed Chinese Americans during the 1950s. Rumors spread among State Department officials of massive passport and visa fraud aimed at getting Chinese from Hong Kong to the United States. While fraud did exist, it was never to the extent immigration authorities believed.[39] Portrayed as heroic allies in the global fight against racist totalitarianism during the early 1940s, Chinese immigrants and Americans were suspected as shock troops for a communist fifth column in the United States during the early 1950s.

The Chinese Confession Program was founded in 1956 within this atmosphere of suspicion and paranoia. Taking advantage of the Cold War-inspired political turbulence of the time, this INS-led program offered a kind of coercive amnesty in which Chinese Americans, usually of politically leftist bent, received asylum if they exposed relatives and friends who might be involved in illegal communist activity in the United States. In the eyes of immigration authorities, illegality and subversion were two sides of the same coin. According to Ngai, the INS' use of confession derived from a traditional law enforcement technique in which confession and testimony against others were exchanged for immunity from prosecution. Unable to rely on documentation to determine which Chinese were in the United States illegally, the INS, Roger Daniels argues, used the "ethically dubious principle" of selective enforcement to weed out who they considered enemies of the state. Ultimately, the INS hoped the confession program would permanently end years of paper immigration from China.[40]

INS investigators worked diligently and patiently to elicit confessions from whole Chinese American families. The line between volunteerism and coercion was rather thin. Families divided over whether to confess or not. INS officials aggressively sought confessions from persons whose names appeared in investigative leads from anonymous phone calls and letters. Additionally, the Chinese were called in for an "informal interview" with INS investigators, in which they were presented with some evidence that suggested fraud in their naturalization status or alleged news that a paper relative, whether close or far, had confessed on them.[41]

Mai Ngai shows how the actual process of confession was rather routine. Confessors answered questions on a standardized form; they confessed their fraudulent claims to citizenship and then listed the names of their true family and paper family members, including their whereabouts. Confessors were asked if they have ever been convicted of a crime, voted in an election, served in the armed forces, belonged to the Communist Party, or believed in "communistic aims."[42]

As routine as the process of confession may have been, Ngai shows how the confession trials of accused paper immigrants could be excruciating. The accused was often presented with charges that were abusive and frivolous, involving crimes allegedly committed years in the past, and were threatened with the possibility of deportation or imprisonment. Families of implicated paper immigrants were humiliated by the fact that they were often subpoenaed to testify against their accused family members.[43]

Scholars disagree on the number of Chinese Americans implicated by the confession program. Ngai argues that 11,336 confessors implicated 19,124 paper immigrants. Xiaojian Zhao offers higher numbers: 13,895 confessors implicating 22,083 paper immigrants.[44] Most confessors successfully received legal status while few Chinese Americans implicated by the confessor program were actually deported.[45]

From the perspective of the INS, the Chinese Confession Program was a great success: it publicly rooted out illegal Chinese immigrants and ended the process of paper immigration that dated back to the nineteenth century. From the perspective of Chinese Americans and immigrants, the confession program of the late 1950s, as well as the Cold War-inspired scrutiny from US authorities beginning in the early part of that decade, represented a step backward. The Chinese Nationalists' failure to protect their country from the spread of communism, the ominous threat to the United States attributed to the PRC after 1949, and the historical legacy of paper immigration reinvigorated American prejudices of Chinese as weak, dangerous, and subversive. Despised as the oriental "other" for decades, accepted into the fold of nations during the Second World War, Chinese Americans and immigrants were once again the racialized other during the early years of the Cold War.[46]

## Notes

1. Lee, "'Where the Danger Lies'," 255.
2. Lee, "'Where the Danger Lies'," 256–7; Daniels, *Guarding the Golden Door*, 17.
3. Jacobson, *Barbarian Virtues*, 28, 73–8; Lee, "'Where the Danger Lies'," 256; Grace Peña Delgado, "Neighbors by Nature: Relationships, Border Crossings, and Transnational Communities in the Chinese Exclusion Era," *Pacific Historical Review* 80, no. 3 (2011): 403–4; Parker, "Citizenship and Immigration Law," 186.
4. Kitty Calavita, "Collisions at the Intersection of Gender, Race, and Class: Enforcing the Chinese Exclusion Laws," *Law & Society Review* 40, no. 2 (2006): 250.
5. Jacobson, *Barbarian Virtues*, 78; Collomp, "Labour Unions and the Nationalisation of Immigration Restriction in the United States," 244.
6. Jacobson, *Barbarian Virtues*, 93.
7. Lee, "The 'Yellow Peril' and Asian Exclusion in the Americas," 541–3; Takai, "Asian Migrants, Exclusionary Laws, and Transborder Migration in North America," 36, 39.
8. Delgado, "Neighbors by Nature," 403–4.
9. Ettinger, "'We Sometimes Wonder What They Will Spring on Us Next'," 163–5.
10. Ibid., 166–7.
11. Takai, "Asian Migrants, Exclusionary Laws, and Transborder Migration in North America," 35, 39.
12. Lee, "The 'Yellow Peril' and Asian Exclusion in the Americas," 546–7; Lee, "'Where the Danger Lies'," 255–9; Calavita, "Collisions at the Intersection of Gender, Race, and Class," 256–7.
13. Ettinger, "'We Sometimes Wonder What They Will Spring on Us Next'," 167.
14. Kennedy, *Freedom from Fear*, 401.
15. Kennedy, *Freedom from Fear*, 401; Xiaohua Ma, "The Sino-American Alliance During World War II and the Lifting of the Chinese Exclusion Acts," *American Studies International* 38, no. 2 (2000): 46–7.
16. Michael H. Hunt, "Pearl Buck–Popular Expert on China, 1931–1949," *Modern China* 3, no. 1 (1977): 34, 39, 51–2.

17 Kennedy, *Freedom from Fear*, 401; Ma, "The Sino-American Alliance During World War II," 46–7.
18 Mae M. Ngai, *Impossible Subjects: Illegal Aliens and the Making of Modern America*. (Princeton, NJ: Princeton University Press, 2004), 203; Daniels, *Guarding the Golden Door*, 150.
19 Ma, "The Sino-American Alliance during World War II," 41–2, 45.
20 Ibid., 49–50.
21 Ibid., 49.
22 Ibid., 44.
23 Ibid., 47; Herring, *From Colony to Superpower*, 576.
24 Kennedy, *Freedom from Fear*, 670; Herring, *From Colony to Superpower*, 575; Ma, "The Sino-American Alliance during World War II," 54–5.
25 Ma, "The Sino-American Alliance during World War II," 51–2.
26 Ibid., 52–3.
27 Ibid., 53.
28 Ibid., 56.
29 Ibid., 57; Ngai, *Impossible Subjects*, 203; Roger Daniels, "Immigration Policy in a Time of War: The United States, 1939–1945," *Journal of American Ethnic History* 25, no. 2/3, *Immigration, Incorporation, Integration, and Transnationalism: Interdisciplinary and International Perspectives* (Winter-Spring, 2006): 109, 115n14.
30 Erika Lee, "Immigrants and Immigration Law: A State of the Field Assessment," *Journal of American Ethnic History* 18, no. 4 (1999): 93: Daniels, *Guarding the Golden Door*, 150–1.
31 Ngai, *Impossible Subjects*, 203.
32 Herring, *From Colony to Superpower*, 575.
33 Ibid., 630–2, 631.
34 Daniels, *Guarding the Golden Door*, 152, 154–5.
35 Ma, "The Sino-American Alliance during World War II," 58.
36 Ngai, *Impossible Subjects*, 204–5.
37 Ibid., 206; Daniels, *Guarding the Golden Door*, 154.
38 Daniels, *Guarding the Golden Door*, 155.
39 Ibid., 155–6.
40 Ibid., 156; Ngai, *Impossible Subjects*, 219–20.
41 Ngai, *Impossible Subjects*, 220.
42 Ibid., 220.
43 Ibid., 223.
44 Daniels, *Guarding the Golden Door*, 157.
45 Ngai, *Impossible Subjects*, 221; Daniels, *Guarding the Golden Door*, 157.
46 Daniels, *Guarding the Golden Door*, 157; Ngai, *Impossible Subjects*, 203, 223.

# 8

# Vietnamese, 1970s

The collapse of South Vietnam in the spring of 1975 confronted the United States with its first transhemispheric refugee crisis in twenty years. In contrast to the last one, the Hungarian refugee crisis of 1956, in which US leaders saw an opportunity to score geopolitical points with relatively little effort (about 15,000 Hungarian refugees were resettled in the United States during the late 1950s), the Vietnamese refugee crisis was fraught with hazard. First, unlike Hungarians, Southeast Asians had little history of immigration to the United States; there was no significant immigration population of Southeast Asians up to the 1970s. Second, it would involve multiple waves of refugees in much larger numbers over an extended period of time. Third, it involved negotiations with an erstwhile enemy state, the Democratic Republic of Vietnam. Fourth, and most important, the flows of Vietnamese and other Indochinese refugees between the mid-1970s and early 1980s came in the wake of a protracted American war in Vietnam that eventually ended in a defeat for the United States. There was one notable similarity between the Hungarian and Vietnamese refugee crises that shaped how the United States addressed the issue of refugee resettlement on US soil: US officials had the advantage of remote control. During the Hungarian refugee crisis, refugees could be screened in camps far from US shores, in countries of first asylum, usually Thailand, and also US military bases in the Philippines and Guam. If refugees were granted admission to the United States, they were then sorted and resettled from military bases in America.[1]

The first challenge for US leaders as Americans viewed the fall of Saigon in April 1975 on their televisions was what to do for the Vietnamese who had supported the US-backed regime of the Republic of Vietnam (ROV, colloquially referred to as "South Vietnam"). The immediacy of the situation seemed to justify the executive branch's reflex of using parole authority to resettle Vietnamese refugees. The need to accommodate refugees from South Vietnam did not completely surprise US leaders. The course of the war by the mid-

1970s made the fall of the ROV seem inevitable. As the fall of Saigon appeared imminent in the spring of 1975, US officials made plans to evacuate nearly 3,900 American citizens and their dependents still in-country, as well as the 17,600 Vietnamese citizens and their families who worked directly for the US government. Yet, as the political situation in Saigon deteriorated precipitously, it quickly became clear that such pre-planned evacuation measures were wholly inadequate for the number of Vietnamese seeking to leave the country. Pressured by advisers to do more to "rescue" former South Vietnamese allies, President Gerald Ford established the Interagency Task Force (IATF) on April 17, 1975. Its role was to prepare for the immediate evacuation and resettlement of the approximately 200,000 Vietnamese whose lives were considered

**FIGURE 8.1** US Policy, *April 2, 1975. Published two weeks before the founding of the Interagency Task Force and four weeks before the fall of South Vietnam, Herblock's depiction of US President Gerald Ford and his Secretary of State Henry Kissinger (with empty briefcase) as inadequately responding to the Vietnamese refugee crisis of 1975 is comparatively inaccurate. Tens of thousands of Vietnamese refugees were resettled on US soil during that year. It was during a second wave of Vietnamese refugees between the late 1970s and early 1980s, by contrast, that the US government was more sluggish in their efforts to resettle displaced persons from Southeast Asia. A Herblock Cartoon, © The Herb Block Foundation.*

most at risk if North Vietnamese communist forces were successful in their final offensive against the Saigon government. Most international observers considered the brewing crisis "an apt conclusion" to the United States' defeat and withdrawal from Vietnam in 1973, and the United States received minimal multilateral cooperation to resettle Vietnamese refugees.[2] Therefore, US policymakers embarked on a plan to permanently resettle on US soil the vast majority of Vietnamese refugees in the spring of 1975. Conducting "Operation New Life," the recently founded IATF coordinated with the Pentagon to send ships to the Vietnamese coast to accept refugees, as well as to expeditiously build relocation processing centers in Guam, the Philippines, Thailand, Wake Island, and Hawaii. Such hasty operations undermined the process of remote control, as it was difficult for US immigration inspectors on the ground to determine whose life was in jeopardy. In sum, during this harried, initial phase of the Vietnamese refugee crisis, many displaced persons who had genuine reason to fear oppression under a socialist-dominated Vietnam were not given admission to the United States, while other refugees with flimsier fears of reprisals made their way through resettlement screening (Figure 8.1).[3]

Through the summer and fall of 1975, 130,000 Southeast Asian refugees were resettled in the United States. The great majority (96 percent) of these displaced persons were Vietnamese, but as many as 5,000 Cambodians, Laotians, and Hmong were also brought to US soil. Most refugees of this first wave boarded cargo ships sent out by the US military and were initially taken to the major processing station on Guam. After the INS officials issued official documents to evacuees, nearly all evacuees were flown to one of four resettlement camps in the United States: Camp Pendleton (California), Fort Chaffee (Arkansas), Fort Indiantown Gap (Pennsylvania), or Eglin Air Force Base (Florida). Once in the United States, evacuees were matched with one of nine voluntary organizations (VOLAGS) whose job it was to coordinate evacuees' eventual resettlement with local sponsors, usually either a private family or a church community. When a refugee family was officially matched and assigned to a sponsor, and after that sponsor committed to provide the refugee family with food, clothing, and shelter in the short term, the refugee family was flown to the resettlement destination. In addition to providing for the basic needs of Vietnamese refugees, sponsors also helped recently resettled evacuees find work, enroll their children in school, and become acquainted with life in the United States. By December 1975, roughly eight months after the Vietnamese refugee crisis had begun, the four relocation centers were closed.[4]

These first-wave Vietnamese shared a relatively strong political connection to the United States even before they were evacuated. Many of them were military officers and professionals who worked in various capacities for US embassies, military bases, and businesses in Vietnam. Demographically,

Vietnamese refugees of 1975 came from the upper and middle classes; they were better educated, tended to be more fluent in English, had advanced occupational skills, were wealthier than most of their countrymen, and were disproportionately Roman Catholic. These demographic factors played an instrumental part in easing the relocation and resettlement of Vietnamese refugees who arrived in the United States immediately after the fall of Saigon.[5] By contrast, the second wave of Vietnamese refugees who made their way to the United States during the late 1970s tended to be poorer, faced horrendous migration experiences, and encountered nativist responses once they arrived on US soil.

There were several factors that caused a second Indochinese refugee crisis. First, the communist regime that led the Democratic Republic of Vietnam (DRV) sought to root out former sympathizers of the South Vietnamese government and others deemed enemies of the state. After taking power nationwide in 1975, the DRV implemented sweeping communist economic, political, and agricultural changes that included the collectivization of farmland, and the forced relocation of citizens from urban to previously uncultivated or heavily damaged rural areas designated as "new economic zones." Additionally, the communist government in Hanoi established "re-education" camps to indoctrinate loyalty to the DRV. Systematic discrimination was rife at these camps. It is estimated that a million Vietnamese were sent to these camps during the late 1970s, including some 200,000 former South Vietnamese military personnel and their families, who routinely faced interrogation and torture.[6]

Second, constant military conflict depleted the nation's resources, kept the DRV leadership in a militant mood, and led to massive outward migration from Southeast Asia during the late 1970s. DRV forces invaded Cambodia in 1979 with the objective of ousting the Khmer Rouge. As this regime was backed by the People's Republic of China (PRC), communist Chinese forces launched a retaliatory invasion against Vietnam in February 1979. Not only did war lead to the expenditure of blood and treasure, it retarded Vietnam's ability to recover from years of conflict. Considering all these factors, internal oppression, war, foreign invasion, as well as stymied infrastructure development and reduced crop yields, Vietnamese of many stripes were "desperate to escape" the country.[7]

Compared to the first wave of displaced persons from Vietnam in 1975, Vietnamese refugees of the second wave were less well-educated and more ethnically diverse. They included persons from ethnic minorities of Southeast Asia, such as the Lao, Cham, Montagnard, and Hmong who had fought alongside the Americans between the 1960s and 1970s. The Hmong, in particular, were trained by the CIA during the Vietnam War to fight communists throughout Southeast Asia. By the late 1970s, many Hmong fled Southeast

Asia as they faced reprisals from and were uprooted by communist forces in Vietnam and Cambodia.

Another notable ethnic minority repressed by Vietnam's socialist regime was the Hoa, Vietnamese of Chinese ancestry living in or around Saigon who faced particular persecution from the socialist regime of Vietnam. Long marginalized because of historical resentment toward China, Hoa were also targeted because of their customary involvement in capitalist trade. Finally, the DRV feared that Hoa were fifth-column agents who sought to weaken Vietnam on behalf of the PRC. Consequently, Hoa businesses were closed and community leaders were imprisoned. The Hoa were also removed from civil service posts, prohibited from practicing other occupations, forced to register with the government, and their food rations were reduced.[8]

Vietnamese refugees had to develop "elaborate and clandestine plans" to flee Vietnam. First there was the danger of being caught by police who closely monitored the movement of people in villages, particularly the children of former South Vietnamese soldiers and US sympathizers. Poet Paisley Rekdal details the various dangers Vietnamese faced as they tried to flee Vietnam:

> Capture meant prison, reeducation camps, or forced conscription into the army, especially for sons of former South Vietnamese servicemen.... Boys could be forced to work patrol units along the Cambodian border, where they might be killed in skirmishes with the Khmer Rouge, while girls were targeted by local police for reeducation camps. Parents wanting to protect their children could be bled dry by bribes paid to officials.[9]

The real danger for Vietnamese evacuees began once they were at sea. First, even after evacuees paid exorbitant bribes to government officials to escape the country, they often fell prey to scams and robberies from crews of naval vessels or people smugglers. Boat people, on small vessels not built for weeks of travel on the open ocean, risked capsizing or starvation. It was not uncommon for entire boatloads of Vietnamese refugees to perish at sea. Piracy was a particular danger. Pirates sought out refugees to steal their money, rape and abduct girls and women, and occasionally kill all aboard by ramming the boat repeatedly until it sank.[10]

While hundreds of thousands of evacuees did manage to escape Vietnam, there was no guarantee they would arrive safely on the shores of an asylum country. Officials of neighboring nations, fearing that the sudden influx of evacuees would strain their country's infrastructure and social services, dispatched coast guard vessels to prevent the landing of refugee boats on their shores. Vessels full of "boat people" were forced to remain at sea for weeks, even months, until they could find a safe place to land or were rescued by passing freighters. For those evacuees who did make landfall, whether at Hong Kong, Thailand, the Philippines, Indonesia, Malaysia, or Singapore, it was common for them to be stranded in makeshift refugee camps for up to a year while they hoped to find sponsorship for resettlement. Families could be broken up as individual family members were relocated to different nations.[11]

The attrition rate of displaced Vietnamese was shocking. One scholar estimates that at least 10 percent, perhaps even half of all escapees, lost their lives. Just as harrowing, it is estimated that fully one-third of all Vietnamese "boat people" fell victim to robbery, rape, or murder. Approximately 400,000 Vietnamese escaped Vietnam between the late 1970s and early 1980s. Rekdal states that stories of being adrift for weeks, of starvation, theft, rape, murder, and even rumors of cannibalism passed down for generations within Vietnamese refugee families.[12]

In contrast to the initial wave of Vietnamese refugees in 1975, who enjoyed a robust American response to their departure from Southeast Asia, the US government responded sluggishly to the second Vietnamese refugee crisis of the late 1970s and early 1980s. "Boat people" could not rely on either US cargo ships or US-sanctioned escape routes. In 1977, Congress responded to the crisis by passing special legislation that allowed nearly 100,000 Indochinese refugees to be admitted into the United States and given permanent residency status.[13] Yet such resettlement measures quickly proved inadequate to demand as tens of thousands of Vietnamese refugees fled Southeast Asia every month by the late 1970s. Nearly 54,000 Vietnamese fled their country in June 1979 alone. That same year witnessed a numerical drop in Vietnamese refugees resettling on US soil when, in accordance with a DRV-UN brokered Orderly Departure Program, the United States pledged to accept 14,000 refugees per month indefinitely. In return, Hanoi was to facilitate the exit of persons associated with the former government and military of South Vietnam as well as promise to curtail the overall flow of refugees from Vietnam. The resettlement of boat people into the United States was eased further by the Refugee Act of 1980, which removed numerical limits and visa preferences that had characterized the US refugee resettlement policy since 1965.[14]

In practical terms, the verdict on US support for the resettlement of Vietnamese refugees is mixed. Initially, in 1975, the US government was quick to respond. Just a few years later, however, during another wave of Vietnamese refugees, US officials were relatively slow to act. Even when they did take steps toward resettling boat people from Southeast Asia, they tread carefully. One aspect of the crisis US leaders were not slow to capitalize on were the diplomatic and political dividends of resettling persons fleeing a communist regime. The United States, sociologist C.N. Le argues, could "implicitly claim a moral victory in that so many Vietnamese were willing to risk their lives to come live in the U.S., rather than stay under communist rule." This symbolic victory was especially poignant for a nation reconciling its loss of the Vietnam War. Similarly, most US media outlets gave positive portrayals of Vietnamese refugees as they fled Southeast Asia, driving home the message of the United States as a land of refuge and freedom.[15]

Still, points in the realm of public diplomacy did not equate to a smooth process of resettlement for Vietnamese refugees in the United States. Military defeat in Vietnam was still an open wound for many Americans in the late 1970s and early 1980s. At a time of persistent economic stagnation and inflation—"stagflation"—some Americans came to resent what they perceived as Vietnamese refugees living generously off of public benefits paid for by taxpayers. Vietnamese refugees faced racially motivated attacks during these politically and personally charged times.[16]

# Notes

1. Daniels, *Guarding the Golden Door*, 215–16; Churgin, "Mass Exoduses," 317.
2. C. N. Le, *Asian American Assimilation: Ethnicity, Immigration, and Socioeconomic Attainment*. (New York: LFB Scholarly Pub., 2007), 35.
3. Ibid.
4. Ibid., 37; Daniels, *Guarding the Golden Door*, 216.
5. Le, *Asian American Assimilation*, 37; Paisley Rekdal, *The Broken Country: On Trauma, a Crime and the Continuing Legacy of Vietnam* (Athens: University of Georgia Press, 2017), 19.
6. Le, *Asian American Assimilation*, 50; Rekdal, *The Broken Country*, 19–20.
7. Le, *Asian American Assimilation*, 50; Rekdal, *The Broken Country*, 19.
8. Le, *Asian American Assimilation*, 50, 51; Rekdal, *The Broken Country*, 19.
9. Le, *Asian American Assimilation*, 51; Rekdal, *The Broken Country*, 19–20.
10. Le, *Asian American Assimilation*, 51; Rekdal, *The Broken Country*, 20–1.
11. Ibid.
12. Le, *Asian American Assimilation*, 51; Rekdal, *The Broken Country*, 21.
13. Cox and Rodríguez, "The President and Immigration Law," 503; Churgin, "Mass Exoduses," 316.
14. Rekdal, *The Broken Country*, 20; Le, *Asian American Assimilation*, 51–2.
15. Le, *Asian American Assimilation*, 58–9.
16. Ibid., 59.

# 9

# Cubans, 1960s–1980

The "relatively liberal" dispositions that had characterized the refugee policies of Western nations like the United States after the Second World War had, by the 1970s, started to give way to more restrictive attitudes. Public antipathy toward Vietnamese refugees was apparent even as the US government made strides to resettle displaced Southeast Asians. Following on the heels of the Vietnamese refugee crisis, the Mariel boatlift crisis of 1980 caused a convergence of public antipathy toward refugees with a renewed opposition to refugee resettlement by the US government.[1]

The US Congress had seemed to learn from the Vietnamese refugee crisis. The visa preference category for refugees, first established by the Hart-Celler Act of 1965, proved totally inadequate for the number of refugees who were eventually resettled in the United States.[2] The Refugee Act of 1980, passed in the wake of the Vietnamese refugee crisis, seemed to prepare a more humane response to displaced persons by broadening the definition of a refugee, who was now defined as not just a person fleeing a communist country but anyone who had a well-founded fear of persecution by the government of their home country. Yet this broadened definition of a refugee did not embody a welcome mat for displaced people, for the Refugee Act of 1980 also circumscribed the executive branch's ability to use parole authority to resettle refugees. This was done to prevent a massive flow of refugees to the United States. Instead, the new act stated that refugee admissions would only be granted on a case-by-case basis. The writers of the new law assumed that there would be relatively few asylum claims directed to the United States—"the odd ballet dancer, tennis player, orchestra member, or political dissident" would be easy to process.[3] This particularist, case-by-case approach to asylum approval was undermined soon after its passage by a longtime enemy of the United States, Fidel Castro.

Since 1959, migration had been a prime "foreign policy tool" in the contentious, and sometimes violent, history of US-Cuban relations. Yet, the migration issue was handled in such a way as to complement the domestic priorities of both governments.[4] There had not been a long history of sustained Cuban migration to the United States up to the mid-twentieth century. That changed suddenly and dramatically during the Cold War, as Cuban refugees quickly comprised one of the largest groups of resettled exiles in the United States. The groundswell of movement followed the overthrow of the US-backed Cuban regime of Fulgencio Batista by Cuban revolutionaries led by Fidel Castro in early 1959. This outward migration had everything to do with Cold War geopolitics. As Castro's regime turned indelibly to socialism and aligned with the Soviet Union during its earliest years in power, many Cubans sought refuge outside of Cuba. Many of them came to the United States.[5]

Successive waves of Cubans were welcomed to US shores during the 1960s and 1970s. An initial group of Cuban exiles fled their country between January 1959 and October 1962. These Cubans tended to come from the island's elite classes. They were business executives or owners of companies, prosperous merchants, sugar mill owners, ranchers, representatives of foreign firms, or professionals. High levels of education were common among these exiles. They left Cuba for political and ideological reasons: the more Castro's regime turned to socialism, the more upper-middle class and elite Cubans fled the country. By the early 1960s, 215,000 exiles had left Cuba during what came to be known as the "golden exile." This number included 14,000 unaccompanied children who were sent to the United States in a program that was dubbed "Operation Peter Pan." Cuban refugees of the early 1960s were overwhelmingly welcomed into the United States because they were considered exiles from communism.[6]

A second wave of Cuban migration took place between the mid-1960s and mid-1970s. This group of exiles contrasted with the first in two distinct ways. One, they tended to be drawn from lower socioeconomic strata of Cuban society: working class and lower-middle class. Two, in contrast to refugees of the "golden exile," who left Cuba because of fundamental opposition to the Castro regime, refugees of the second wave were driven by economic and familial pressures. They hoped for better jobs and sought to join family members who had already emigrated to the United States.[7]

Even though Cuban exiles of the second wave were not driven by ideological motives, the US government did not miss the opportunity to capitalize on their departure from Cuba. In 1961, the Kennedy administration created the Cuban Refugee Program (CRP) to provide benefits to Cuban exiles as they resettled in the United States. A few years later, in 1966, the Cuban Adjustment Act (CAA) conferred distinct privileges to Cuban exiles seeking to enter the United States. The law gave the US attorney general "discretionary authority" to grant exemptions to Cuban nationals from the national immigration quotas that had been established by the Hart-Celler Act of 1965. The CAA offered preferential treatment to Cuban exiles in two distinct ways. First, the discretionary authority allowed Cuban exiles legal permanent residency status after only a year's residence in the United States. And, second, there was no cutoff date for the privilege of resettlement, in contrast to other refugee acts that limited how long displaced persons from other countries (such as Vietnam) had to resettle in the United States. In practical terms, the laws offered Cuban exiles substantial economic assistance, employment support networks, bilingual education courses, and programs to validate professional titles. In ideological terms, the CRP and the CAA were oblique foreign policy statements that simultaneously condemned the Castro regime while also welcoming Cuban exiles and resettling them into US society as quickly as possible. For the rest of the decade and into the 1970s, the US government regularly renewed support to subsidize the resettlement of Cuban refugees.[8]

Crucially, while the US government had relative control over the welcoming response they afforded Cuban exiles of the 1960s and 1970s, it had less control over the diplomatic tensions that caused successive waves of Cuban migration to the United States. As the remainder of this chapter will discuss, Fidel Castro twice manipulated (first in 1965 and most especially in 1980) US refugee law for his own diplomatic and domestic ends. On September 28, 1965, his government announced that Cubans with relatives in the United States would be allowed to leave Cuba from the port of Camarioca. If that was not surprising enough for the US government, Castro also invited Cuban exiles to come by sea to pick up family members who had been stranded in Cuba since the suspension of commercial flights between the two countries after the Cuban Missile Crisis of October 1962. So began the Camarioca refugee crisis of 1965, the "dress rehearsal" for the Mariel boatlift crisis fifteen years later.[9]

If Castro's motives were to set off a diplomatic crisis in late 1965, he succeeded. Kelly Greenhill, a political scientist, attributes two factors behind Castro's decision to open Camarioca harbor to Cubans who wanted to leave the country. Neither of those reasons had to do with humanitarian concerns. First, pertaining to domestic concerns, Castro opened Cuba's borders to expel political dissidents with close ties to the Cuban exile community in Miami, Florida. Second, Castro wanted to show how he could easily disrupt US refugee policy.[10]

The Lyndon B. Johnson administration (1963–9) was at "sixes and sevens" over how to respond to the opening of Camarioca. It worried about the potential political, logistical, and economic problems associated with the sudden influx of Cuban exiles. It also worried about looking weak in response to Castro's gambit.[11] Therefore, in a calculated move to show American generosity toward refugees, Johnson, on the same day that he announced and publicly signed the Hart-Celler Act in front of the Statue of Liberty (October 3, 1965), stated that the United States would welcome Cuban exiles to US shores. With this statement, the US government was committed to accept as many Cubans as Castro would permit to leave. Privately, Johnson officials felt they had no choice but to accept Cuban refugees. For a half decade the US government had cited Cuban emigration barriers as proof of the corruption of Castro's regime, the logic being that Cuba could only keep its nationals by preventing them from leaving the island. The only way for the Johnson administration to maintain the political high ground was to take in all Cubans exiles who came to the United States. Johnson officials believed that failing Cuban refugees would allow Castro to embarrass the United States by pointing to the hypocrisy of a land of immigrants spurning the entry of Cubans.[12]

Within a week of Johnson's public statement in front of Lady Liberty, it became clear to US officials that thousands, perhaps tens of thousands, of Cubans planned to make their way to the United States. On October 10, 1965, a series of secret negotiations between the two governments began that would soon normalize the migration flow. A Memorandum of Understanding between the United States and Cuba was publicly announced the following month, which established a coherent system for the movement of Cuban refugees to the US shores and resulted in Castro closing the port of Camarioca. Between October and November 1965, 80,000 Cubans entered the United States. The next month, December 1965, an open-ended airlift program—nicknamed "freedom flights"—was begun to facilitate resettlement of Cuban exiles. Scholars disagree on exact numbers, but by the time the freedom flights were discontinued in 1973, they had relocated anywhere from 270,000 to 340,000 Cubans to the United States.[13] Castro learned a valuable lesson from the Camarioca exile crisis: skillful manipulation of US leaders' fear of looking hypocritical about refugee policy could provide space in which he could dump domestic opponents onto American shores.[14]

Six hundred and thirty thousand Cubans had migrated to the United States by the time the freedom flights ended in 1973. Between 1959 and the mid-1970s, successive presidential administrations willingly resettled Cuban exiles in the United States as a part of its anticommunist, anti-Castro foreign policy. The US government encouraged, assisted, and sponsored mass migration out of Cuba for at least three reasons: it seemed to demonstrate foreign peoples' desire to flee communist governments, the flight of wealthy and educated Cubans would weaken the Cuban government, and resettled Cubans in the United States would serve as a beacon of anti-Castro agitation.[15]

While tensions in US-Cuban relations remained on a low simmer during most of the 1970s, Cuba's domestic problems and prejudices—not the welcoming hand of the United States—laid the groundwork for the Mariel boatlift crisis of 1980. First, social and economic changes in Cuba such as rapid urbanization and a decline in the rural population encouraged Cuban migration.

Another factor was a decline in the Cuban economy. The 1970s were years of economic stagnation for Cubans; 1978 was the only positive year of economic growth for the nation. Between 1978 and 1979, the rate of economic growth fell from 9.4 percent to 4.3 percent. The growth rate fell further, to 3.0 percent, in 1980. National productivity sank as people stopped showing up for work, and by 1980 there were nationwide shortages in food and housing.[16]

The Castro regime tried to address this economic shortfall by taking the unprecedented step of inviting Cubans exiles to return to Cuba to visit family members. Eventually, over 100,000 Cubans would enter Cuba. Castro's primary motivation behind the "visitas de la comunidad" (visitas) was the hope that visiting exiles would bring in much needed hard currency, the circulation of which would revitalize the Cuban economy and improve Cuba's ability to purchase desperately needed goods on the world market. In this sense, Castro's goal was accomplished: Cuban Americans spent $100 million in Cuba by 1979. There were unintended consequences of the visitas, however; the visible prosperity of Cuban-Americans showcased the poverty of Cubans still living under Castro's regime. This stark contrast bred resentment among Cubans and added to their desire to leave Cuba.[17]

A breakdown in diplomacy also led to the Mariel boatlift crisis. Upon entering office, the new administration of Jimmy Carter (1977–81) hoped to find some kind of rapprochement with Cuba. Toward that end, in 1977, the United States and Cuba agreed to open "interest sections." Since there was no official US recognition of Castro's government there were no embassies or ambassadors exchanged between the two countries in Havana and Washington, DC. In the absence of official diplomatic relations, the interest sections established a direct line of communication between the United States and Cuba for the first time in sixteen years.[18]

As promising as this opening of dialogue may have appeared, the Carter administration was not quick to laud the development. Carter faced two pressures. First, many Americans opposed opening relations with Cuba and, second, there were broader, geopolitical concerns that subsumed any positive progress in renewed diplomacy. In 1977, the same year the interest sections were established, Cuba sent military support to Ethiopia in its war against the neighboring nation of Somalia. Ethiopia had been a US ally for decades until a socialist coup overthrew its government in the mid-1970s. Somalia had aligned itself with the Soviet Union since the 1960s, but with the changing calculus of Cold War politics and the closer Ethiopia moved toward socialism, the Somalis moved to forge an alliance with the Americans. Loath to see the failure of a fledgling socialist nation in the Horn region of Africa and recognizing the opportunity to indirectly snub US Cold War interests, Castro jumped at the chance to support Ethiopia. The Ogaden War between Ethiopia and Somalia quickly ended by March 1978, but hardliners in the Carter administration believed no substantive discussion on US-Cuban issues—like immigration—should begin until Castro withdrew his troops from East Africa. This hardline condition represented a missed opportunity to relieve pressure between the United States and Cuba. By the end of 1978, the diplomatic spirit that had led to the founding of the interest sections had been squandered.[19]

The failure of rapprochement was exacerbated a year later by the issue of hijacking. Starting in late October 1979, an increasing number of Cubans had been forcibly hijacking Cuban vessels to the United States. According to a hijacking treaty from 1973, US authorities were obliged to apprehend and prosecute hijackers. But in the diplomatic staring contest between the United States and Cuba, the US government instead immediately paroled hijackers upon their arrival on US shores and took no action to prosecute them. Castro's government viewed this sheltering of Cuban hijackers as "inflammatory" while the Carter administration gave little consideration to what consequences might ensue from such an action.[20]

As early as January 1980, various US intelligence agencies warned Washington, DC, that Castro was planning another Camarioca-like expulsion of Cuban exiles. On February 21, 1980, the US State Department learned that the Cuban government was discussing re-opening Camarioca harbor and hoped to pressure the Carter administration to allow more Cubans to immigrate to the United States. A few weeks later, on March 8, Castro publicly expressed the possibility of another Camarioca and criticized the Carter administration for giving asylum to Cuban hijackers. On April 1, 1980, Castro hinted that he might respond to the hijacking crisis by opening Cuban borders if the US government continued to grant asylum to Cuban hijackers. Despite the warnings, the US State Department gave little credence to Castro's threats. Instead, it informed the interest section in Havana to brief Cuban officials on the Refugee Act of 1980, which was to go into effect in April 1980. The new law allowed admittance of 1,000 Cubans per month during fiscal year 1980. US diplomats believed the new law would adequately accommodate the exiles Castro expelled from Cuba.[21]

There were multiple reasons why the Carter administration did not take seriously the warnings it was receiving from its intelligence agencies. The long 1979 (February 1979 to April 1980) witnessed some of the biggest challenges to US foreign interests in the history of the nation. First, the Western-backed shah (ruler) of Iran was overthrown and an anti-American, Islamic Republic was established. Soon thereafter, in November 1979, Iranian students demonstrating against the United States stormed the US embassy in Tehran and apprehended over sixty American military and civilian personnel, the great majority of whom would be held hostage in Iran for the next 444 days. A clandestine military operation launched in April 1980 by Carter to rescue the hostages failed abysmally. Next, the Somoza family dynasty that ran Nicaragua and had been backed by the Americans since the 1930s was overthrown by an assortment of nationalist groups led by the left-wing Sandinistas. The Sandinista regime that took power aligned themselves with other socialist nations like the Soviet Union and, notably, Cuba. Finally, the Soviet Union invaded Afghanistan to prop up an unpopular socialist government in the capital of Kabul, seemingly visible evidence that US containment policy was threatened.

Amid all of these diplomatic troubles, President Carter and his advisers did not give much heed to the warnings from their intelligence agencies nor did they take seriously Castro's threats that he would reopen Cuban borders. Additionally, the Carter administration was trapped by its own Cold War logic when it assumed that Cubans only wanted to leave Cuba to escape Castro's socialist government. By viewing the situation unidimensionally, the US government failed to recognize how economic factors and desires for family reunification also drove emigration. Hubris and neglect also explain Carter's lack of response. Administration officials with the task of dealing with Cuba believed the assignment beneath them, not within their purview, or the problem of some other department. Essentially, by the late 1970s, Cuba had become a backwater of US Cold War concerns, but Castro and Cuba would soon be on the front pages of America's newspapers.[22]

The triggering event of what became known as the Mariel boatlift crisis began on April 1, 1980, the same day that Castro announced that he may be forced to open the borders for would-be exiles. On that day six Cubans crashed a bus through the front gates of the Peruvian embassy in Havana. Such attempts to flee Cuba by breaking into the grounds of Latin American embassies started as early as the spring of 1979. Much to Castro's annoyance, Peru's government granted political asylum to the gatecrashers and rebuffed repeated appeals to have the six placed under Cuban custody. Soon thereafter, Castro announced that anyone who wanted to leave the country should go to the Peruvian embassy, from where he would permit them to depart to any country that would take them. Castro's government was surprised and embarrassed when, over the span of three days, 10,000 Cubans—many of them shouting "freedom, freedom, freedom"—rushed to the embassy. The rapidly escalating crisis also came to the attention of the UNHCR, which was committed to assisting the "free emigration of peoples."[23] Two weeks later, on April 19 and 21, Castro announced that Cuban exiles could travel to the port of Mariel by sea to pick up not only the original refugees who sought asylum two weeks prior, but anyone else who wanted to leave. He even directly contacted the Cuban exile community in Miami to encourage its members to come and pick up their relatives. Within three days, between April 21 and 24, over 1,000 boats had sailed to Cuba.[24]

The Mariel boatlift crisis occurred at a time when the US public was souring on the idea of refugee resettlement in the United States. While rates of immigration had been low during the first half of the 1970s, between 1976 and 1980 almost 2.5 million immigrants had arrived in the United States along with several hundred thousand Indochinese refugees. Public polls by 1979 and 1980 revealed that half to two-thirds of Americans either opposed additional refugee inflows or favored an immigration freeze until unemployment fell. This hostility to immigrants and refugees was particularly strong in Florida, where residents wanted the boatlift stopped or diverted away from the state.[25]

Past refugee crises from Cuba had afforded the US government an easy opportunity to embarrass Castro's government. By welcoming exiles from socialist countries, the United States simultaneously lauded liberal democracy and criticized socialism.[26] By contrast, the Carter administration's response to the Mariel boatlift was so "slow, confused, and incompetent" that any political and foreign diplomatic capital that may have come from accepting Cuban exiles was quickly subsumed by prejudice domestically and bitterness internationally.[27]

Part of this shift had much to do with how the Carter administration responded to the Mariel crisis in particular; it also indicated a larger shift in how the United States faced refugee crises in general. Between the late 1940s and late 1970s, the United States was generally welcoming to the idea of resettling refugees on US soil. It will be recalled, however, that this welcome mat had conditions (see Chapter 3), such as a unilateral definition of who could be defined as a refugee and the use of resettlement as a tool of foreign policy against socialist nations. Nevertheless, the United States resettled more refugees in the thirty years after the Second World War than at any other time in its history.

The passage of the Refugee Act of 1980 marked a shift in this welcoming approach to refugees. The new law discontinued the standard policy that facilitated the en masse resettlement of groups of exiles from communist countries. Thereafter, refugees could only gain admission into the United States on an individual, case-by-case basis. Some of this shift had to do with interbranch competition over refugee policy—Congress trying to temper the president's use of parole authority (again, see Chapter 3). But it also had to do with the political, social, and economic costs of resettling refugees in the United States. In the throes of a prolonged economic recession during the 1970s, Americans increasingly opposed the prospect of their government offering asylum to displaced foreigners. It was notable, for example, that the CRP, which dated back to the Kennedy administration, was closed in 1981, not long after the Mariel crisis ended.[28]

Like Lyndon Johnson before him, Carter faced the quandary of matching political rhetoric with refugee policy. Accepting displaced persons from socialist countries was the baseline of US refugee policy, especially Cubans, and with them the chance to embarrass the hated Castro regime. Carter's pledge as a presidential candidate to infuse respect for human rights into the conduct of US foreign policy only amplified the drive to admit Cuban exiles in toto. But these political and humanitarian factors were complicated by, first, the new Refugee Act of 1980, which called for a more controlled, bureaucratic system of refugee processing. Carter's response was also influenced by a US public that did not want large numbers of Cubans exiles resettled in the United States. The result, according to immigration historian Roger Daniels, was "strenuous vacillation" in the Carter administration's approach to the Mariel boatlift.[29]

If the point of history education is to learn from past mistakes, then Carter did not heed the Camarioca crisis from fifteen years before. Like Johnson, Carter (on May 5, 1980) made a bold statement that the United States would welcome Cuban exiles with "open arms." And like Johnson before him, Carter faced immediate blowback for these remarks. Instead of being viewed as a statement in accord with the humanitarian posture that US refugee policy customarily tried to extol, Carter's welcoming words were viewed as an explicit encouragement for those persons wishing to leave Cuba. Carter's welcome statement was complicated further by an issue of semantics. In his public address of May 8, Carter referred to Cuban exiles as *refugees*, which suggested that his administration would look kindly upon the idea of resettling Cubans coming to US shores en bloc, despite the fact that the new Refugee Act of 1980 disallowed such automatic granting of asylum. Instead, under the new law, those arriving at US shores were "asylum seekers," denoting the fact that each exile would need to receive permission to enter the United States. Rounding out the confusion emanating from the Oval Office, on May 13, 1980—five days after the "open arms" address—Carter reversed his welcoming stance and took actions to halt the boatlift (Figure 9.1).[30]

The sheer volume of Cuban exiles seeking admission into the United States precluded any quick solution to what Carter officials now had to admit was a full-blown refugee crisis. By early June 1980, 100,000 Cubans had arrived in the United States. The new Refugee Act proved completely inadequate to meet this rush of exiles. The Carter administration had no time to individually evaluate and admit refugees; instead, it relied on the reflex of parole authority to face the crisis. In a purely bureaucratic move—likely aimed at saving face amid the boiling crisis—the INS stipulated in May 1980 that Cuban exiles coming from the port of Mariel ("Marielitos") were not refugees or asylees, but rather "entrants (status pending)."[31]

It would take three months of negotiations for the United States to provide a proposal that persuaded Castro to close the port of Mariel, namely that migration talks would be linked to a future broader agenda of normalizing diplomatic relations. Diplomatically, the boatlift crisis came to an end on

**FIGURE 9.1** Bay of People, *May 7, 1980. Nearly twenty years beyond the Bay of Pigs fiasco, in which a US-backed force of Cuban exiles who invaded Cuba failed to overthrow Fidel Castro's socialist government, Castro employed a novel form of diplomatic retaliation: the sudden expunging of undesirable Cubans to US shores. A Herblock Cartoon,* © The Herb Block Foundation.

September 26, 1980, when the Cubans closed the port of Mariel, but politically and socially, the crisis was ongoing.[32]

By the time the port of Mariel was closed, public polls in the United States showed that three-fourths of Americans viewed Cubans refugees as bad for the nation.[33] Much of this antipathy toward the Marielitos had to do with where they resettled. Unlike Vietnamese refugees who had been dispersed throughout the United States because of official resettlement policies that sought to avoid overburdening certain cities with significant numbers of refugees, Marielitos predominantly resettled in South Florida. Nearly half of the over 260,000 Vietnamese who lived in the United States in 1980 resided in eight metropolitan areas across three states and districts: Los Angeles-Long Beach, Orange County, San Jose, San Diego, and San Francisco in California, New Orleans, Louisiana, Houston, Texas, and the Washington, DC, area.[34] By contrast, the great majority of the nearly 125,000 Marielitos who were admitted to the United States in 1980 came to reside in Florida. This problem of resettlement distribution was new and represented an oversight by the Carter administration. In the past, US authorities, cognizant of potential political blowback in the electorally significant state of Florida, designed the freedom flight airlift program (1969–73) to distribute and resettle Cubans outside of the state.[35]

Marielitos also faced a harsh response from American and Cuban-Americans for their alleged burden on public resources and their alleged dispositions to crime. According to historians, the arrival of thousands of Cuban exiles caused a division within the Cuban-American community of South Florida. Older Cuban exiles tended to be white and came from the middle or upper-middle classes. By contrast, Marielitos were racially mixed (40 percent of them were Afro-Cuban), were minimally educated, younger, less likely to speak English, had fewer family and social networks in the United States, and were working class. Two other distinctions were noteworthy: Marielitos had no recollection of pre-revolution Cuba and the Cuban-American community was far less accommodating and welcoming to them than they had been to earlier waves of exiles.[36]

The over 124,700 individuals who made up the third, Mariel wave of Cuban migration to the United States were comprised of four groups: ex-political prisoners and dissidents who were pressured to leave by the central government; "social undesirables" defined to include petty criminals, mentally unstable persons, homosexuals, and juvenile delinquents; "antisocial" persons which were defined to include religious evangelists (such as Jehovah's Witnesses), alcoholics, prostitutes, and vagrants; and finally, individuals with family members already living in the United States who had expressed a desire to leave Cuba.[37] Far from being safely shepherded to exile, Marielitos were hounded out of Cuba and made scapegoats of political, social, and economic tensions within Cuban society. They were considered counterrevolutionaries and traitors and faced mob attacks. They were called "worms" ("gusanos/gusanas") and "scum" ("escoria").[38] In *Cubamerican*, a documentary on Cuban migration, an elderly Cuban woman critical of the exiles stated in 1980 that Marielitos were "all betrayers of the country and they should all leave. We don't want them here. What we want here are revolutionaries."[39] Some presumptive exiles were besieged in their homes and prevented from leaving by surrounding mobs, leading to the death of those trapped inside. According to one Marielita, Mirta Ojita, Cuba "was the closest it [had] ever been to a civil war. People turned against their neighbors, their friends, even their relatives."[40] Castro himself publicly depicted Marielitos as enemies of the state: "Whoever lacks revolutionary blood. Whoever lacks a mind that adapts itself to the ideas of the Revolution. Whoever lacks heart to adapt to the effort and the heroism of the Revolution. We don't want them! We don't need them!"[41]

Scholars of the Mariel crisis differ on how much agency, even blame, they attribute to Castro. They tend to agree that he opened up the port to relieve Cuba's domestic, economic, and social pressures by getting rid of those citizens who were deemed counterrevolutionaries, thereby freeing up jobs and housing units, especially for thousands of returning soldiers from military campaigns in Africa. Between April and September 1980, Castro artfully "crafted" a series of events that essentially internationalized what had begun as a domestic political and economic crisis in Cuba into a diplomatic, political, economic, and social headache for the United States. Castro exploited American "rhetorical grandstanding" on the acceptance of Cuban refugees by suddenly foisting a wave of exiles on the United States. US leaders had a choice of how to respond, and neither option was totally palatable. They could deny admittance of Cuban migrants, which would have undermined their posturing of the United States as a haven for refugees fleeing communist countries. Such a choice, US leaders feared, would make the United States look weak in the face of Castro's government. Or, US leaders could admit Cuban exiles, an option that could excite a nativist backlash among Americans and would raise difficult issues such as the expense of refugee resettlement.[42]

Some scholars such as Kate Dupes Hawk and Margarita Cervantes-Rodríguez ascribe more sinister motives to Castro: infiltrating Cuban agents into the United States, disrupting the Cuban exile community in Miami, increasing criminal activity in the United States, and putting a financial burden on the US authorities by having to apprehend or incarcerate criminals and the mentally insane among the Cuban exiles. Essentially, these scholars argue that Castro was using exiles as political tools against enemy countries such as the United States. Additionally, Hawk contends that Castro launched the boatlift crisis to "pay back" the Carter administration for not lifting the US trade embargo on Cuba and that he was emboldened further by the lack of response from the Carter administration to the exile crisis.[43] Hawk concludes that the Mariel boatlift was part of Castro's "continuous war on the United States" and likened the multi-month crisis in 1980 to other significant invasions of the United States: Pearl Harbor and September 11.[44]

Readers will have to decide for themselves whether they find such arguments convincing, hyperbolic, or something in-between. Historical agency is a fickle thing. Events of the past can easily drag along persons in their crosscurrents just as easily as individuals of the past believe (and are believed to) push along historical events. Specifically, while it may seem clear that Castro orchestrated much of what became the Mariel boatlift crisis, this should not be confused with his ability to conduct the event as it transpired. Conductors do not play music after all, it is the musicians they lead who do. And embarrassment can work two ways. Just as Castro played the Mariel boatlift crisis to embarrass the United States, the sheer number of Cubans who sought to leave Cuba embarrassed his government. In reaction, the regime quickly organized mobs "reminiscent of the Nazi pogroms" to harass, harangue, and in some cases physically harm those who sought to leave Cuba.[45]

This stigma against Marielitos crossed the water into the United States and led to a resurgent nativism against Latino immigrants. Domestically, the Mariel boatlift crisis occurred at a time of economic recession and high inflation, an ongoing hostage crisis in Iran, and a US presidential campaign. The arrival of Cuban exiles also coincided with a wave of crime in South Florida perpetuated by gangs of Hispanic origin. US politicians and media started to attribute this outbreak of crime to the arrival of Marielitos.[46] The dispersal of Marielitos to "resettlement camps" across the country—as opposed to countries distant from US shores—would only reinforce the notion of Marielitos' inherent aberrance.[47] The backlash of white Americans against Marielitos in South Florida took such forms as a voter referendum in Dade County to revoke a bilingual ordinance that had been passed in the early 1970s.[48] The "Mariel stigma" had a very real effect on how Marielitos assimilated into US society. Cubans exiles of 1980 had higher rates of incarceration and institutionalization than older Cuban-American refugees. They had less access to education and had stunted social and economic advancement compared to older members of the Cuban-American exile community.[49] This anti-Marielito backlash in South Florida played a part in a nationwide antipathy toward immigrants that prompted sweeping legislative changes in US immigration policies during the 1980s and 1990s.[50]

By giving refuge to exiles, the United States perpetuated bad relations with Cuba; by weaponizing exiles for internal and foreign diplomatic ends, Cuba alienated itself further from the United States. In sum, successive waves of Cuban exiles have undermined US-Cuban relations for years and pitted US opposition to communism against Castro's coercion of Cubans and his manipulation of US refugee policy.[51]

Yet, in contrast to the Cuban immigration between 1959 and 1973, the Mariel crisis showed that just as refugees could be used as foreign policy tools to suit US foreign policy interests, so could refugees also be used against US foreign policy interests. The United States was not alone in rooting its refugee policy in its foreign policy, and just as the act of admitting displaced people was a political statement, the displacing of people carried political repercussions.[52] In the span of two decades, from the Camarioca crisis of 1965 to the Mariel crisis of 1980, Castro manipulated an exile crisis to expel domestic critics and embarrass the United States. This external manipulation was buttressed by blindspots in legislative reform to US refugee policy. In the effort to make the United States a place of refuge for all displaced people, not just those from communist nations, the Refugee Act of

1980 failed to account for the economic and social—not just the political and diplomatic—factors that lead to emigration. In short, US refugee policy was trapped by its Cold War logic. Persons fleeing political persecution were not the same as those seeking better economic opportunity. But the 1980 act, and subsequent legislation, did not make this distinction—to the regret of many hundreds of thousands of would-be refugees who followed the Mariel crisis.[53]

When refugees served as "political metaphors of alleged communist oppression," there was a little interpretive gray area in which US officials could recognize that the Cold War was not the sole explanation for the displacement of foreign peoples.[54] This shortcoming created the condition by which Marielitos were viewed as aberrant by both the Cuban and US governments. It also laid the foundations for shortsightedness when it came to later refugee crises from Central America (see Chapter 10). For Americans and their leaders, the bitter legacy of the Mariel boatlift was to squelch the non-ideological spirit that underlined the Refugee Act of 1980 and to revive a parochial, political, non-humanitarian approach to persons seeking asylum within the United States.[55]

# Notes

1. Loescher, "The International Refugee Regime," 362.
2. Zolberg, "Reforming the Back Door," 320.
3. Cox and Rodríguez, "The President and Immigration Law," 506–7; Rosenblum and Salehyan, "Norms and Interests in US Asylum Enforcement," 683–4; Jorge I. Domínguez, "'Cooperating with the Enemy' U.S. Immigration Policies toward Cuba," in *Western Hemisphere Immigration and United States Foreign Policy*, ed. Christopher Mitchell (University Park, PA: The Pennsylvania State University Press, 1992), 31–88, p. 73; Churgin, "Mass Exoduses," 318.
4. Cervantes-Rodríguez, *International Migration in Cuba*, 155, 169; Engstrom, *Presidential Decision Making Adrift*, 4.
5. Lorena G. Barberia, "U.S. Immigration Policies Toward Cuba," in *Debating U.S.-Cuban relations: Shall We Play Ball?*, ed. Jorge I. Domínguez, Rafael Hernández, and Lorena Barberia (New York: Routledge, 2012), 180.
6. Silvia Pedraza, *Political Disaffection in Cuba's Revolution and Exodus* (New York: Cambridge University Press, 2007), 3, 5–6; Cervantes-Rodríguez, *International Migration in Cuba*, 161 and 168.
7. Pedraza, *Political Disaffection in Cuba's Revolution and Exodus*, 5–6.
8. Cervantes-Rodríguez, *International Migration in Cuba*, 170, 171–2; Barberia, "U.S. Immigration Policies Toward Cuba,"183; Tienda and Sánchez, "Latin American Immigration to the United States," 50.

9   Kelly M. Greenhill, *Weapons of Mass Migration: Forced Displacement, Coercion, and Foreign Policy* (Ithaca, NY: Cornell University Press, 2010), 83–4, 89.
10  Ibid., 84.
11  Ibid.
12  Ibid., 85–6.
13  Ibid., 86–7, 87n61; Cervantes-Rodríguez, *International Migration in Cuba* 161; Greenhill argues for the lower figure, Cervantes-Rodríguez argues for the higher figure.
14  Greenhill, *Weapons of Mass Migration*, 89.
15  Cervantes-Rodríguez, *International Migration in Cuba*, 161; Barberia, "U.S. Immigration Policies Toward Cuba," 180, 182, 183.
16  Cervantes-Rodríguez, *International Migration in Cuba*, 158, 172; Engstrom, *Presidential Decision Making Adrift*, 5–6, 46; Greenhill, *Weapons of Mass Migration*, 89–90.
17  Engstrom, *Presidential Decision Making Adrift*, 46–7; Greenhill, *Weapons of Mass Migration*, 89–90; Cervantes-Rodríguez, *International Migration in Cuba*, 173.
18  Engstrom, *Presidential Decision Making Adrift*, 43–4.
19  Ibid., 44–6.
20  Greenhill, *Weapons of Mass Migration*, 89–90; Engstrom, *Presidential Decision Making Adrift*, 48.
21  Kate Dupes Hawk, et al., *Florida and the Mariel Boatlift of 1980: The First Twenty Days* (Tuscaloosa: University of Alabama Press, 2014), 41–2, 44; Greenhill, *Weapons of Mass Migration*, 91, 104–5.
22  Hawk, et al., *Florida and the Mariel Boatlift of 1980*, 41–2, 44; Greenhill, *Weapons of Mass Migration*, 91, 104–5; Engstrom, *Presidential Decision Making Adrift*, 197.
23  Dominguez, "Cooperating with the Enemy," 72–3; Jose Enrique Pardo, *Cubamerican* (San Francisco: Ño Productions, 2012), 1.03–1.04; Hawk, et al., *Florida and the Mariel Boatlift of 1980*, 29; Greenhill, *Weapons of Mass Migration*, 92.
24  Greenhill, *Weapons of Mass Migration*, 92–3; Pardo, *Cubamerican*, 1.03–.04.
25  Greenhill, *Weapons of Mass Migration*, 94–5.
26  Cervantes-Rodríguez, *International Migration in Cuba*, 175.
27  Dominguez, "Cooperating with the Enemy," 77.
28  Barberia, "U.S. Immigration Policies Toward Cuba," 183–4.
29  Daniels, *Guarding the Golden Door*, 206; Greenhill, *Weapons of Mass Migration*, 95.
30  Greenhill, *Weapons of Mass Migration*, 95, 97, 98.
31  Ibid., 100; Churgin, "Mass Exoduses," 318; Daniels, *Guarding the Golden Door*, 206.
32  Greenhill, *Weapons of Mass Migration*, 103.

33  Ibid.
34  Le, *Asian American Assimilation*, 54 and 55.
35  Greenhill, *Weapons of Mass Migration*, 88.
36  Hawk, et al., *Florida and the Mariel Boatlift of 1980*, 233–4; Gastón A. Fernández, "Race, Gender, and Class in the Persistence of the Mariel Stigma Twenty Years After the Exodus from Cuba," *The International Migration Review* 41, no. 3 (2007): 604, 605–7; Martinez and Stowell, "Extending Immigration and Crime Studies: National Implications and Local Settings," 176; Pedraza, *Political Disaffection in Cuba's Revolution and Exodus*, 7, 154–5.
37  Fernández, "Race, Gender, and Class in the Persistence of the Mariel Stigma," 604–5.
38  Pardo, *Cubamerican*, 1.07.07–41; Pedraza, *Political Disaffection in Cuba's Revolution and Exodus*, 7.
39  Pardo, *Cubamerican*, 1.05.02–10.
40  Ibid., 1.04.37–49, 1.04–.05.
41  Ibid., 1.05.38–55.
42  Cervantes-Rodríguez, *International Migration in Cuba*, 173–4; Greenhill, *Weapons of Mass Migration*, 77.
43  Cervantes-Rodríguez, *International Migration in Cuba*, 175; Hawk, et al., *Florida and the Mariel Boatlift of 1980*, 30–3, 39–40.
44  Hawk, et al., *Florida and the Mariel Boatlift of 1980*, 252.
45  Ibid., 30, 333.
46  Fernández, "Race, Gender, and Class in the Persistence of the Mariel Stigma," 609, 610, 611, 612; Maddux, "Ronald Reagan and the Task Force on Immigration, 11981," 202.
47  Fernández, "Race, Gender, and Class in the Persistence of the Mariel Stigma," 605–6, 611.
48  Hawk, et al, *Florida and the Mariel Boatlift of 1980*, 235.
49  Fernández, "Race, Gender, and Class in the Persistence of the Mariel Stigma," 604, 605–6, 620–1.
50  Martinez and Stowell, "Extending Immigration and Crime Studies," 178–9.
51  Pedraza, *Political Disaffection in Cuba's Revolution and Exodus*, 283–4.
52  Engstrom, *Presidential Decision Making Adrift*, 4.
53  Ibid., 197; Maddux, "Ronald Reagan and the Task Force on Immigration," 202.
54  Engstrom, *Presidential Decision Making Adrift*, 5; Ira J. Kurzban, "A Critical Analysis of Refugee Law," *University of Miami Law Review* 36 (September 1982): 866–7.
55  Barberia, "U.S. Immigration Policies Toward Cuba," 183–4; Daniels, *Guarding the Golden Door*, 206.

# 10

# Central Americans, 1980s–1990s

There are two broad tendencies that underline the history of US refugee policy: the desire to protect human rights and the desire to promote foreign policy goals. Sometimes, as in the case of Vietnamese refugees, these two tendencies complemented each other; at other times, as in the case of Jewish refugees, these two tendencies conflicted.[1] Of the four major refugee crises the United States dealt with during the twentieth century, none of them were so obviously tied to US foreign policy interests than the Central American refugee crisis of the 1980s and 1990s.[2] None of the past crises were so affected by different ideas of who constituted a refugee; and in no other refugee crisis did US public opinion play such an instrumental role in shaping US refugee policy.

As with past refugee crises, war caused the flight of Central Americans to the United States. Starting in the early 1960s, left-wing, socialist, and nationalist groups formed in Central America. They had various—and often conflicting—goals, but their primary objective was the ouster of oppressive, and often US-backed, regimes. Some of these regimes had been in power since the 1930s, such as the Somoza family dynasty in Nicaragua. By 1979, the dominant insurgent group in Nicaragua, the Sandinistas, successfully overthrew the regime of Anastasio Somoza. Political conservatives in the United States feared that Cuban-style socialism was spreading throughout Central America.[3] Similar socialist-nationalist insurgencies cropped up and waged war on right-wing military regimes in Guatemala and El Salvador. Those governments, with the staunch support of the Americans, were able to hold on, but a decade of bloody civil war-ravaged Central America.[4]

Upon entering office in January 1981, the Ronald Reagan administration (1981–9) became "obsessed" with the belief that the Soviet Union and

Cuba were attempting to spread their influence throughout the Western Hemisphere. It did not help that the Sandinistas were vocally anti-American.[5] To prevent another "Nick-a-wog-wha," as the head of the CIA, William Casey, pronounced Nicaragua, the US government sent vast amounts of military aid to the governments of El Salvador and Guatemala, both of which faced left-wing insurgencies.[6] El Salvador, a historically poor and stratified society in which 2 percent of the population dominated the country, received $5 billion in aid from the United States during the 1980s. Great expense did not result in greater security. The Salvadoran army squandered most of the money it received from the United States, while government troops and paramilitary death squads—some members of which were trained by the Americans— prowled the tiny country killing about 70,000 peasants, teachers, union organizers, and church workers. Congress asked few questions of the Reagan administration and the civil war in El Salvador did not wind down until 1992.[7]

Nicaragua was not spared from Reagan's gaze. In that country, which was under the Sandinista government, US leaders were forced to become more artful—and conniving— in their attempts to roll back socialism. Reagan was convinced that the Sandinistas were a front for the Cubans and Soviets, pointing to their harassment of political opponents and blocking of promised free elections in Nicaragua.[8] But the question for Reagan officials was how to discredit and ultimately remove the Sandinistas from power while limiting direct US involvement. Less than a decade after US withdrawal from Vietnam, the prospect of direct military intervention by American troops was completely unpalatable for the United States. An *indirect* form of intervention was utilized instead. In 1981, Reagan authorized William Casey, the director of the CIA, to organize an anti-Sandinista force called the contrarevolucionarios, or simply *contras*. The contra army numbered anywhere between 10,000 to 20,000 Nicaraguans, most of whom were veterans of the old Somoza dynasty. Publicly, Reagan lauded the contras as "freedom fighters" who fought in a noble struggle against the Sandinistas. Locally, the contras committed atrocities against their countrymen comparable to the actions of the death squads in El Salvador. Privately, the Reagan administration had to work some legal legerdemain to get the dollars to US proxies in Central America. Congressional law disallowed the allocation of foreign aid to military groups aspiring to overthrow governments that were at peace with the United States (no state of war technically existed between the Americans and the Sandinistas). Casey convinced lawmakers that the contras, instead of attempting to oust the Sandinista government, were actually working to interdict Sandinista military aid to left-wing insurgents in El Salvador. Secretly, Reagan signed an order authorizing contra aid for the purpose of deposing the Sandinista government.[9]

For Reagan and his advisers, there was more at stake than rolling back socialism. Holding the line in Central America was presented to Reagan as a chance to expunge, to exorcize, the "humiliating memory" of the Vietnam War, and to reestablish US credibility as a champion of anticommunism.[10] Despite Reagan's dire warnings about the potential spread of communism in the Western Hemisphere and the need for greater US involvement in Latin America, the American public was apathetic. Public polls seemed to show that the average citizen was indifferent to who dominated the region, as long as American troops were not killed in combat. This helps to explain why military aid and support to such groups as the contras in Nicaragua and the death squads in El Salvador became the standard policy of the Reagan administration.[11] The initial American indifference to affairs in the wider region is all the more striking when one considers the role public opinion played in the Central American refugee crisis.

This literal change of opinion was rooted in Reagan's "not-so-covert" wars in Nicaragua. During the 1980s, Central America was at the center of a larger political and even emotional debate among US leaders and citizens about the nation's proper role in the world.[12] Between 1981 and 1984, as the war in Nicaragua grew, Reagan came to see that nation of less than 4 million people (by comparison, the population of Los Angeles in 1985 was over 10 million) as a major front in the struggle against communism.[13] But other Americans were not so certain. Unconvinced that the Sandinistas posed a fundamental threat to US national security, and unconvinced that the contras were the protagonists (and not the antagonists) in the Cold War drama playing out in Nicaragua, more and more Americans came to oppose further US involvement there.[14] In 1984, the US press reported that the CIA, in an attempt to aid the contra war effort, had mined Nicaraguan ports to deny fuel imports from reaching the Sandinista regime. Belying the notion that the Reagan administration was not trying to oust the Nicaraguan government, a huge credibility gap opened up between the executive and legislative branches. It did not help that 4,000 US troops staged military operations in Honduras in the summer and fall of 1983 to intimidate the Sandinistas. Already wary that US funds sent to the contras were being used to overthrow the Sandinistas, in October 1984 Congress passed the Boland amendment, which cut off funding to the contras.[15] Reagan responded by instructing his advisers to develop a strategy that would "help these people [the contras] keep body and soul together."[16] So was laid the groundwork for one of the most significant political scandals in American history: the Iran-Contra Affair.

Simultaneously, US foreign policy created another scandal in Central America during the 1980s, and that pertained to the issue of displaced persons. The same US foreign aid that propped up the death squads in El Salvador and the contras in Nicaragua created the conditions that displaced hundreds of thousands of Salvadorans and Nicaraguans; the same foreign policy initiatives that led to US support of the death squads in El Salvador and the contras in Nicaragua, shaped how US leaders responded to the arrival of Salvadoran and Nicaraguan refugees. For example, the Salvadoran military's aggression against its own people, an aggression that utilized US arms and money, led to the mass exodus of Salvadorans. In the effort to safeguard the region from communism, US involvement in Central America during the 1980s actually destabilized the internal security of foreign nations.[17]

Policy shaped the Reagan administration's response to the Central American refugee crisis, but so did precedent. Entering office just months after the end of the Mariel boatlift crisis, Reagan and many other Americans believed Carter had bungled the Cuban exile problem of 1980 and were certain that if the "Soviet-Cuban-Nicaraguan axis" were successful in spreading communism through the region, then the numbers of refugees from Cuba who entered the United States would be "child's play" compared to what would come next.[18] Underlying these arguments was a presumption that communist regimes produced mass emigration flows by oppressing their peoples. Ergo, if US officials wanted to tamp down on the inflow of refugees, and public polls of the time seemed to show that this was what the American public wanted, then their designs to prevent the spread of communism in the Western Hemisphere were justified. This argument also had a complementary effect: for those who were concerned about undocumented refugee flows to the United States, supporting Reagan's foreign policy in Central America made sense; for those who were concerned about the spread of communism in Central America, Reagan's concerns about the flow of refugees were credible. In sum, during the 1980s, US foreign policy concerns directly influenced US refugee policy.[19]

Such views of communist regimes as producers of refugees because of their inherently oppressive nature had informed US refugee and foreign policy since the early Cold War. For the Reagan administration, this thinking was enhanced by recent criticism of the much-maligned Carter presidency. Before she was appointed by Reagan to serve as US ambassador to the United Nations, Jeanne Kirkpatrick, a political scientist, argued in an article well-regarded by political conservatives like Reagan, that Carter's human rights policies had undermined friendly authoritarian regimes while they indirectly encouraged totalitarian regimes. According to Kirkpatrick's schema, authoritarian (which was to say non-communist) regimes at least had the possibility of eventually turning to democratic governance, while totalitarian (which was to say communist) regimes had no hope of becoming democracies. Recent events seemed to bear out Kirpatrick's assertion. Had not Castro's totalitarian government made a mockery of the Carter administration by expelling tens of thousands of Cuban exiles in 1980? By contrast, Kirkpatrick argued, well-supported authoritarian governments would not necessarily become net exporters of refugees. For Reagan and his advisers, the conclusion was simple: support anticommunist regimes in Central America, for it would prevent the spread of communism and the flow of refugees.[20]

Ironically, the political violence that US foreign aid abetted in Central America resulted in the kinds of refugee flows Reagan officials feared most.[21] Statistical data from El Salvador demonstrates how violence drove Salvadoran refugee flows to the United States. There was a fourteenfold increase in political murder from 1,000 Salvadorans killed in 1979, to 8,000 in 1980, to 14,000 in 1981. El Salvador's military and paramilitary groups carried out most of the violence. It was not just murder that drove emigration, but other forms of violence such as torture, rape, disappearances, and destruction of crops and property. Most of the violence was random, designed to terrorize the population into submission. It was often assumed by El Salvador's government that peasants who lived near guerrilla-controlled areas of the country were supporters of the rebels; therefore, these bystanders were considered "legitimate targets." Political terror had a second function beyond punishing alleged rebel sympathizers. It was used to convince peasants to never support the rebels.[22]

The government's use of military sweeps, which focused on moving civilians out of areas in which rebel groups were thought to operate, also spurred emigration. Such actions left many Salvadorans homeless and generated refugees. Finally, forced recruitment of young men, by either government or rebel forces, accelerated the refugee crisis and helped explain why young men comprised the large majority of Salvadorans who fled to the United States.[23]

Definitionally, displaced people from El Salvador easily met the internationally recognized definition of a refugee as a person who was fleeing oppression from their home government. But there were two caveats that explain why Salvadoran refugees were largely blocked from resettling in the United States, one political, the second terminological. For the Reagan administration, only communist countries produced refugees. El Salvador's government was not only non-communist, but it and the United States were making herculean efforts to make sure it never became communist. Second, it was not always clear what *primarily* drove Salvadorans to flee their country: political violence or structural want—oppression or poverty. The international refugee regime, which included the United States after passage of the Refugee Act of 1980, was predisposed to assist victims of the former but was more nebulous in its response to the latter. When considering the resettlement of refugees, can political violence be separated from poverty as causes of displacement? The Central American refugee crisis of the 1980s and 1990s demonstrated the difficulty of delineating such a separation.[24]

The United Nations and the United States responded in different ways to this definitional blind spot in refugee policy. The UNHCR, utilizing a broad definition of a *political refugee*, supported tens of thousands of Central American refugees in camps in Costa Rica, Honduras, and Mexico. By contrast, the United States, defining many refugees from Central America as *economic migrants*, rejected the great majority of asylum applicants. But, politically, US refugee policy viewed displaced persons differently. While only 2 percent of Salvadorans who applied for asylum were granted it, 87 percent of asylum applicants from Nicaragua were granted sanctuary by the INS. The US State Department, which administered political asylum, regularly advised the INS to reject asylum cases of Salvadorans and Guatemalans, which they did, at an average rate of 98 percent. US officials justified this imbalanced rate of approval by using a Cold War-inspired, foreign policy-focused definition of a refugee. Since displaced Salvadorans were not persecuted because of their religion or race; because they were not coming from the Middle East, and because they were not living under a communist regime, their asylum applications were rejected. Fleeing generalized violence, civil war, and poor economic conditions was not enough to gain entry into the United States. In making this case, US officials worried that an overly flexible asylum policy that would lead to a massive influx of asylum seekers.[25] No consideration was given to how US foreign aid may have contributed to refugee flows.

The Reagan administration's foreign policy shaped this asylum policy. To grant asylum to droves of Salvadoran refugees would have embarrassed the government of El Salvador, which was staunchly supported by the Americans. Additionally, to have allowed Salvadoran refugees into the United States would have been tantamount to admitting internationally that the Central American governments the United States was supporting were brutalizing their own people, an admission that would have called into question the morality of US foreign policy. By contrast, admitting refugees from Nicaragua was an easy win for the Reagan administration: it embarrassed the Sandinista regime and confirmed Reagan officials' belief that only communist nations forcibly displaced people.[26]

By 1984, the same year that Congress passed the Boland amendment, more than 1.2 million Salvadorans had been displaced, out of a population of 5 million. Half of those refugees, representing nearly 25 percent of El Salvador's total population, made their way to the United States. As substantial numbers crossed the border, the INS used detention centers and built tent cities to house the refugees. The hope was that detention would deter others from coming. There was no other way to do so; the legal process for gaining asylum was nearly impossible to surmount.[27]

Under the new system of asylum established by the Refugee Act of 1980, in which refugees had to apply for asylum individually, asylum seekers from

Central America were obliged to prove that the violence they experienced was *exceptional* in ways anticipated by US asylum law. The application process and asylum hearings were influenced by the larger political considerations of the Cold War. US government lawyers argued against granting asylum to many Central American refugees by asserting that individual experiences of violence were cases of generalized suffering that was attributable to criminal factors instead of political factors.[28] Asylum applicants, criminal anthropologist Susan Bibler Coutin argues, faced a "frightening type of [a] catch-22": if a refugee escaped to the United States this was used as evidence against their appeal for asylum, as it suggested that by escaping their lives were never really in danger.[29] By contrast, if a refugee was killed, the danger was proven, and the foundation was established for approval of asylum—which of course was a moot point since the person was dead. Reminiscent of the bizarre, puritanical form of justice meted out to accused witches in colonial Massachusetts during the early 1690s, one INS attorney at an asylum hearing asked an applicant who had been threatened by guerrilla forces in El Salvador, "But they in fact didn't kill you?" In short, being alive was evidence against an applicant's appeal for asylum.[30]

Reagan officials argued that Central American refugees flowed to the United States for economic, not political, reasons. Domestic critics of US refugee policy, and Reagan's foreign policy in Central America, asserted otherwise.[31] Starting in the early 1980s, a grassroots movement took shape to challenge the Reagan administration's handling of the growing refugee crisis from Central America. Many church-based congregations declared themselves "sanctuaries" for displaced people from El Salvador and Guatemala. These activists pressured the US government to grant temporary status to Central Americans either through executive or legislative action.[32]

The *Sanctuary* movement's brand of political dissent was deeply rooted in a history of protesting the ethics of American law. Like adherents of the Civil Rights Movement, Sanctuary activists predominantly emerged from faith-based communities and utilized methods of nonviolence to broadcast their message. Like most antiwar activists during the Vietnam War, supporters of the Sanctuary movement called for a US foreign policy that was non-interventionist and peaceable. And like participants in the Underground Railroad during the pre-Civil War period, Sanctuary activists sheltered displaced persons from danger and shepherded them to safety.[33]

Some sanctuary churches gained experience sheltering displaced persons during the Vietnamese refugee crisis of the late 1970s. Churches were central in resettlement efforts by directly sponsoring refugee families or by contributing to church-affiliated agencies working with refugees. For Sanctuary supporters, honoring the personhood of each refugee was paramount. As one participant recounted, "When such a refugee stands at the church door requesting assistance, there is no preliminary inquiry into the merits of one's claim to the status of refugee as defined by the United States immigration law. There is only an unconditional invitation and welcome extended to the person in need."[34] In addition to civilly disobeying the Reagan administration's official policy on Central American refugees, the Sanctuary movement presented a significant challenge to the assumption that government was sovereign over immigration policy. Instead, the movement contended, there were values that transcended laws.[35]

The Sanctuary movement attracted a wide range of supporters from civic-minded groups and citizens who were normally indifferent to foreign policy issues joined. Most of the groups that joined were religious in nature, but they also included students, teachers, Hispanic organizations, human rights groups, and legal guilds.[36] While only a small portion of the US population ever directly supported the Sanctuary movement, its growth paralleled an increased awareness among Americans of the plight of Central American refugees during the 1980s. Newspapers ran front-page stories on refugees, municipal governments held local ballots to declare cities as sanctuaries for refugees, church bulletin boards detailed the harrowing experiences refugees endured, and, most especially, the rapidly increasing physical presence of Central Americans in the United States brought the issue of refugee policy to the forefront of public and political conversations.[37] For some Americans, this awareness resulted in a renewed humanitarian concern for refugees that replaced the erstwhile indifference that public polls recorded in the early part of the 1980s.[38]

The Sanctuary movement was founded in Tucson, Arizona, in March 1982. By the following year there were forty-five Sanctuary churches and synagogues throughout the country and 600 secondary Sanctuary groups that provided endorsement and support. The process by which Sanctuary advocates provided protection for Central American refugees has been dubbed by historian Lars Schoultz as "a contemporary underground railroad."[39] Activists smuggled refugees across the US-Mexico border and drove them to nearby cities—Tucson, San Antonio, Los Angeles—from which refugees were transported to different churches and families across the continent. Refugees were provided food, shelter, and transportation along the way. Once at their destination, movement-affiliated churches and synagogues took responsibility for the refugees for up to a year, arranging for housing, food, education and literacy training, jobs, health care, and legal services.[40]

The movement was founded and initially driven by humanitarian concern for the Central American refugees who were unable to obtain asylum in the United States. Soon, however, the humanitarian focus moved into the political realm, as activists called into question US foreign policy in Central America, the nature of the regimes governing the countries from which the refugees fled, and the reasons why these refugees were denied asylum. Individual refugee testimonials given publicly to shine a light onto US policy in Central America, and to confront the injustice of asylum denial hastened the politicization of the refugee issue. These testimonials provided a "deeper perspective," and a more direct criticism of the Reagan administration's actions in the region.[41]

The Sanctuary movement continued to grow during the mid-1980s. By early 1985, 150 churches throughout the country offered sanctuary to Central American refugees, and the movement in general received the endorsement of eighteen national religious denominations and commissions. INS officials, increasingly frustrated by movement activities, began to arrest Sanctuary activists in Texas and Arizona as early as 1984. This official crackdown only increased the growth of the movement. By mid-1985 there were 250 declared sanctuaries, including churches as well as colleges, universities, municipalities, and even entire states (New Mexico). By 1987 there were over 420 Sanctuary groups, including 305 churches, forty-one synagogues, twenty-four cities, and fifteen universities.[42]

For Jewish Americans, who were activists in the Sanctuary movement, the Central American refugee crisis had disturbing parallels to the Jewish refugee crisis of the 1930s. The belief that the Roosevelt administration could have done more to rescue European Jews from the Nazis provided a powerful impetus to challenge the Reagan administration's regular rejection of Salvadoran and Guatemalan asylum seekers. In the words of Evely Laser-Shlensky, who served as the social action chair of the Southwest Region of the New Reform Movement during the 1980s, the "Sanctuary movement walks a prophetic path when it confronts a government that is using its power callously and carelessly in its dealing with Central American refugees, people whose presence here is a testimony to the human rights of the countries to whom we supply arms and military training." Activists such as Laser-Shlensky chafed at the discriminatory way in which the US government admitted Nicaraguans refugees, who came from a country led by a socialist regime, while turning down asylum appeals from Salvadorans and Guatemalans, who fled countries whose central governments were supported by the United States.[43] In political terms, the Sanctuary movement represented a moral and religious challenge to US foreign relations and refugee policy; in practical terms, it helped thousands of Salvadorans and Guatemalans escape the danger of deportation.[44]

The yawning gap between the Cold War principles that drove Reagan's refugee policy and the humanitarian principles Reagan's critics believed should define US refugee policy spawned a direct, multiyear challenge to the Reagan, and later Bush, administrations. The *American Baptist Church v. Thornburgh* case (the ABC case) embodied this challenge. Brought forward in 1985, the class action lawsuit involved scores of churches, religious organizations, legal groups, and refugees.[45] Customarily, the INS granted admission to around one-fourth of asylum applications between the 1970s and 1990s. The great majority of those admitted into the United States were individuals who fled socialist countries such as the Soviet Union, Poland, Cuba, Vietnam, Laos, Cambodia, and China.[46] It was this discrimination in favor of refugees from socialist countries that formed the basis for the plaintiffs' argument in the ABC case, which held that Salvadoran and Guatemalan asylum seekers were treated unfairly compared to refugees from socialist countries. The ABC plaintiffs sought to correct this disparity by having it be officially acknowledged that the wars taking place in El Salvador and Guatemala were civil wars instead of fights against communism.[47] In broad political terms, changes in terminology would have questioned the Reagan administration's motives for supporting the Salvadoran and Guatemalan governments. In specific, legal terms, such a change in terminology could potentially clear a way for displaced people from El Salvador and Guatemala to be defined—and admitted—as refugees of political violence.

The ABC case arose at a time when the wars in El Salvador and Guatemala stalled and the extent of human rights abuses in those countries were well known. Depending on how the ABC case was settled, it had the potential to greatly embarrass the US government as being complicit in the destruction of nations and the displacement of hundreds of thousands of people.[48] The ground continued to shift under the Reagan administration's official approach to the Central American refugee crisis when the US Supreme Court, in a 1987 decision, *INS v. Cardoza-Fonseca*, ruled that the standard which had been applied in asylum adjudication had been too restrictive. A "well founded fear" for one's life should be, the court stated, standard enough to justify non-refoulement. While the US government continued to reject a large share of asylum applicants from El Salvador and Guatemala, in a continued attempt to legitimize their support of right-wing military regimes in the region, the 1987 Supreme Court decision represented a real check on the executive branch's refugee policy. If applicants were *physically present* in the United States, they could use the provisions of judicial review or seek systematic relief through class action litigation.[49] At a stroke, the government was placed in a defensive posture and the ABC plaintiffs were invigorated.

The ABC case culminated on January 31, 1991, in an out-of-court settlement between the administration of George H.W. Bush (1989–93) and the ABC plaintiffs. Prior to settling, the Bush administration had tried, and failed, to have the case dismissed by a federal district court. In the face of evidence pointing to the inconsistent application of the asylum process based on country or origin, the government decided to permit reopening of all the previously adjudicated claims. This unprecedented action by the Bush administration was taken to spare the government embarrassment from a potential court ruling that would declare the US asylum adjudicatory process as inherently unfair. Strikingly, as part of the settlement agreement, the US government admitted that "foreign policy and border enforcement considerations are not relevant to the [asylum] determination." The INS was required to reopen asylum cases for 250,000 Guatemalan and Salvadoran refugees who had previously been denied asylum. The settlement liberated asylum hearings "from foreign policy tutelage" by prohibiting the consideration of diplomacy in the evaluation of future asylum claims.[50]

The Sanctuary movement scored a redeeming victory with the ABC case, but the settlement did not represent the end of the Central American refugee crisis. Symbolically, the ABC settlement was a direct blow to the Reagan administration's Cold War-driven refugee policy. Practically, however, the ABC settlement's victory was tempered by the huge backlog of cases that quickly developed. Additionally, the changing geopolitical context caused by the end of Central America's wars and the collapse of the Soviet Union during the early 1990s dramatically altered the nature of the refugee issue. With the Cold War ended, the major justification for safe haven in the United States was moot.[51] Instead of ending, however, the Central American refugee crisis transformed into a new problem for the United States: a permanently displaced population of refugees temporarily residing on US soil far away from their home countries.

In late November 1990, just two months before the ABC case was settled, President Bush signed into law a new immigration act, a part of which created the Temporary Protected Status program (TPS). It allowed the attorney general to give temporary resident status to refugees. Essentially, the Bush administration was reviving the executive branch's use of parole authority to resolve refugee issues. Not content to rewind the clock back to a time when the legislative branch had little influence over refugee resettlement, Congress qualified the TPS "to replace the nontransparent use" of parole authority by placing temporary resident status on a time-fixed basis: renewable periods of eighteen months. The new program granted safe haven to applicants who entered the United States prior to mid-September 1990 while fleeing life-threatening conditions such as civil wars and natural disasters. Under the TPS, the generalized violence that was once used as evidence to deny Central American asylum applicants permanent residence in the United States was now recognized as legitimate grounds to allow refugees into the country. Salvadorans were granted TPS protection after peace accords ended the war in El Salvador in 1991; Guatemalan refugees would not be granted TPS status until the civil war ended in their home country in 1996.[52]

A different type of insecurity for Central American refugees in the United States set in during the 1990s—a permanent "sense of temporariness."[53] When the TPS system expired in 1992, it was replaced by the Deferred Enforced Departure (DED), which extended the eligibility date for temporary status from 1990 to 1996. While temporary status applicants were assured that their deportation was deferred, it was not resolved.[54]

The settlement of asylum cases, paradoxically, was complicated by peace returning to Central America in the 1990s as it became difficult for applicants to claim that they would face persecution if they were deported to their home countries. And since Salvadoran and Guatemalan asylum applicants had to have entered the United States prior to 1990 to qualify for the benefits of the ABC settlement, by the mid-1990s it was questionable if Salvadorans, for example, who entered the United States after the end of El Salvador's civil war could benefit from the conditions of the ABC settlement. Ironically, for an international refugee regime that had been forged in the Cold War and, arguably, built as a geopolitical weapon in the vast ideological arsenal of the "First World" against the "Second World," the post-Cold War era was a quandary. Refugee flows were more likely to result from ethnic, communal, and religious conflicts. International troubles were increasingly fueled by the increasing availability of arms, sharp socioeconomic divisions, and human rights abuses.[55]

This "legal limbo" of permanent temporariness for Central American refugees experienced was complicated further by changes to US immigration laws during the mid-1990s. Far from stemming the flow of refugees, the end of the Cold War witnessed a surge of displaced persons to the United States, notably from Haiti and Cuba. First the Bush administration, and then the administration of Bill Clinton (1993–2001), interdicted Haitian and Cuban asylum applicants at sea in order to preempt any legal claims of due process once on US soil. The *INS v. Cardoza-Fonseca* decision of 1987 had stipulated that asylum applicants could receive permanent status if they were *physically present* in the United States. In 1995, the US government implemented regulatory changes limiting the right to appeal asylum rulings. A year later, Congress passed the Illegal Immigration Reform and Immigrant Responsibility Act (IIRIRA), which shortened the time limit for new asylum applications, imposed broader asylum detention provisions, and expedited the removal of rejected applicants.[56] The IIRIRA closed off other forms of legalization for Salvadoran and Guatemalan asylum applicants. Additionally, the law allowed a "cancellation of removal" (essentially, a person's deportation) but only if applicants could prove that they had had continuous presence in the United States for at least ten years. This made recent arrivals deportable. Also, hardship to a US citizen or legal permanent resident spouse, parent, or child was no longer considered grounds to cancel the removal of an asylum applicant. In addition, the new law imposed an annual cap of 4,000 cancellation of removals, which would come nowhere near resolving the backlog of approximately 300,000 ABC plaintiffs whose asylum cases were still pending in the mid-1990s. Finally, the law created a "stop-time" rule by which a Notice to Appear in court would represent the stoppage of the clock that was accruing time toward the requisite ten years of residence.[57]

In contrast to the harsh resettlement provisions of the IIRIRA, the US government passed the Nicaraguan Adjustment and Central American Relief Act (NACARA) in 1997. Responding to pressure from Central American governments concerned about the loss of remittances and the social effects of deportations, as well as immigrant rights groups and immigrants themselves, NACARA sought to correct what was considered two decades' worth of executive branch discrimination against Central American asylum seekers. NACARA incorporated earlier eligibility dates and thus allowed the population affected by the ABC settlement and TPS to remain in the United States. It was a remarkable turnaround considering the highly restrictive immigration measures passed less than a year before. The reform was especially noteworthy because it recognized displaced Salvadorans and Guatemalans— previously defined as economic migrants—as deserving of protection because of the lives they had created in the United States and because of the circumstances of their departure from their home countries. Yet NACARA was not a complete victory for Salvadoran and Guatemalan asylum applicants. The legal requirement to demonstrate a criterion of "extreme hardship" for asylum approval was more difficult at a time when Central America was not obviously embroiled in Cold War-inspired conflicts. By contrast, Nicaraguan applicants found it much easier to gain legal permanent resident status. The Cold War was over, but its ideology still affected US asylum policy: Nicaraguan asylum seekers enjoyed a smoother application review process than their Salvadoran and Guatemalan counterparts. The latter two groups' process "was lengthier, more expensive, more cumbersome, and less certain." Implemented to relieve the backlog of ABC claimant cases, the NACARA program itself was burdened with a huge backlog of cases by 2001.[58]

Despite backlogs and delayed asylum approvals, was the Central American refugee crisis that began in the early 1980s resolved by the early 2000s? The answer must be delayed to consider the strange coda of displacement and violence that was apparent by the turn of the twenty-first century. Passed into law just a few months before and in tandem with the IIRIRA of 1996, the Anti-Terrorism and Effective Death Penalty Act (AEDPA) expanded the range of crimes that could result in deportation. Notably, for Salvadoran and Guatemalan asylum seekers, the laws' preexisting focus on criminal histories "trumped" the circumstances of their departure from home countries, as well as their work histories, family ties, and periods of residency in the United States. Therefore, delayed amnesty became dangerous. Had Salvadoran and Guatemalan asylum applicants been granted asylum between the 1980s and early 1990s, many of them could have been naturalized citizens whose children would not have been subject to new deportation policies passed in 1996. Even as asylum laws allowed Salvadoran and Guatemalan asylum applicants to remain in the United States, hardening immigration laws—a result of growing public concern over undocumented immigration and crime (see Chapter 11)—led to legal revision that facilitated the US government's ability to deport noncitizen felons to *countries of origin* in Central America. But here is the rub: most of the noncitizen felons of Salvadoran and Guatemalan background had never been to Central America; they had entered the United States as young people with their families during the 1980s. As these persons were not officially defined as refugees upon their entry into the United States, and since Central America's civil wars had been over for years, the rule of non-refoulement was not considered a block on their deportation.[59]

Unfortunately, it was not so clear that peace had been restored in Central America by the early 2000s. Nicaragua's civil war ended in 1990, El Salvador's in 1992, and Guatemala's in 1996, yet each of those nations still bore the "scars and open wounds of traumatized societies."[60] Each of these nations was burdened by weak government institutions, rampant corruption, intense urban poverty, overpopulation, and neglect by the international community. Gang warfare and drug smuggling added to the problems of these benighted countries.[61] Much of this history of violence was the legacy of US Cold War foreign policies in the region. By myopically focusing on combating left-wing insurgencies, US policymakers did not consider how warfare would retard the structural characters of the three nations. Consequently, in the years since the end of the civil wars, many former combatants—some of whom gained positions of power—had more incentive to make profits illicitly than to do the hard work of building credible forms of governance. And as the region was pushed to the back of US diplomatic priorities in the early twenty-first century, Central American criminals—some of whom were high officials—enjoyed a rate of impunity witnessed in few other places, even in war zones.[62] In such a political vacuum, "the line between criminal and political violence" was blurred. Many former combatants of the civil wars—contras and Sandinistas in Nicaragua, for example—now use old weapons (AK 47s are easy to get a hold of across the region) to engage in criminal activities in the present: kidnapping, bank robbery, and murder.[63]

Central American gangs, known as *marabuntas* (or *maras* for short), represented "the most serious challenge" to peace in the region since the civil wars of the 1980s. While such gangs as MS 13 or Mara 18 have grown in power and influence in the power vacuums of El Salvador in particular, these gangs actually have their roots in the immigration and deportation policies of the United States. They "spawned" in the ghettos of American cities, notably Los Angeles; started out as young gangs, and then "migrated" to Central America, where they transformed into powerful, cross-border crime networks.[64]

As stated earlier, the IIRIRA and the AEDPA in 1996 facilitated the process of deportation. Noncitizens who were sentenced to a year or more in prison would now be repatriated to their countries of origin. Foreign-born American felons could be stripped of their citizenship and expelled once they served their prison terms. The list of deportable crimes was increased to include minor offenses such as drunk driving and petty theft. Consequently, investigative journalist Ana Arana argues, "between 2000 and 2004, an estimated 20,000 young Central American criminals, whose families had settled in the slums of Los Angeles in the 1980s after fleeing civil wars at home, were deported to countries they barely knew."[65] As early as the late 1990s, the gangs of Central America had grown in numbers to the tens of thousands; their size increased to anywhere between 70,000 and 100,000 after the turn of the century as the United States exported noncitizen felons to Central American countries whose national populations numbered less than 7 million. Local governments in Central America, which were focused on rebuilding their nations after years of civil war, were soon engulfed in new civil wars with gangs that profited

**FIGURE 10.1** Hecho en Estados Unidos, 2017. *In this illustration by graphic artist Eric J. García, a central, heavily tattooed figure representing the notorious Mara Salvatrucha 13 (MS-13), a gang of Salvadoran immigrants founded in 1980s Los Angeles (hence, "made in the United States"), perpetuates the myriad factors underlying the Central American refugee crisis of the late twentieth century: violence, poverty, drugs, fear. Yet the background figure, Uncle Sam, also contributes to the refugee crisis by denying Lady Liberty's attempt to grab the outstretched hand of a refugee desperately trying to climb a wall into the United States. Eric J. García, 2017.*

substantially from drug smuggling, human trafficking, and sex trafficking. Gangs controlled and terrorized whole neighborhoods of Central American capitals such as San Salvador.[66]

US Cold War policies in Central America abetted civil wars that devastated the region and caused waves of refugees to flock to the United States. The precarious legal limbo some of those refugees—Salvadoran and Guatemalan especially—were subjected to kept them in the shadow of deportation even as they made lives in the United States. Despite peace in their home countries, changes to US immigration and asylum law perpetuated the fear of deportation and undermined the national rebuilding of Nicaragua, El Salvador, and Guatemala. Ironically, the nature of gang violence, which is devoid of any explicitly political motives, undermined appeals for asylum by Central American applicants. Going full circle from the 1980s to the early 2000s, Coutin states, the "risk of becoming a victim of violence is deemed outside the protections promised by political asylum [in the United States]."[67] This begs the question: is the Central American refugee crisis over? Hardly (Figure 10.1).

## Notes

1. Rosenblum and Salehyan, "Norms and Interests in US Asylum Enforcement," 681.
2. Schoultz, "Central America and the Politicization of U.S. Immigration Policy," 159, 217–18.
3. Herring, *From Colony to Superpower*, 858.
4. Michael Shaller, "Reagan and the Cold War," in *Deconstructing Reagan: Conservative Mythology and America's Fortieth President*, ed. Kyle Longley, et al. (Armonk, NY: Routledge, 2007), 3–40, p. 26.
5. Herring, *From Colony to Superpower*, 886; Shaller, "Reagan and the Cold War," 24.
6. Shaller, "Reagan and the Cold War," 26.
7. Ibid.
8. Ibid.
9. Ibid., 26–7; Herring, *From Colony to Superpower*, 889.
10. Shaller, "Reagan and the Cold War," 25; Herring, *From Colony to Superpower*, 886.
11. Shaller, "Reagan and the Cold War," 25.
12. Herring, *From Colony to Superpower*, 884, 889.
13. Ibid., 889.
14. Ibid., 890.
15. Ibid., 889–90.
16. Ibid., 890; Shaller, "Reagan and the Cold War," 27.

17 Sassen, "Beyond Sovereignty," 13, 17n14; Kleven, "Why International Law Favors Emigration over Immigration," 85 and 85n49.
18 Schoultz, "Central America and the Politicization of U.S. Immigration Policy," 157–8.
19 Ibid., 159, 218.
20 Herring, *From Colony to Superpower*, 886; W. D. Stanley, "Economic Migrants or Refugees from Violence? A Time-series analysis of Salvadoran Migrants to the United States," *Latin American Research Review* 22, no. 1 (1987): 148.
21 Stanley, "Economic Migrants or Refugees from Violence?," 146.
22 Ibid., 135, 136; Susan Bibler Coutin, "Falling Outside: Excavating the History of Central American Asylum Seekers," *Law & Social Inquiry* 36, no. 3 (2011): 575–6.
23 Stanley, "Economic Migrants or Refugees from Violence?," 137, 145.
24 Ibid., 133, 144.
25 Gallagher, "The Evolution of the International Refugee System," 590, 592; Coutin, "Falling Outside," 574, 576–7.
26 Coutin, "Falling Outside," 574–5.
27 Ibid., 576; Churgin, "Mass Exoduses," 319.
28 Coutin, "Falling Outside," 574, 577.
29 Ibid., 577.
30 Ibid.
31 Schoultz, "Central America and the Politicization of U.S. Immigration Policy," 167.
32 Coutin, "Falling Outside," 577.
33 Ignatius Bau, *This Ground is Holy: Church Sanctuary and Central American Refugees* (New York: Paulist Press, 1985), 20; Norma Stoltz Chinchilla, Nora Hamilton, and James Loucky, "The Sanctuary Movement and Central American Activism in Los Angeles," *Latin American Perspectives* 36, no. 6 (2009): 119–20.
34 Bau, *This Ground is Holy*, 13.
35 Ibid., 180, Chinchilla, et al., "The Sanctuary Movement and Central American Activism in Los Angeles," 102.
36 Schoultz, "Central America and the Politicization of U.S. Immigration Policy," 210–11; Chinchilla, et al., "The Sanctuary Movement and Central American Activism in Los Angeles," 102.
37 Schoultz, "Central America and the Politicization of U.S. Immigration Policy," 218–19.
38 Chinchilla, et al., "The Sanctuary Movement and Central American Activism in Los Angeles," 102; Salehyan and Rosenblum, "International Relations, Domestic Politics, and Asylum Admissions in the United States," 108–15.
39 Schoultz, "Central America and the Politicization of U.S. Immigration Policy," 211.
40 Chinchilla, et al., "The Sanctuary Movement and Central American Activism in Los Angeles," 105–6.

41  Ibid., 106, 123.
42  Ibid., 107.
43  Ibid., 114, 119–20.
44  Ibid., 119–20, 122.
45  Rosenblum and Salehyan, "Norms and Interests in US Asylum Enforcement," 684; Chinchilla, et al., "The Sanctuary Movement and Central American Activism in Los Angeles," 118.
46  Ester E. Hernandez, "Relief Dollars: U.S. Policies Toward Central Americans, 1980s to Present," *Journal of American Ethnic History* 25, no. 2/3 (2006): 231, 241n15.
47  Ibid., 231.
48  Coutin, "Falling Outside," 580–1.
49  Churgin, "Mass Exoduses," 319.
50  Ibid., 321; Rosenblum and Salehyan, "Norms and Interests in US Asylum Enforcement," 684; Chinchilla, et al., "The Sanctuary Movement and Central American Activism in Los Angeles," 118.
51  Coutin, "Falling Outside," 581.
52  Churgin, "Mass Exoduses," 320; Adam B. Cox and Cristina M. Rodríguez, "The President and Immigration Law Redux," *The Yale Law Journal* 125, no. 1 (2015): 118; Coutin, "Falling Outside," 580–1; Hernandez, "Relief Dollars," 227–8.
53  Hernandez, "Relief Dollars," 228.
54  Churgin, "Mass Exoduses," 320; Coutin, "Falling Outside," 582.
55  Coutin, "Falling Outside," 582; Loescher, "The International Refugee Regime," 362.
56  Rosenblum and Saleyhan, "Norms and Interests in US Asylum Enforcement," 684.
57  Coutin, "Falling Outside," 582–3.
58  Salehyan and Rosenblum, "International Relations, Domestic Politics, and Asylum Admissions in the United States," 107, 119n4; Coutin, "Falling Outside," 583–5; Hernandez, "Relief Dollars," 232.
59  Coutin, "Falling Outside," 585–8; Stumpf, "The Crimmigration Crisis," 383.
60  Ana Arana, "The New Battle for Central America," *Foreign Affairs* 80, no. 6 (2001): 88.
61  Ibid., 88.
62  Ibid., 97–8.
63  Ibid., 89.
64  Ibid., 98–100.
65  Ibid., 100.
66  Ibid., 98, 101.
67  Coutin, "Falling Outside," 590.

# 11

# Mexicans, 1980s–2000s

Economic liberalism is the bedrock of US economic prosperity.¹ Since the end of the Second World War in 1945, US leaders have tied their goal to maintain global peace with a desire to spread economic liberal values. US leaders believed global peace was only sustainable if it rested upon global wealth, and that capitalist economic systems were the only credible basis upon which global prosperity could thrive. If capitalism was the basis upon which global prosperity would be built after the Second World War, then the United States was the model nation for others to emulate. Moreover, the US economy would serve as the foundation for global capitalist growth: the US dollar was established as the basis for foreign exchange and trade, and US economic aid was central to reconstruction and development efforts.

The US desire to rebuild and foster global peace and prosperity was not driven simply by generous and altruistic goals but by two other goals. First, preventing another world war and, second, and most relevant to this chapter, maintaining US economic prosperity. After 1945 most American leaders believed that Second World War was caused in part by the global economic depression of the 1930s. Now in the post-war period, if it was assumed that the bedrock of global peace and prosperity was not just the political leadership of the United States but especially the health of the US economy, then US capital investment abroad was essential. Not only was US foreign investment deemed necessary for the American economy, but it was also considered instrumental in developing "Third World" nations—nations in which, it was feared by US leaders, that the socioeconomic factors abounded for political instability: poverty and overpopulation.

The question for US leaders in the post-war era was what formula must "Third World" nations use to reach a level of prosperity that resolved their socioeconomic problems, which—for countries like Mexico—tended to spur along immigration to the United States? During the 1950s and early 1960s, US economists such as Walt Rostow propagated the idea of *modernization theory* to lay out a path to prosperity. The theory rested on the idea that all nations' economies could modernize in a similar fashion: by mechanizing agricultural production, poorer nations would meet the food subsistence of their peoples and produce enough surplus products for export. Those exports would bring in desperately needed capital that would help that nation industrialize, thereby producing jobs in non-agricultural sectors. Such economic diversification, along with a healthy dose of foreign investment (not just in the form of capital but also in the shape of technology and knowledge transfers), would see "Third World" nations enter a "take-off" stage, during which they would develop enough to resolve their issues of overpopulation and poverty.[2]

US leaders took for granted that the US economy would always be robust enough to serve as a backstop for the global economy and that US investment into foreign economies would uplift "Third World" nations and set them on a path of capitalist development modeled after the United States. The edifice of optimism started to crumble by the 1970s, just thirty years after the end of the Second World War. As the US economy faltered in that decade, an under-recognized—if essential—factor upon which US prosperity had been built came under sharp public critique: Mexican migration to the United States. During subsequent years, American leaders wrestled with the twin challenge of revitalizing the US economy while restricting Mexican migration. The effort to meet the first challenge led to a doubling down of liberal economic strategies and goals that resulted in an *even deeper* penetration of US economic interests into underdeveloped nations like Mexico. Such penetration actually exacerbated the factors that caused Mexican migration. This neoliberal turn was paralleled by an effort to slow Mexican migration and enhance regulation of the international border between the United States and Mexico. Such restrictionist efforts also exacerbated the social, legal, and political marginalization of Mexican migrants. In short, since the 1970s, the US economic prosperity that was to foster global peace and development has in fact created the conditions that cause undocumented Mexican migration to the United States.

Mexican migrant workers had always been in high demand by American employers. Between 1942 and 1964, the Bracero program between the United States and Mexico imported Mexican migrant laborers to primarily work in the agricultural sector of the American southwest. Mexican migrants not only worked in agriculture but heavy industry. Employers preferred Mexican migrants because they could pay them cheaply and were largely unobligated to provide on-the-job protections and services that nonmigrant workers were legally required to have. Immigration laws of the 1920s drastically diminished European immigration and completely barred Asian immigration, so Mexican migrant labor helped fill this void. Finally, Mexico's close proximity to the United States played a role in US businesses preferring to use Mexican migrant laborers, as the return of those migrants—whether voluntary or coerced—to their home country was quite easy. The demand for Mexican migrants did not slacken after the Bracero program was cancelled in 1964. Indeed, by the end of the 1960s rates of Mexican immigration were reaching record levels. Undocumented Mexican migration doubled during the decade in response to US labor demands.[3] Rates of legal Mexican immigration continued to grow during the 1970s and 1980s: 680,000 during the former decade and 3 million during the latter decade. Data on undocumented migration is never clear because of the surreptitious nature of avoiding legal entrance into the United States but there are estimates that 800,000 undocumented Mexican migrants crossed the border during these years.[4]

As Mexican migration numbers rose, so did fear and anger among American citizens about the presence of Mexican migrants in US society. Fears rose within the American public of an "invasion" of "illegal" Mexican migrants, and this fear was often stirred up by the media. By the late 1970s, it was apparent that there was a great deal of public and media dissatisfaction with what was considered the federal government's inability to control its borders.[5] Such public pressure resulted in the formation of the Select Commission on immigration and Refugee Policy (SCIRP) in 1978 by the Carter Administration (1977–81). Among other things, SCIRP was tasked with developing a solution to the problem of undocumented Mexican migration to the United States. The commission's final report of March 1981 framed immigration regulation in terms of national security by recommending stronger law enforcement at the border, sanctions on US employers who knowingly hired undocumented laborers, and a path to permanent resident status for undocumented migrants—which provides access to citizenship—who had resided in the United States for a fixed period of time (refer to Chapter 2 for discussion of the various domestic constituencies the SCIRP report hoped to satisfy with its recommendations).[6]

The dramatic rise in Mexican migration numbers and the subsequent increase of public anxiety did not exist in isolation. First, the apprehension occurred amid a protracted economic downturn, and second, it followed a long historical response of ambivalence and antipathy among Americans toward nonwhite immigrants.

High rates of inflation and nearly a decade-long recession impacted the US economy during the 1970s. High rates of unemployment and inflation and elevated energy (oil) prices made the 1970s tough economic years for Americans. Partly because of the simultaneously stagnant economy which suffered from high inflation—"stagflation"—but also in response to the proliferation of liberal sociopolitical reforms, such as the Civil Rights Movement, from the mid-1950s to the early 1970s, American politics took a decided conservative turn from the late 1970s to the 1980s. This occurred as rates of undocumented Mexican migration reached historic highs.[7]

A period of sustained economic growth since the early 1960s came to an end. In this context of economic insecurity, a latent nativism was reborn. This nativism was at a low ebb during the 1960s, as indicated by the eradication of discriminatory quotas in immigration law with the Hart-Celler Act of 1965 and the relative absence of public concern about rising rates of undocumented Mexican migration.[8] Amid rising unemployment, inflation, and oil prices, Americans again became alarmed about undocumented Mexican migration. The 1970s was a time of "belt-tightening, anxiety, and suspicion."[9]

Americans' renewed anxiety over immigration in the 1970s was not driven solely by the economic downturn. Historical antipathy and ambivalence among Americans toward immigrants were also important. American prejudice toward immigrants stretches back to the colonial period, but in the latter half of the twentieth century two demographic and socioeconomic factors underlined Americans renewed anxiety about immigration. The Hart-Celler Act of 1965 dramatically changed the demographics of immigration to the United States by ending a bar on Asian immigration that had its foundation in the 1880s. As a result, after 1965, Asian immigration to the United States skyrocketed: by over 3,800 percent in the decade after Hart-Celler went into effect in 1968. While Western Hemisphere immigration had a numerical ceiling with Hart-Celler, continuous demand for especially Mexican migrant laborers was *a*—but not *the*, as we shall see—prime reason why Mexicans migrated to the United States in record numbers after 1965.[10] European immigration to the United States declined during the same years that Latin American and Asian immigration rose. This trend has been attributed to two factors: recovering post-war economies in Europe closed the gap in wage differentials between European countries and the United States (European immigrants would no longer receive markedly higher wages in the United States) and the US economy's increased demand for unskilled laborers. Most of these unskilled workers were from impoverished "Third World" nations in Asia and Latin America, where standardized education was less available. For US employers, unskilled laborers could be paid less and exploited more than skilled, educated workers. This increasing demand for unskilled migrant laborers after 1965 reflected a larger neoliberal shift in the US economy, from a primarily production-based economy to a service-based economy.[11] An ancillary factor that helps to explain the rise of Asian and Latin American immigration to the United States was the massive population growth many nations of these regions experienced during the latter half of the twentieth century. Mexico's population, for example, doubled between the 1950s and 1970s. And like other underdeveloped nations, there was an insufficient growth in education and job creation to complement this population growth.[12]

The cruel contrast between overpopulation and underdevelopment goes a long way in explaining the surge of immigration to the United States from countries like Mexico after the 1960s.

Americans in the 1970s and 1980s would not have necessarily been cognizant of these larger demographic and socioeconomic shifts and immigration streams as they took place. Yet the shifts were perceptible in how Americans *felt* about and reacted to immigration. It is no coincidence that American nativism resurged during the same years that rates of immigration to the United States among nonwhite Asians and Latin Americans rose. It is economic stagflation and demographic and socioeconomic shifts in immigration that help us understand the sharp American public reaction against Mexican undocumented migration after the 1970s.

As with America's deep-seated ambivalence toward immigration, the neoliberal reforms that were put into place after the 1970s did not occur in a void. Neoliberalism was a political-economic agenda of the late twentieth century that sought to broaden international capitalist exchange by relaxing trade barriers (tariffs and subsidies) and spurring investment in foreign countries. This expansion in trade coincided with innovations in communication (the internet and the smartphone). The free movement of people was considered an important part of neoliberalism, as it was believed that an adequate supply of migrant laborers was essential for meeting the demand of global consumers.

Liberalizing trade and investment has a long history in US-Mexican relations. During the late nineteenth century, American corporations had a robust presence in major Mexican industries such as railroads and mining.[13] This neo-colonial economic relationship simultaneously created and reinforced the asymmetry between the United States and Mexico. In the decades after the Second World War, however, this neo-colonial relationship based on liberalized economic principles related to their rights of foreigners to own territory and wealth of a sovereign nation started to shift away from US investments in mining and railroads to manufacturing. Hundreds of US corporations had subsidiaries operating in Mexico's manufacturing sector by the start of the twenty-first century.[14] Mexico was transitioning from an investment destination for US businesses to a site of production of American goods. This process of globalization was not distinct to the United States and Mexico. Yet the long history of asymmetry between these two countries, the sharp contrast between the "First World" and the "Third World," reified the subordinate status of Mexico to the United States and Mexicans to Americans.

This US transition away from investment abroad to production abroad, from trade liberalism to economic globalization, was not just driven by a desire to curb Mexican immigration, but primarily to increase profits. Not only were American firms relocating manufacturing operations to Northern Mexico, but they were also relocating to Caribbean and Asian countries. American manufacturing firms did this, first, to avoid high taxes and union pressures for better wages and benefits in the United States and, second, to take advantage of the lower wage scales and working conditions standards in developing countries. What made this process of globalization truly *global* was that innovations in transportation and communications technology allowed companies to transfer labor-intensive assembly to areas of the world where wages were much lower than they were in the United States. The lucrative stages of production, such as administration, inventory control, research and development, and marketing, were kept in the United States. Essentially, globalizing US corporations were *migratizing* foreign workers within their home countries.[15]

This drive toward globalization was ramped up by the economic downturn of the 1970s and early 1980s, as waves of industrial plants closed and millions of manufacturing jobs were either exported or eliminated from the US economy. "From the point of view of industry," two analysts argue, "globalization was not just a search for better conditions of production but also a realignment of power between workers and investors."[16]

To get the full picture of how globalization abetted Mexican migration, however, it is important to recognize how Mexico also made a neoliberal turn in the latter half of the twentieth century. Mexico enjoyed years of rapid economic growth from 1940 to 1970. The Bracero program existed during most of that thirty-year period, in which a giant agribusiness economy was constructed on both sides of the border. It was an economic sector that relied on a constant supply of cheap labor from the interior of Mexico.[17]

During these same years of growth, however, Mexico became increasingly dependent on foreign loans. Between 1950 and 1972, Mexico's foreign debt grew at an average annual rate of 23 percent, reaching $11 billion by the latter year. Mexico suffered from a chronic balance-of-payments problem; in other words, Mexico was not making enough money annually to pay its bills. This worsening situation helps explain why, starting in the late 1960s, Mexican leaders liberalized their economic policies by allowing the establishment of maquilas. The Mexican North became "a gigantic assembly operation."[18]

Between the 1940s through the 1960s, Mexican leaders liberalized economic protections on Mexican agricultural workers. Mexico's central government eliminated subsidies to small agricultural producers in response to pressure from multinational agribusiness corporations in the United States and international lenders which warned Mexico City about ever-rising debts. Small producers who were increasingly vulnerable to international competition for their agricultural products, such as corn and beans, began to abandon their farm plots and joined the migration streams going north.[19] Ironically, Mexico's neoliberal turn of the mid-twentieth century only made the Mexican state and its poorer citizens more economically vulnerable. Statist policies such as subsidies, now removed, migratized many Mexican laborers who were once self-sustaining workers. And the evisceration of the Mexican agricultural sector increased Mexico's dependency. Between the 1940s and 1960s, Mexico's agricultural sector adequately provided the basic food staples—corn, beans, wheat—demanded by the nation's rapidly growing urban population. The production of these staple crops started to fall behind the rate of Mexico's population growth by the 1970s. The Mexican government responded by starting to import basic food supplies. It was clear by the 1980s that such contingency measures were not working as disease, malnutrition, and poverty joined economic underdevelopment, regular economic downturns, currency crises (1982 and 1988), and overpopulation as prevailing causes of Mexican migration to the United States.[20]

Border enforcement measures became more stringent during the late 1980s and early 1990s as the permanent population of Mexican immigrants in the United States grew and as the rate of undocumented Mexican migration to the United States persisted.[21] Notable examples of such efforts were the grand sweeps of "illegals" by US Border Patrol agents along border regions. "Operation Hold the Line" of September 1993 saw 450 Border Patrol agents sweep a 20-mile area of the border around El Paso, Texas. Similar sweep operations took place in the San Diego area in 1994 ("Operation Gatekeeper") and along the Arizona-Mexico borderland in 1996 ("Operation Safeguard"). These actions were successful in reducing unauthorized border crossings, but only in the short term. The limits of this "Maginot-Line strategy" soon became clear: suppressing the flow of illegal border crossings in one area simply directed it elsewhere, often to more remote and dangerous parts of border regions.[22]

The proportion of migrants passing through non-traditional areas doubled during the 1990s in response to enhanced border sweep operations by the Border Patrol. Customarily, migrants would enter the United States through high-volume passageways such as those that connected Tijuana and San Diego or Ciudad Juárez and El Paso. Starting in the late 1980s, however, migrants increasingly traveled through sparsely populated, arid regions of the border in the wake of the IRCA and especially in response to border sweep operations. Consequently, a growing number of migrants died while attempting to enter the United States. The number of migrant fatalities was negligible before 1986; by contrast, nearly 500 migrants were dying annually in the early 2000s.[23] Migrant fatalities are usually attributable to exposure, but also to road accidents and fatal conditions in trucks, vans, and shipping containers.[24] The "illegalization" of Mexican migrants in US society and the lethality of border crossing between the mid-1980s and the mid-1990s has been the ultimate result of immigration laws and enforcement practices that criminalize undocumented migrants and marginalize their traditional migration pathways.

The North American Free Trade Agreement (NAFTA) of 1994 was a culmination of neoliberal efforts to expand trade and investment. For US leaders, heady with the success of the liberal-democratic model that the end of the Cold War seemed to highlight, NAFTA represented an attempt to achieve financial hegemony throughout the Western Hemisphere. While the principle of globalization relies on the free movement of capital, information, and people, architects of NAFTA believed they could construct a trade agreement that would curb, not abet, Mexican migration to the United States. American leaders hoped they could keep out Mexican laborers as they relaxed barriers to trade by simultaneously *unbundling* the free movement of people from definitions of globalization and *re-asserting* the United States' sovereign right to control borders and restrict immigration.[25]

There has been a great deal of scholarly and public debate about NAFTA's successes and failures. NAFTA has been unquestionably successful in expanding North American trade: a 400 percent increase in intra-regional trade, from $290 billion in 1993 to $1.1 trillion in 2012. Roughly $1 *billion* worth of goods and services cross the US-Mexico border *daily*. Mexico is the second largest export market for the United States. Production chains between Canada, Mexico, and the United States have become intertwined, basically meaning that assembly and production costs are shared and profits enjoyed in all three countries. Cross-border investment has grown rapidly which has led to job growth in all three countries. NAFTA has even been credited with a boom in tourism, which for Mexico has resulted in billions of tourist dollars. On the face of it, NAFTA has succeeded in making Mexico a more modern nation.[26]

Underneath the superficial layer, beyond the broad, macroeconomic measures, however, NAFTA has placed Mexico and especially poor Mexicans in a perilous state. Per capita income growth has just barely doubled over the past twenty years, rising in 2014 dollar terms from $4,500 (1994) to $9,700 (2012), or an average yearly rate of just 1.2 percent. That is below per capita rates of other major Latin American countries. And while intra-regional trade has risen, that has not resulted in job growth within Mexico. Production at the border maquilas (manufacturing plants where workers *assemble* durable goods such as automobiles with pre-made parts in border towns) is stagnant, resulting in the creation of relatively few *new* jobs. Maquilas were created to tamp down on Mexican migration to the United States. If more jobs were created in Mexico, it was believed, then Mexicans would have less need to go to the United States for work. It did not work out that way. In fact, maquilas destabilized the Mexican economy and made Mexico even more economically dependent on the United States than it already was. Mexico became a "direct appendage" of US manufacturing.[27] Between 1994 and 2014 the maquila industry created just 700,000 jobs, as 20 *million* Mexicans entered the job market during those same twenty years.[28] Because maquilas are not *production* sites where parts and technology are created and innovated, it helps explain why Mexican wages are stagnant, especially when compared to US wages, which are much higher.[29] Whereas the dramatic increase in trade because of NAFTA created 23 million US jobs between 1994 and 2008, Mexican jobs have fallen victim to the forces of globalization—to the very economic phenomenon that created them in the first place. One estimate shows that 30 percent of maquila jobs have been lost since the 1990s, as US assembly subsidiaries have moved to nations in Asia where wages are even lower.[30] In this sense, Mexico is going through a simultaneous process of *underdevelopment* and *deindustrialization*: the establishment of subsidiary, US owned, export-oriented assembly plants in Mexico has undermined the growth of entrepreneurial enterprises among native industries, while the stagnation and decline in manufacturing employment is showing the limits of maquila-led industrialization. Instead of working to modernize the Mexican economy, globalizing industrialization has only continued Mexico's dependence upon larger, developed economies such as the United States.[31]

NAFTA and neoliberalism have made Mexico and Mexicans more vulnerable to the disruptive influences of globalization, which is especially evident in Mexico's agricultural sector. As Mexico entered the free trade agreements, Mexican farmers were fully exposed to the harsh realities of globalizing free trade competition. They were no match for the productivity and automation of commercialized agriculture in the United States. Such free trade competition displaced many Mexican farmers, as their products could not compete on the global market or even in many domestic markets. This inability to survive in a globalizing, transnational marketplace made it increasingly difficult for Mexicans to stay on their farms and led many to migrate northward to scratch out livings as a "nomadic mass of migrant workers."[32]

This further explains why the number of Mexican nationals entering the United States has jumped during the twenty years since the creation of NAFTA, from 6.2 million in 1994 to 12 million in 2013. Over 2 million Mexican workers lost their jobs just between 1994 and 1996. In short, not only has NAFTA failed in its goal of ending Mexican migration to the United States by creating more jobs in Mexico, but it has also exacerbated the migration issue by devastating Mexico's agricultural economy and displacing its citizens.[33]

Around 15 million Latino and Asian immigrants entered the United States between 1980 and 1995. About one-third of legal immigrants and about half of undocumented migrants went to California, where, during these same years, economic recession led to federal and state cuts to welfare, education, and social services. During the 1980s and early 1990s, periods of low job confidence, pessimism about future economic prospects, worries about inflation, and conditions of the statewide economy bedeviled California residents. The late 1980s witnessed an economic resurgence in the Golden State, but the consequent optimism in growth dissipated by 1994 amid cutbacks in defense spending, the departure of industries from California, and the fallout from technological transformations in many business sectors (see "creative destruction" in Introduction).[34]

This combination of economic insecurity and racial anxiety culminated in Californians' passage of Proposition 187 (Prop 187) in November 1994.[35] It was designed to prevent undocumented immigrants living in the state from accessing a variety of publicly funded social services, including health care and education.[36] Social service providers such as teachers, social workers, and doctors were essentially deputized as immigration inspectors, forcing them to identify to local law enforcement officials the individuals who had entered the country illegally. "Here was legislation," immigration scholar George Sanchez states, "that tied issues of crime and immigration into a tidy package and allowed voters to voice nativist fears in the anonymous sanctity of the voting booth[.]"[37] The measure helped to redefine the illegality of Mexican immigrants by claiming that the people of California were "suffering" economic hardship and higher rates of crime because of the presence of illegal aliens.[38] By describing illegal aliens as threats to California, Prop 187 was both the result of and the cause of nativist rhetoric that had increasingly criminalized the act of undocumented migration in the years following passage of the IRCA in 1986. Foreign nationals in the United States were not simply illegal, they were a threat—both to society and individual citizens. The development of such "alien terminology" helped to rationalize the harsh treatment of Mexican immigrants.[39] Prop 187 was ultimately struck down by a US District Court in California in late 1995, just a year after California voters passed it. Yet its social and legal legacy was immediately apparent as a Republican-controlled US Congress in turn passed legislation in 1996 that reflected the same fear and xenophobia of Prop 187 (see Chapter 2 for discussion of 1996 laws).

Public fear and anxiety about Mexican immigration receded during the late 1990s, as the United States enjoyed robust economic growth with low unemployment rates and significant job growth. Suddenly immigrant labor was in high demand, and the US public seemed to convert from opposition to an embrace of immigrants.[40]

Interestingly, the 1980s and 1990s witnessed a broad improvement in diplomatic relations between the United States and Mexico even as the issue of immigration created friction between the two nations. Compared to the diplomatic tensions of the first half of the twentieth century, US-Mexican relations during the Second World War and the Cold War were positively ebullient. Mexico joined the alliance against the Axis powers and supplied the Western nations with valuable raw materials (notably oil). During the Cold War Mexico was squarely in America's backyard alliance of the Western Hemisphere. While the United Mexican States was anything but a free and fair republic, governed for decades by a single political party—the Institutional Revolutionary Party (PRI)—that at times oppressed its own people (notably during a massacre of hundreds, perhaps even thousands, college students at an anti-government rally in Mexico City in October 1968), Mexico from the American perspective was a reliable, non-communist redoubt in a region directly threatened by Soviet and Cuban infiltration. Harmonious relations were strained by economic downturns in both countries during the 1970s, which exacerbated the problem of Mexican immigration, but especially during the 1980s, as the Reagan administration begrudgingly helped Mexico resolve its currency crisis of 1982. Mexican criticism of Reagan's interventionist policies in Central America (see Chapter 10) did not help either.[41]

Diplomatic repair was underway by the late 1980s, as the Mexican president Carlos Salinas (1988–94) purposefully moved Mexico in a neoliberal direction, most notably by brokering NAFTA. Evidence of this new harmony in US-Mexican relations was apparent when the Clinton administration gave generous assistance to Mexico when it was struck by another currency crisis in late 1994. Immigration continued to bedevil diplomatic relations, however, as California's Prop 187 fomented protest from political action groups in Mexico and Mexican consular officials in the United States. There was an uptick in Mexican-American voter registration as Mexican-Americans came to appreciate how their growing voting power could block such nativist measures as Prop 187.[42]

As a new century dawned, an auspicious moment arose for both governments to resolve what had become the perennial problem of their diplomatic relationship: immigration. Mexico's economy had recovered from the doldrums of the mid-1990s. In 2000, after more than seventy years in power, the PRI lost at the voting polls and conceded power to an opposition party. The new president, Vincente Fox, who, on the campaign trail (which significantly included stops north of the border) publicly committed to protecting the interests of all Mexicans, those 100 million who lived within the nation's borders and the 20 million who lived in the United States. Likewise, north of the border, the US economy was humming along. Latinos, the fastest-growing minority group in the American electorate by the turn of the century, were appealed to by presidential aspirants who tried out their Spanish-speaking skills from the stump. The US media declared the year 2000 the "year of the Latino."[43]

During the first year of the administration of George W. Bush (2001–9), the US and Mexican governments attempted comprehensive immigration reform that included a temporary worker program as well as an initiative to legalize undocumented Mexican workers. A booming US economy, which not coincidentally caused an upsurge in undocumented Mexican immigration to the United States, was behind this moment of detente.

The terrorist attacks of September 11, 2001, undermined the progress made in these negotiations. The subsequent focus for the Bush administration was national security and anti-terrorism laws.[44] The events of 9/11 only heightened nativist fears of Mexican immigrants; therefore, after September 2001, efforts were accelerated to militarize the US-Mexico border as well as to heighten restrictions on immigration.[45] The border was now considered both a "protective seal" against terrorists and a "porous threat" because of undocumented immigrants.[46] The first step toward this end was the consolidation and centralization of border enforcement agencies into the Department of Homeland Security in November 2002.

The US government broadened its immigration restriction authority beyond the confines of the physical boundaries after 9/11. New regulations between 2002 and 2006 allowed immigration officials to expeditiously return undocumented migrants found within 100 miles of the border up to fourteen days after their actual crossing.[47] Such processes of "expedited removal" blurred the line between the perimeter and interior of the United States.[48] Increased surveillance was another element of post-9/11 border crossings. The Border Security Act of May 2002 required foreign nationals to have machine-readable passports to enter the United States,[49] and the Real ID Act of May 2005 required state motor vehicle agencies and other institutions responsible for issuing identification documents to verify that license holders were legally authorized to be in the United States.[50] These new, "mundane" methods of mass surveillance were combined with tried-and-true internal enforcement efforts of immigration regulation as the newly created Immigration and Customs Enforcement Agency (ICE), founded in March 2003. ICE promptly conducted sweeping raids looking to deport undocumented immigrants.[51]

The stated purpose of this legislation was to enforce the border security of the United States from terrorist threats. Yet the principal effect of such acts and legislation has been to "terrorize" immigrant workers. Indeed, in the post-9/11 United States, border security was fused with anti-terrorist measures even though none of the 9/11 terrorists had crossed the US-Mexico border. Nonetheless, since the early 2000s the "illegal alien" has been likened to the foreign terrorist (Figure 11.1).[52]

Even as the post-9/11 era saw a novel move toward deterritorialized surveillance, concrete, territorially bound measures toward border security were also implemented. The Bush administration signed into law the Secure Fence Act in October 2006, which authorized the construction of 670 miles of reinforced wall along the US-Mexico border. Such an effort to physically block undocumented Mexican migrants from entering the United States

**FIGURE 11.1** *A female protester against the Sensenbrenner Bill holds a sign that attempts to dispel the notion that undocumented immigrants were synonymous with foreign terrorists. Getty Images: David S. Holloway.*

was not without precedent. For decades, the US-Mexico border region has been shaped into a "densely militarized space" with all kinds of new and old interdiction technologies: fences, walls, vehicle barriers, vehicle checkpoints, ground sensors, and electronic surveillance towers.[53] In 1991, a 10-foot-high wall (eventually expanded to 14 feet) of thin corrugated steel was constructed along 7 miles of the border from the ocean inland, between San Diego and Tijuana. The wall's purpose, like the border sweeps of the early 1990s, was to keep out undocumented migrants and to channel their migration routes through more isolated and dangerous areas. Mexican leaders viewed the wall as an insult and criticized the administration of George H.W. Bush (1989–93) for constructing it while simultaneously trying to economically integrate the United States and Mexico—efforts that were eventually finalized in NAFTA. Additionally, critics of this border wall highlighted the irony between the collapse of the Berlin Wall in November 1989, which effectively represented the end of the Cold War, and the United States building a wall along the border of one its closest—proximately, culturally, economically, historically—neighbors.[54]

While the IIRIRA of 1996 had empowered the US government to construct barriers along other parts of the border, legal hurdles as well as opposition from various domestic groups prevented further border wall construction outside of San Diego until the early 2000s. The Secure Fence Act of 2006 provided a new impetus for border wall construction. By 2009, the first year of the administration of Barack Obama (2009–17), there were over 100 miles of wall built along the Texas-Mexico border and 70 miles along the Arizona-Mexico border despite opposition from environmental groups, human rights groups, academics, landowners on the border, and Mexican leaders.[55]

The border wall issue was weaponized politically when Donald Trump announced his intention to campaign for the US presidency in 2016. He shocked and awed Americans in July 2015 by likening all Mexican immigrants to drug dealing criminals: "When Mexico sends its people, they're not sending the best"; "They're not sending you, they're sending people that have lots of problems and they're bringing those problems. They're bringing drugs, they're bringing crime. They're rapists and some, I assume, are good people, but I speak to border guards and they're telling us what we're getting."[56] Trump boldly declared that if elected president, he would build a "big" and "beautiful" border wall that would keep Mexican immigrants out of the United States. He even stated that he would get Mexico to pay for the construction of the wall. The border wall issue was a primary plank of the Trump campaign by the fall of 2016.

Trump won the presidency and pursued his effort to build a wall, facing opposition from human rights groups, landowners along the border, US lawmakers, and Mexican leaders. The Trump administration attempted to secure funding from Congress when it became clear by 2018 that he could not follow through on his promise to "get Mexico to pay for it." The border wall issue grew so contentious that negotiations over a federal budget broke down, leading to a government shutdown between December 2018 and January 2019. After that time, the Trump administration tried to cobble together border wall construction money by re-directing defense appropriations. Such actions have raised questions about executive overreach and legal impropriety. Some funding was also raised by private donors.[57] By the end of 2020, the Trump administration claimed to have fulfilled its promise to build a wall by citing the ostensible completion of 450 miles of border construction.[58] Less than ten percent (40:450) of this wall represents new construction, while the great majority of the construction has replaced older, extant fencing.[59] The irony of a global business tycoon sponsoring a garish symbol of illiberalism would have been rich indeed if the reality of apprehension, deportation, and family separation of Mexican and Central American immigrants since 2017 were not so egregious.

Globalization was promoted to encourage economic integration between the United States and Mexico. Instead, it exacerbated the conditions that led to increased migration across the border by undocumented Mexican migrants. US immigration law and border enforcement policies became stricter and more sophisticated as Mexican migration to the United States reached new highs between the 1980s and early 2000s. The increasingly restrictive nature of US border security measures and immigration laws have worked not only to marginalize the Mexican immigrant's place within US society but also to reduce the basic human rights of Mexican nationals who attempt to enter the United

**FIGURE 11.2** "Illegal Love," 2013. *Eric García's fictional movie poster highlights the tragically non-fictional dynamic that underscores the Mexican immigration crisis of the late 20th, early 21st centuries: Uncle Sam's economic dependence on the undocumented migrant worker. Getty Images: Eric J. García.*

States as undocumented migrants. The tensions between economic globalization and "illegal" immigration go a long way toward explaining the contemporary heavy-handed and misguided attempts at border security (Figure 11.2).

# Notes

1. Portions of this chapter were originally published by the author in *Understanding and Teaching Contemporary US History Since Reagan*, ed. Kimber M. Quinney and Amy L. Sayward. Reprinted by permission of the University of Wisconsin Press. © 2022 by the Board of Regents of the University of Wisconsin System. All rights reserved.
2. Alan McPherson, *Intimate Ties, Bitter Struggles: The United States and Latin America since 1945* (Washington, DC: Potomac Books, 2006), 25.
3. Chavez, *The Latino Threat*, 7; Zolberg, "Reforming the Backdoor," 318–20; Lemay, *Anatomy of a Public Policy*, 21–4; Richard C. Jones, "Immigration

Reform and Migrant Flows: Compositional and Spatial Changes in Mexican Migration After the Immigration Reform Act of 1986," *Annals of the Association of American Geographers* 85, no. 4 (1995): 715; Massey, "America's Immigration Policy Fiasco," 8.

4  Jorge Durand and Douglas Massey, *Miracles on the Border* (Tucson: University of Arizona Press, 1995), 2.
5  Lemay, *Anatomy of a Public Policy*, 25; Chavez, *The Latino Threat*, 23, 28–9; Zolberg, "Reforming the Back Door," 322; Dunn, *The Militarization of the U.S.-Mexico Border*, 1.
6  Lemay, *Anatomy of a Public Policy*, 36; Dunn, *The Militarization of the U.S.-Mexico Border*, 36; Zolberg, "Reforming the Back Door," 323.
7  Dunn, *The Militarization of the U.S.-Mexico Border*, 35; Zolberg, "Reforming the Back Door," 322–3; Lemay, *Anatomy of a Public Policy*, 21–4.
8  Lemay, *Anatomy of a Public Policy*, 11.
9  Angela P. Harris, "Equality Trouble: Sameness and Difference in Twentieth-Century Race Law," *California Law Review* 88, no. 6 (2000): 1999.
10 Lemay, *Anatomy of a Public Policy*, 13; Zolberg, "Reforming the Back Door," 318–20.
11 George J. Borjas, *Friends or Strangers: The Impact of Immigrants on the US Economy* (New York: Basic Books, 1990), 46, 49–52, 117–19, 121–3.
12 David Bennett, *The Party of Fear: From Nativist Movements to the New Right in American History* (New York: Knopf Doubleday), 370; Fitzgerald, *A Nation of Emigrants*, 36–8.
13 Cf. Montoya, *Risking Immeasurable Harm*, Ch 1.
14 Gilbert Gonzalez and Raul Fernandez, "Empire and the Origins of Twentieth Century Migration from Mexico to the United States," *Pacific Historical Review* 71, no. 1 (2002): 48.
15 Fernández-Kelly and Massey, "Borders for Whom?," 100.
16 Ibid.
17 Gonzalez and Fernandez, "Empire and the Origins of the Twentieth Century Migration from Mexico to the United States," 48.
18 Ibid., 45–9.
19 Ibid., 49.
20 Ibid., 49–50; Cervantes-Rodríguez, *International Migration in Cuba*, 154; Riosmena and Massey, "Pathways to El Norte," 11–12; Kelly Lytle Hernández, "Mexican Immigration to the United States," *OAH Magazine of History* 23, no. 4 (2009): 27.
21 One study shows that around 1 to 3 million unauthorized persons were present in the United States in the late 1980s, and that the net flow of illegal aliens ranged from 200,000 to 300,000 persons per year. George Borjas, "The Economics of Immigration," *Journal of Economic Literature* 32 (December 1994): 1669.
22 Andreas, "Open Markets, Closed Border," 65; Gallegos, "Border Matters," 1734–5.

23 Fernández-Kelly and Massey, "Borders for Whom?," 110–11.
24 See Luis Alberto Urrea's, *The Devil's Highway, A True Story* (New York: Back Bay Books, 2004) for grisly accounts of the danger of border crossing in remote areas. "Death by sunlight, hyperthermia, was the main culprit. But illegals drowned, froze, committed suicide, were murdered, were hit by trains and trucks, were bitten by rattlesnakes, had heart attacks." 19; Gallegos, "Border Matters," 1771n241.
25 Sassen, "Beyond Sovereignty," 9, for unbundling and reasserting; Gordon, "People Are Not Bananas," 1114; Gallegos, "Border Matters," 1735; Fernández-Kelly and Massey, "Borders for Whom?," 99–104.
26 Carla Hills, "NAFTA's Economic Upsides, The View from the United States," *Foreign Affairs* 93, no. 1 (2014): 122–7, 123–4; Jorge Castañeda, "NAFTA's Mixed Record," *Foreign Affairs* 93, no. 1 (2014): 134–7.
27 Andreas, "Open Markets, Closed Border," 59–60.
28 Castañeda, "NAFTA's Mixed Record," 137–8.
29 Castañeda, "NAFTA's Mixed Record," 138; M. Angeles Villarreal and Ian F. Fergusson, "NAFTA at 20: Overview and Trade Effects," *Congressional Research Service*, 2014, 19.
30 Stephen W. Hartman, "NAFTA, the Controversy," *The International Trade Journal* 25, no. 1 (2010): 16–17.
31 Gonzalez and Fernandez, "Empire and the Origins of Twentieth Century Migration from Mexico to the United States," 54; Hartman, "NAFTA, the Controversy," 21.
32 Hartman, "NAFTA, the Controversy," 19; Gonzalez and Fernandez, "Empires and the Origins of Twentieth Century Migration," 54–7; Villarreal and Fergusson, "NAFTA at 20," 17–18; Andreas, "Open Markets, Closed Border," 61; Gallegos, "Border Matters," 1761; Gordon, "People Are Not Bananas," 1115; Riosmena and Massey, "Pathways to El Norte," 11–12, 29.
33 Cacho, "The People of California are Suffering," 392; Castañeda, "NAFTA's Mixed Record," 139. Jennifer Gordon offers figures on increasing Mexican migration levels in the wake of the passage NAFTA that follow a different timeline by asserting that between 1990 and 2000, the population of foreign-born Mexicans in the United States doubled, from 4.3 million to 9.2 million, peaking at 11.6 million in 2008 (Gordon, "People Are Not Bananas," 1115). Huyen Pham argues that these numbers hit 11.8 million by January 2007 and decreased to 11.6 million in Jan 2008. Other data used by Pham shows that undocumented Mexican immigration numbers reached 11.9 million by March 2008. Pham, "When Immigration Borders Move," 1126–7.
34 Cacho, "The People of California are Suffering," 389; Barkan, "Return of the Nativists?," 244–5.
35 Cacho, "The People of California are Suffering," 389.
36 Monica W. Varsanyi, "Immigration Policy Activism in U.S. States and Cities: Interdisciplinary Perspectives," 1–2.
37 Sanchez, "Face the Nation," 1011–12.
38 Cacho, "The People of California are Suffering," 393, emphasis mine.

39  Johnson, "Aliens and the U.S. Immigration Laws," 268–9.
40  Chavez, *The Latino Threat*, 36–7; Barkan, "Return of the Nativists?," 265–6.
41  Rosenblum, "Moving Beyond the Policy of No Policy," 106.
42  Ibid., 106–7, 110–11; Arturo Santamaría Gómez and James Zackrison, "Politics without Borders or Postmodern Nationality: Mexican Immigration to the United States," *Latin American Perspectives* 30, no. 2 (2003): 78.
43  Rosenblum, "Moving Beyond the Policy of No Policy," 112–13.
44  Giovagnoli, "Overhauling Immigration Law," 2; Fitzgerald, *A Nation of Emigrants*, 60–2; Chavez, *The Latino Threat*, 37; Rosenblum and Gorman, "The Public Policy Implications of State-Level Worksite Migration Enforcement," 115.
45  Chavez, *The Latino Threat*, 23, 38–9; see Alan D. Bersin, "Lines and Flows: The Beginning and End of Borders," *Brooklyn Journal of International Law* 37, no. 2 (March 2012): 394–6, for a countervailing view which holds that 9/11 was a shock that changed how immigration was viewed.
46  Gallegos, "Border Matters," 1748; Davies, "Latino Immigration and Social Change in the United States," 379; Karen C. Tumlin, "Suspect First: How Terrorism Policy Is Reshaping Immigration Policy," *California Law Review* 92, no. 4 (2004): 1173–239.
47  Bersin, "Lines and Flows," 395–6.
48  Shachar, "Territory Without Boundaries," 811, 817–18.
49  Ibid., 824, 827, 835.
50  Rosenblum and Gorman, "The Public Policy Implications of State-Level Worksite Migration Enforcement," 119.
51  Coleman and Kocher, "Detention, Deportation, Devolution and Immigrant Incapacitation in the US," 230; Fernández-Kelly and Massey, "Borders for Whom?," 108.
52  Fernández-Kelly and Massey, "Borders for Whom?," 108; Chavez, *The Latino Threat*, 38–9; Stumpf, "The Crimmigration Crisis," 385, 395. It is worth noting that the 9/11 terrorists were all in the United States legally on student, tourist, or business visas.
53  Coleman and Kocher, "Detention, Deportation, Devolution and Immigrant Incapacitation in the US," 229.
54  Dunn, *The Militarization of the U.S.-Mexico Border*, 66–7; Andreas, "Open Markets, Closed Border," 63–4. A sign soon appeared on the San Diego-Tijuana wall, with the words, "Welcome to the New Berlin Wall."
55  Denise Gilman, "Seeking Breeches in the Wall: An International Human Rights Law Challenge to the Texas-Mexico Wall," *Texas International Law Journal* 46 (Spring 2011): 258–60.
56  *Fox News Channel*, "Trump Stands by Statements on Mexican Illegal Immigrants, Surprised by Backlash," Published July 4, 2015, updated December 20, 2015; accessed January 5, 2021. Trump stands by statements on Mexican illegal immigrants, surprised by backlash | Fox News.

57  *The Washington Post*, "Trump Ramps up Border-Wall Construction Ahead of 2020 Vote," Published February 6, 2020; accessed January 5, 2021. Trump's border wall: How many miles have been built? - Washington Post.
58  There is even a website dedicated to tracking the construction progress of "Trump's Wall," https://www.trumpwall.construction/; accessed January 5, 2021.
59  *Washington Examiner*, "Trump hits 450-mile goal for 2020 border wall construction," Published January 5, 2021; accessed January 5, 2021. Trump hits 450-mile goal for 2020 border wall construction (washingtonexaminer.com).

# Conclusion

Is the United States a "nation of immigrants?" Present-day readers may be surprised to find that the positive use of this phrase, denoting a nation that welcomes the tired, poor, and hungry to forge a nation of one common people, has been relatively recent. *A nation of immigrants* was used between the mid-1960s and mid-1980s in a complimentary way to describe the long history of immigration to the United States. John F. Kennedy's A Nation of Immigrants (published posthumously in 1964) and the liberal turn in immigration policy that resulted in the Hart-Celler Act of 1965 (see Chapter 2) helped popularize the positive use of the phrase. There was some irony here. Kennedy and other Democratic leaders of his generation used the phrase to celebrate all the distinct contributions immigrants—most of whom came from Europe—had contributed to the United States. Had Kennedy's paean to immigration been published twenty years later, even just ten years later, as Asian and Latin American immigration to the United States started to reach new highs, one is left to wonder if the book might have warned of a foreign flood rather than extolled the presence of noncitizens in US history. Aside from the momentary blip between the 1960s and 1980s, "a nation of immigrants" was used in a derisive fashion, usually by restrictionists—whether they were elected leaders, academics, or social scientists—to appeal for stronger curbs on immigration. Otherwise, the argument went, foreign hordes would invade the land and permanently and negatively change US society.[1]

In recent decades this anti-immigrant sentiment has coalesced around the birthright citizenship movement. Rooted in a time of social frustration that led to passage of the IRCA in 1986, the birthright citizenship movement argues that citizenship should be granted on a consensual basis, by choice and assent, rather than automatically granted upon a person's birth on US soil. This notion of consensual citizenship can be persuasive upon first impression as it asserts that choice, not coercion, should determine a person's membership into a polity. The movement can claim historical legitimacy by connecting its sentiments for voluntary citizenship with the original designs of the framers of the Constitution, who purposefully abrogated their tradition of perpetual British citizenship (see Chapter 1). When one looks closer at the fruit on the tree of birthrighters as well as the company they keep, however, it is clear that the movement seeks more nefarious ends, and that its ideology owes less to the liberalism of the 1780s than to the illiberalism of the 1920s.[2]

The birthright citizenship movement claims not to oppose immigration. Its advocates publicly laud the achievements and assimilation of past waves of immigrants to the United States. By contrast, they argue that more-recent waves of foreigners, notably Mexicans, are invading the United States and leeching off of the nation's wealth. Such arguments represent a modernized version of the claims made by immigration restrictionists like Henry Cabot Lodge during the late nineteenth and early twentieth century. Adding insult to injury, these modern-day restrictionists believe that noncitizens are taking advantage of US citizenship laws to *anchor* themselves in US society. The children born of immigrants on US soil—whether those immigrants are legally in the United States or not—become US citizens. It is the "automatic" nature of citizenship that most angers birthrighters.[3]

There are antecedents to the birthright movement in American history. During the late nineteenth century and early twentieth century, restrictionists viewed children born of Chinese immigrants in the United States as "accidental" or "technical" citizens, in contrast to "real"—presumably Northern and Western European-derived—Americans. Immigration restrictionists began to challenge the notion of *jus soli* citizenship shortly after passage of the Fourteenth Amendment in 1868, claiming that the novel method for creating citizens was antithetical to American values. In fact, *jus soli* was not a new concept at all, but rather an idea dating back to the colonial period, when English common law accorded citizenship rights to anyone born *of the land*. It was during the early years of the new republic, however, that race and citizenship were interlinked, precluding any apprehension American whites at the time may have had about the fact that the great majority of enslaved Blacks were born on US soil by the late eighteenth century (see Chapter 1).[4]

Despite the Fourteenth Amendment's reversion to *jus soli* in US citizenship law, in the 1880s and 1890s state governments chose to interpret the *jus soli* as applying to native-born Blacks and whites only. Restrictionists argued that *jus sanguinis* (or, by the blood) should be the standard for granting citizenship because the Chinese were considered too culturally different to make good US citizens. The US Supreme Court spurned this argument in 1898 when it ruled in *U.S. v. Wong Kim Ark* to preserve the extension of *jus soli* to anyone born on US soil, even if that person's parents were themselves not citizens of the United States.[5]

Like their restrictionist predecessors, birthrighters of the 1990s and early 2000s feared the social consequences of immigration, such as an alleged eventuality of overpopulation. Birthrighters claimed that immigrants "love to have kids" and were "breeding like cattle," while native-born Americans were "getting swamped" and their nation would soon be "taken over."[6] Also, like restrictionists of the past, birthrighters have tried to revise US citizenship laws to block US citizenship to the children of immigrants. More than twenty resolutions or amendments to other pieces of legislation were introduced in Congress since the early 1990s to disallow the *jus soli* citizenship to children of undocumented immigrants. While all of these legislative efforts have failed, they have succeeded in stimulating xenophobia and nativism in US society during the opening decades of the twenty-first century.[7]

Conservative journalist James Goldsborough spoke for many birthrighters in 2000 when he expressed alarm at the rising levels of immigration to the United States during the latter half of the twentieth century. For Goldsborough, immigration was disrupting people's access to education, jobs, welfare, and livelihoods. These problems were exacerbated by the concept of "citizen children," children of immigrants who were US citizens. Americans must revise everything they had customarily believed about immigration, Goldsborough concluded. They have to realize that the uncontrolled flow of foreigners was tearing the nation apart. "If the United States owes its very identity to immigration," Goldsborough stated, "it is time to recognize the hazards of unreasonable and uncontrolled immigration."[8] Instead of approbation, then, "a nation of immigrants" is a term of revulsion for some Americans in the twenty-first century.

It only takes a cursory glance at immigration statistics throughout US history to get a sense that by and large the nation certainly does include a substantial portion of foreign-born persons. Statistically, then, the United States is indeed a nation of immigrants. Empirically, however, the real point of contention between advocates and critics of *a nation of immigrants* revolves around the fundamental question of whether immigration has been a complement or a detriment to the historical development of the United States. Unfortunately, immigration historian Mai Ngai explains, such juxtaposing questions are problematic because, in the process of boiling down discussions over immigration to a net gain or net loss, they tend to elicit simplistic answers. Broad, xenophobic condemnations of where immigrants come from, what they bring, and who they are have informed generations of immigration restrictionists. And yet xenophilists tend to commit the same error in their support for immigrants, just in the opposite direction. Both extremes, Ngai states, use immigrants "as a screen onto which [Americans] project their own aspirations and frustrations about American democracy." Essentially, this interplay between immigrants-as-good versus immigrants-as-bad "falsely posits" noncitizens as inherently separate from US society. And it is this "we" versus "them" duality that reifies the nationalism that threatens, encumbers, surveilles, apprehends, and deports immigrants.[9]

Perhaps a better way to understand the nature of immigration in US history is to conceive of the nation as a stage in which different foreign peoples cooperate and conflict with one another. A nation of peoples rather than a nation of immigrants, some persons who were born on US soil, some newly arrived, some recently naturalized, some marginalized. It is a new type of melting pot. Not the one acclaimed during the late nineteenth century as the harmonious, national body composed of the assimilated foreign masses, but instead, as immigration historian Elliott Barkan states, a melting pot that "has been profoundly shaped by the centuries-long interaction of . . . victors, victims, and vanquished."[10]

This book has tried to debunk some of the common shibboleths associated with immigration to the United States. First, despite what many critics of immigration claim, the United States does not have a policy of open borders. If anything, the late twentieth, early twenty-first century represents the most-restrictionist period in US immigration history. It has never been so hard for an immigrant to enter and remain in the United States as it has been since the 1980s. Second, immigration historians tend to fly over the long history of US immigration policy and situate the start of comprehensive legal restriction in the late nineteenth century, most commonly with the Chinese Exclusion cases of the 1880s and 1890s. Instead, immigration law scholars show us that colonial and US lawmakers have been concerned with how to regulate the inflow of "foreigners" (a term that did not just refer to origins in a distant land, but also held economic, legal, and religious characteristics) for centuries. Third, the United States has a problematic legacy of being a safe haven for generations of immigrants and refugees. Some immigrants have found refuge and escape in the United States. Other immigrants to the United States, however, have found a place of danger and vulnerability. Various factors shaped the historically ambivalent response Americans have had toward foreigners. This book shows that foreign policy was a factor that indelibly fed that ambivalence.

The United States is in a new type of cold war. Instead of the ideological struggle with the Soviets and Chinese that consumed most of the second half of the twentieth century, Americans are now embroiled in an existential crisis among themselves over what immigration represents for the nation. The arguing points include the nature of border enforcement, the distribution of public services, the multilingual nature of US society, and the concept of US citizenship. There seems to be no end in sight for this acrimonious debate. No bridge over the troubled waters of partisanship that roil the United States in the twenty-first century.

This confusion and contention have been at the root of how the United States has historically formulated its immigration policy, and that confused and contentious nature has affected its foreign relations with immigrant and refugee-sending nations—largely for the worse. The decisions of lawmakers and policymakers within the halls of Congress and the White House, the corridors of foreign ministries, and the offices of consular officials, shape the pathways of millions of foreign persons. These millions have occupied various holes, hovels, hiding places, and shanties to get into the United States over the centuries. Some work dangerous, poorly compensated jobs to provide for families in distant, beleaguered home regions. Some tolerate exploitative employers to avoid public scrutiny of their documentation status. Some live in the shadows of US society to avoid apprehension and, perhaps, deportation. Some attempt to cross desolate parts of border regions to avoid immigration authorities. Some put themselves at the mercy of human traffickers to avoid US border restrictions.

Perhaps historical empathy can offer a pathway through our present immigration cold war. Scholars of history education have given considerable attention to defining historical empathy. All of them tend to agree that it should rest on a cognitive (intellectual, objective) understanding of why the past developed the way it did. The aspiration to concretely report the past has long been a foundation upon which the historical profession was built, finding its basis in Leopold von Ranke's "so often and approvingly quoted" statement from the 1830s: the job of the historian is to report history "how it actually was" (*wie es eigentlich gewesen*).[11]

What education scholars tend to disagree on is whether affective (emotive, subjective) understanding is, first, possible, and second, desirable to cultivate in the learning of history. Can scholars and students of history inhabit the mind of personages from the past to understand what history *felt* like? Can we understand fear, loss, happiness, sadness, displacement, death, and combat? Decades after von Ranke, another German historian, Wilhelm Dilthey, suggested that we can. In his 1883 essay, "Construction of the Historical World," Dilthey argued that a "total awareness of a mental state" is the basis upon which a true understanding of human affairs must be conducted.[12] Dilthey never discounted the importance of an intellectual understanding of the past, but he did assert that rational explanations of human history were bland and incomplete without attempting to attend to the feelings of people who lived through the past. In short, affective experience and feeling were just as, perhaps more, important than cognitive understanding. "[I]in certain circumstances," Dilthey stated, "life itself succeeds in penetrating its own depth to an extent which surpasses the power of a [Thomas] Carlyle and achieves a highly developed understanding of others which even [Leopold von] Ranke cannot equal."[13]

Dilthey risked becoming mystical in his positioning of historical empathy when he claimed that students of history, through historical analysis, can re-experience the past. He even suggested that the limitations of the historical observer's experience—which presumably forms the bedrock of that observer's ability to empathize with a person from the past (e.g., one cannot know what is was like to be a soldier unless they themself have been a soldier)—need not be a hindrance to historical empathy. Even if the observer cannot totally, cognitively understand the past, their ability to feel and to know what it is like to feel—whether that be a feeling of prosperity or poverty, gain or loss—can open for the observer "a wide realm of possibilities which do not exist within the limitations of [their] real life." Even as the student of history is "limited by the reality of life," the limits of their experiences, they are "liberated by historical understanding." Dilthey goes so far as to say that the observer can "re-live" the experience of someone from the past: "I [can] transpose myself into the circumstances[.]"[14]

Most historians, including this one, have no lived experience of being an immigrant or a refugee. We have no analogous memory comparable to fleeing one's home, placing your life into the hands of someone you barely know, much less knowing them well enough to know if they are trustworthy. For historians to assume they can re-live the experience of the undocumented worker and the displaced person borders on condescension. Nevertheless, there is something to Dilthey's coupling of intellectual and emotive forms of historical empathy. His refusal to boil down the history of human life to cognitive retellings of the past reminds us of something we often miss as students of history. Human affairs are comprised of humans. And humans are not all one thing. They are neither completely rational, objective beings, nor are they completely irrational, emotive personages.

If we can accept that broad historical trends such as immigration are driven by humans making decisions, with each of those decisions driven by cognitive *and* affective forces, then we can start to historically empathize and understand why immigration happens. And if we can come to appreciate the cognitive and affective forces underlying immigration, then we can realize that solutions to immigration must, to be lasting, be instilled with cognitive and affective motives.

Most of us will never understand what it is like to be an immigrant or a refugee. Can we at least try?

# Notes

1 Donna R. Gabaccia, "Nations of Immigrants: Do Words Matter?" *The Pluralist* 5, no. 3 (2010): 9, 15–24; Tichenor, "The Politics of Immigration Reform in the United States," 342–3.

2 Robin Jacobson, "Characterizing Consent: Race, Citizenship, and the New Restrictionists," *Political Research Quarterly* 59, no. 4 (2006): 645, 653. It is notable that during the mid-1980s a spate of English-only referendums were voted upon by the American electorate across a host of US states, especially

those with high percentages of Spanish-speaking residents: Florida, California, Arizona, Colorado, and Texas. During these same years lawmakers from the South—Virginia, Indiana, Tennessee, Kentucky, Arkansas, Mississippi, North Carolina, South Carolina, and Georgia—petitioned the US Congress to adopt an English-only amendment. Zaragosa Vargas, *Crucible of Struggle: A History of Mexican Americans from Colonial Times to the Present Era*. (New York: Oxford University Press, 2011), 354–5.

3  Jacobson, "Characterizing Consent," 647–52.
4  Parker, "Citizenship and Immigration Law," 190; Martha Menchaca, "The Social Climate of the Birthright Movement in the United States," *Chicana/ Latina Studies* 12, no. 2 (Spring 2013): 33–4.
5  Jacobson, "Characterizing Consent," 646; Menchaca, "The Social Climate of the Birthright Movement in the United States," 34.
6  Jacobson, "Characterizing Consent," 649–52.
7  Menchaca, "The Social Climate of the Birthright Movement in the United States," 33.
8  Goldsborough, "Out-of-Control Immigration," 99–101.
9  Ngai, "No Human Being is Illegal," 291–2.
10  Barkan, et al., "Comment: Searching for Perspectives," 145–6.
11  Ernst Breisach, *Historiography: Ancient, Medieval, and Modern*, 2nd ed. (Chicago, IL: The University of Chicago Press, 1994), 233.
12  H. P. Rickman, ed. and trans., *W. Dilthey: Selected Writings* (Cambridge: Cambridge University Press, 1976), 181.
13  Ibid., 182.
14  Ibid., 227, 228. Dilthey's understanding of affective empathy may not sound so far fetched when one considers how psychology researchers, from Theodor Lipps in 1906 to Frans de Waal in 2009, have investigated a person's ability to innately understand the experiences of another person. Alfred Adler (1870–1937), an under-appreciated researcher in psychology who was a contemporary to and is often overshadowed by Sigmund Freud, coined the phrase *Gemeinschaftsgefühl* to describe what he believed was a person's inherent ability to empathize with another. By way of explaining *Gemeinschaftsgefühl*, Adler utilized a quote from an unattributed English author: "To see with the eyes of another, to hear with the ears of another, to feel with the heart of another." S. Kathleen La Voy, Matthew J. L. Brand, and Collin R. McFadden, "An Important Lesson from Our Past with Significance for Our Future: Alfred Adler's *Gemeinschaftsgefühl*," *The Journal of Individual Psychology* 69, no. 4 (Winter 2013): 280–93.

# Selected Bibliography

Abrams, Kerry. "Plenary Power Preemption." *Virginia Law Review* 99, no. 3 (2013): 601–40.
Acuña, Rodolfo. *Corridors of Migration: The Odyssey of Mexican Laborers, 1600–1933*. Tucson: University of Arizona Press, 2007.
Adelman, Jeremy and Stephen Aron. "From Borderlands to Borders: Empires, Nation States and the Peoples in Between in North American History." *American Historical Review* 104, no. 3 (1999): 814–41.
Aguila, Jaime. "Mexican/U.S. Immigration Policy Prior to the Great Depression." *Diplomatic History* 31, no. 2 (2007): 207–25.
Alfaro-Velcamp, Theresa and Robert H. McLaughlin. "Immigration and Techniques of Governance in Mexico and the United States: Recalibrating National Narratives through Comparative Immigration Histories." *Law and History Review* 29, no. 2 (2011): 573–606.
Allerfeldt, Kristofer. "'And We Got Here First': Albert Johnson, National Origins and Self-Interest in the Immigration Debate of the 1920s." *Journal of Contemporary History* 45, no. 1 (2010): 7–26.
Andreas, Peter. "U.S.-Mexico: Open Markets, Closed Border." *Foreign Policy*, No. 103 (Summer, 1996): 51–69.
Arana, Ana. "The New Battle for Central America." *Foreign Affairs* 80, no. 6 (2001): 88–101.
Arana, Ana. "How the Street Gangs Took Central America." *Foreign Affairs* 84, no. 3 (2005): 98–110.
Baker, Susan Gonzalez. "The 'Amnesty' Aftermath: Current Policy Issues Stemming from the Legalization Programs of the 1986 Immigration Reform and Control Act." *The International Migration Review* 31, no. 1 (1997): 5–27.
Balderamma, Francisco E. and Raymond Rodríguez. *Decade of Betrayal: Mexican Repatriation in the 1930s*. Albuquerque: University of New Mexico Press, 1995.
Ball, Simon. J. *The Cold War: An International History, 1947–1994*. London: Arnold Publishers, 1998.
Bankston, III, Carl L. and Danielle Antoinette Hidalgo, eds. *Immigration in U.S. History*. Pasadena: Salem Press, 2006.
Barberia, Lorena G. "U.S. Immigration Policies Toward Cuba." In *Debating U.S.-Cuban Relations: Shall We Play Ball?*, edited by Jorge I. Domínguez, Rafael Hernández, and Lorena Barberia, 180–200. New York: Routledge, 2012.
Barilleaux, Ryan J. "The President, 'Intermestic' Issues, and the Risks of Policy Leadership." *Presidential Studies Quarterly*, 15, no. 4 (1985): 754–67.
Barkan, Elliott Robert. "Return of the Nativists? California Public Opinion and Immigration in the 1980s and 1990s." *Social Science History* 27, no. 2 (2003): 229–83.

Barkan, Elliott Robert, Jon Gjerde, and Erika Lee. "Comment: Searching for Perspectives: Race, Law, and the Immigrant Experience [with Responses]." *Journal of American Ethnic History* 18, no. 4 (1999): 136–66.

Basch, Linda, et al. *Nations Unbound: Transnational Projects, Postcolonial Predicaments, and Deterritorialized Nation States*. New York: Routledge, 1993.

Bau, Ignatius. *This Ground is Holy: Church Sanctuary and Central American Refugees*. New York: Paulist Press, 1985.

Bean, Frank, et al., eds. *At the Crossroads: Mexico Immigration and U.S. Policy*. Lanham: Rowman and Littlefield, 1997.

Bean, Jonathan, ed. *Race and Liberty in America: The Essential Reader*. Lexington: University Press of Kentucky, 2009.

Behnken, Brian D. and Simon Wendt, eds. *Crossing Boundaries: Ethnicity, Race, and National Belonging in a Transnational World*. Lanham: Lexington Books, 2013.

Bennett, David. *The Party of Fear: From Nativist Movements to the New Right in American History*. New York: Knopf Doubleday, 1990.

Benton-Cohen, Katherine, "Other Immigrants: Mexicans and the Dillingham Commission of 1907–1911." *Journal of American Ethnic History* 30, no. 2 (Winter 2011): 33–57.

Bersin, Alan D. "Lines and Flows: The Beginning and End of Borders." *Brooklyn Journal of International Law* 37, no. 2 (March 2012): 389–406.

Borjas, George J. *Friends or Strangers: The Impact of Immigrants on the US Economy*. New York: Basic Books, 1990.

Borjas, George J. "The Economics of Immigration." *Journal of Economic Literature* 32, no. 4 (December 1994): 1667–717.

Breisach, Ernst. *Historiography: Ancient, Medieval, and Modern*, 2nd edn. Chicago: The University of Chicago Press, 1994.

Breitman, Richard and Allan J. Lichtman. *FDR and the Jews*. Cambridge. MA: The Belknap Press of Harvard University Press, 2013.

Buff, Rachel Ida, ed. *Immigrant Rights in the Shadows of Citizenship*. New York: New York University Press, 2008.

Cacho, Lisa Marie. "The People of California are Suffering: The Ideology of White Injury in Discourses of Immigration." *Cultural Values* 4, no. 4 (2000): 389–418.

Calavita, Kitty. *U.S. Immigration Law and Control of Labor, 1820–1924*. New York: Academic Press, 1984.

Calavita, Kitty. *Inside the State: The Bracero Program, Immigration, and the INS*. New York: Routledge, 1992.

Calavita, Kitty. "U.S. Immigration Policy: Contradictions and Projections for the Future." *Indiana Journal of Global Legal Studies* 2, no. 1 (1994): 143–52.

Calavita, Kitty. "Collisions at the Intersection of Gender, Race, and Class: Enforcing the Chinese Exclusion Laws." *Law & Society Review* 40, no. 2 (2006): 249–81.

Calderón-Zaks, Michael. "'Debated Whiteness Amid World Events: Mexican and Mexican American Subjectivity and the U.S.' Relationship with the Americas, 1924–1936." *Mexican Studies/Estudios Mexicanos* 27, no. 2 (2011): 325–59.

Carens, Joseph H. "Aliens and Citizens: The Case for Open Borders." *The Review of Politics* 49, no. 2 (1987): 251–73.

Casteñeda, Jorge. "NAFTA's Mixed Record." *Foreign Affairs* 93, no. 1 (2014): 131–41.

Cervantes-Rodríguez, Margarita. *International Migration in Cuba: Accumulation, Imperial Designs, and Transnational Social Fields*. University Park: Pennsylvania State University Press, 2010.

Charles, Patrick J. "Recentering Foreign Affairs Preemption in *Arizona v. United States*. Federal Plenary Power, the Spheres of Government, and the Constitutionality of SB 1070." *Cleveland State Law Review* 60, no. 1 (2012): 133–58.

Chavez, Leo R. *Covering Immigration: Popular Images and the Politics of the Nation*. Berkeley: University of California Press, 2001.

Chavez, Leo R. *The Latino Threat: Constructing Immigrants, Citizens, and the Nation*. Stanford: Stanford University Press, 2008.

Chinchilla, Norma Stoltz, Nora Hamilton, and James Loucky. "The Sanctuary Movement and Central American Activism in Los Angeles." *Latin American Perspectives* 36, no. 6 (2009): 101–26.

Chomsky, Aviva, Barry Carr, and Pamela Maria Smorkaloff, eds. *The Cuba Reader: History, Culture, Politics*. Durham: Duke University Press, 2003.

Chow, Misuzu Haninara and Kiyofuku Chuma. *The Turning Point in US-Japan Relations: Hanihara's Cherry Blossom Diplomacy in 1920–1930*. New York: Palgrave Macmillan, 2016.

Churgin, Michael J. "Mass Exoduses: The Response of the United States." *The International Migration Review* 30, no. 1 (1996): 310–24.

Clarke, John. "Turning Inside Out? Globalization, Neo-Liberalism, and Welfare States." *Anthropologica* 45, no. 2 (2003): 201–14.

Coffey, Kendall. "The Due Process Right to Seek Asylum in the United States: The Immigration Dilemma and Constitutional Controversy." *Yale Law & Policy Review* 19, no. 2 (2001): 303–39.

Coleman, Mathew and Austin Kocher. "Detention, Deportation, Devolution and Immigrant Incapacitation in the US, Post 9/11." *The Geographical Journal* 177, no. 3 (2011): 228–37.

Collomp, Catherine. "Labour Unions and the Nationalisation of Immigration Restriction in the United States, 1880–1924." In *Migration Control in the North Atlantic World: The Evolution of State Practices in Europe and the United States from the French Revolution to the Inter-War Period*, edited by Andres Fahrmeir, Olivier Faron, and Patrick Weil, 237–52. New York: Berghahn Books, 2003.

Conley, Ellen Alexander. *The Chosen Shore: Stories of Immigrants*. Berkeley: University of California Press, 2004.

Conway, Dennis. "Are There New Complexities in Global Migration Systems of Consequence for the United States 'Nation-State'?" *Indiana Journal of Global Legal Studies* 2, no. 1 (1994): 31–44.

Cook-Martín, David and David Fitzgerald. "Liberalism and the Limits of Inclusion: Race and Immigration Law in the Americas, 1850–2000." *The Journal of Interdisciplinary History* 41, no. 1 (2010): 7–25.

Council on Foreign Relations. *Survey of American Foreign Relations*, edited by Charles Howard. New Haven: Yale University Press, 1929.

Coutin, Susan Bibler. "Falling Outside: Excavating the History of Central American Asylum Seekers." *Law & Social Inquiry* 36, no. 3 (2011): 569–96.

Cox, Adam B. and Cristina M. Rodríguez. "The President and Immigration Law." *The Yale Law Journal* 119, no. 3 (2009): 458–547.

Cox, Adam B. and Cristina M. Rodríguez. "The President and Immigration Law Redux." *The Yale Law Journal* 125, no. 1 (2015): 104–225.

Dallek, Robert. *Flawed Giant: Lyndon Johnson and His Times, 1961–1973.* Oxford: Oxford University Press, 1999.

Daniels, Roger, "Immigration since World War II: The Need for a New Paradigm." *Polish American Studies* 55, no. 1 (Spring, 1998): 37–43.

Daniels, Roger. *Guarding the Golden Door: American Immigration Policy and Immigrants Since 1882.* New York: Hill and Wang, 2004.

Daniels, Roger. "Immigration Policy in a Time of War: The United States, 1939–1945." *Journal of American Ethnic History* 25, no. 2/3, *Immigration, Incorporation, Integration, and Transnationalism: Interdisciplinary and International Perspectives* (Winter-Spring, 2006): 107–16.

Daniels, Roger, James T. Patterson, and Otis L. Graham. *Debating American Immigration, 1882-Present.* Lanham: Rowman & Littlefield Publishers, 2001.

Davies, Ian. "Latino Immigration and Social Change in the United States: Toward an Ethical Immigration Policy." *Journal of Business Ethics* 88 (2009): 377–91.

Dawley, Alan. *Changing the World: American Progressives in War and Revolution.* Princeton: Princeton University Press, 2003.

Dear, Michael. *Why Walls Won't Work: Repairing the US-Mexico Divide.* New York: Oxford University Press, 2013.

De Genova, Nicholas. "Migrant Illegality and Deportability in Everyday Life." *Annual Review of Anthropology* 31, no. 1 (2002): 419–47.

Delgado, Grace Peña. "Neighbors by Nature: Relationships, Border Crossings, and Transnational Communities in the Chinese Exclusion Era." *Pacific Historical Review* 80, no. 3 (2011): 401–29.

DeSipio, Louis. "A Return to a National Origin Preference? Mexican Immigration and the Principles Guiding U.S. Immigration Policy." *Perspectives on Politics* 9, no. 3 (2011): 567–9.

"Developments in the Law: Immigrant Rights & Immigration Enforcement." *Harvard Law Review* 126, no. 6 (2013): 1565–682.

Dinnerstein, Leonard and David M. Reimers. "John Higham and Immigration History." *Journal of American Ethnic History* 24, no. 1 (2004): 3–25.

Domínguez, Jorge I. "'Cooperating with the Enemy' U.S. Immigration Policies Toward Cuba." In *Western Hemisphere Immigration and United States Foreign Policy*, edited by Christopher Mitchell, 31–88. University Park: The Pennsylvania State University Press, 1992.

Domínguez, Jorge I., Rafael Hernández, and Lorena Barberia, eds. *Debating U.S.-Cuban Relations: Shall We Play Ball?* New York: Routledge, 2012.

Dunn, Timothy. *The Militarization of the US-Mexico Border, 1978–1992: Low Intensity Conflict Doctrine Comes Home.* Austin: University of Texas at Austin, 1996.

Durand, Jorge, and Douglas Massey. *Miracles on the Border.* Tucson: University of Arizona Press, 1995.

Eastman, John C. "From 'Plyler' to 'Arizona': Have the Courts Forgotten about 'Corfield v Coryell'?" *The University of Chicago Law Review* 80, no. 1 (2013): 165–99.

Engstrom, David W. *Presidential Decision Making Adrift: The Carter Administration and the Mariel Boatlift.* New York: Rowman & Littlefield, 1997.

Espiritu, Yến Lê. *Body Counts: The Vietnam War and Militarized Refuge(es).* Berkeley: University of California Press, 2014.

Ettinger, Patrick. "'We Sometimes Wonder What They Will Spring on Us Next': Immigrants and Border Enforcement in the American West, 1882-1930." *Western Historical Quarterly* 37, no. 2 (2006): 159–81.

Fahrmeir, Andres, Olivier Faron, and Patrick Weil, eds. *Migration Control in the North Atlantic World: The Evolution of State Practices in Europe and the United States from the French Revolution to the Inter-War Period*. New York: Berghahn Books, 2003.
Feingold, Henry L. *Bearing Witness: How America and Its Jews Responded to The Holocaust*. Syracuse: Syracuse University Press, 1995.
Fernandez, Gastón A. *The Mariel Exodus: Twenty Years Later*. Miami: Ediciones Universal 2002.
Fernández, Gastón A. "Race, Gender, and Class in the Persistence of the Mariel Stigma Twenty Years After the Exodus from Cuba." *The International Migration Review* 41, no. 3 (2007): 602–22.
Fernandez, Raul. *The Mexican American Border Region: Issues and Trends*. Notre Dame: University of Notre Dame Press, 1989.
Fernández-Kelly, Patricia and Douglas S. Massey. "Borders for Whom? The Role of NAFTA in Mexico-U.S. Migration." *The Annals of the American Academy of Political and Social Science* 610, (March 2007): 98–118.
Fitzgerald, David. *A Nation of Emigrants: How Mexico Manages its Migration*. Berkeley: University of California Press, 2009.
Flores, John H. *The Mexican Revolution in Chicago: Immigration Politics from the Early Twentieth Century to the Cold War*. Urbana: University of Illinois Press, 2018.
Foley, Neil. *The White Scourge: Mexicans, Blacks, and Poor Whites in Texas Cotton Culture*. Berkeley: University of California Press, 1997.
Foner, Nancy. "Immigration Past & Present." *Daedalus* 142, no. 3 (Summer 2013): 16–25.
Forbath, William E. "Politics, State-Building, and the Courts, 1870–1920." In *The Cambridge History of Law in America, Three Volumes*, edited by Michael Grossberg and Christopher Tomlins, 643–96. Cambridge and New York: Cambridge University Press, 2008.
Fragomen, Austin T. "The Illegal Immigration Reform and Immigrant Responsibility Act of 1996: An Overview." *The International Migration Review* 31, no. 2 (1997): 438–60.
Gabaccia, Donna R. "Nations of Immigrants: Do Words Matter?" *The Pluralist* 5, no. 3 (2010): 5–31.
Gallagher, Dennis. "The Evolution of the International Refugee System." *International Migration Review* 23, no. 3 (1989): 579–97.
Gallegos, Gabriela A. "Border Matters: Redefining the National Interest in U.S.-Mexico Immigration and Trade Policy." *California Law Review* 92, no. 6 (2004): 1729–78.
Gerstle, Gary. *American Crucible: Race and Nation in the Twentieth Century*. Princeton: Princeton University Press, 2001.
Gibney, Mark. "In Search of a US Refugee Policy." In *The United States and Human Rights*, edited by David Forsythe, 52–74. Lincoln: University of Nebraska Press, 2000.
Gilman, Denise. "Seeking Breeches in the Wall: An International Human Rights Law Challenge to the Texas-Mexico Wall." *Texas International Law Journal* 46 (Spring 2011): 258–93.
Gimpel, James and James Edwards, Jr. *The Congressional Politics of Immigration Reform*. Boston: Longman, 1999.
Giovagnoli, Mary. "Overhauling Immigration Law: A Brief History of Basic Principles of Reform." *Immigration Policy Center*, February 14, 2013.

Goldsborough, James. "Out-of-Control Immigration." *Foreign Affairs* 79, no. 5 (2000): 89–101.

Gómez, Arturo Santamaría and James Zackrison. "Politics without Borders or Postmodern Nationality: Mexican Immigration to the United States." *Latin American Perspectives* 30, no. 2 (2003): 66–86.

Gonzalez, Gilbert G. "Mexican Labor Immigration, 1876–1924." In *Beyond La Frontera: The History of Mexico-U.S. Immigration*, edited by Mark Overmyer-Velázquez, 28–50. New York: Oxford University Press, 2011.

Gonzalez, Gilbert G. and Raul Fernandez. "Empire and the Origins of the Twentieth Century Migration from Mexico to the United States." *Pacific Historical Review* 71, no 1 (2002): 19–57.

Goodman, Adam. *The Deportation Machine: America's Long History of Expelling Immigrants*. Princeton: Princeton University Press, 2020.

Gordon, Jennifer. "People Are Not Bananas: How Immigration Differs from Trade." *Northwestern University Law Review* 104, no. 3 (2010): 1109–45.

Gratton, Brian and Emily Klancher Merchant. "Immigration, Repatriation, and Deportation: The Mexican-Origin Population in the United States, 1920–1950." *The International Migration Review* 47, no. 4 (2013): 944–75.

Gratton, Brian and Emily Klancher Merchant. "An Immigrant's Tale: The Mexican American Southwest 1850 to 1950." *Social Science History* 39, no. 4 (2015): 521–50.

Grayson, George, *The United States and Mexico: Patterns of Influence*. New York: Praeger, 1984.

Greenhill, Kelly M. *Weapons of Mass Migration: Forced Displacement, Coercion, and Foreign Policy*. Ithaca: Cornell University Press, 2010.

Grossberg, Michael and Christopher Tomlins. *The Cambridge History of Law in America, Three Volumes*. Cambridge and New York: Cambridge University Press, 2008.

Gutiérrez, David G. "'Sin Fronteras?': Chicanos, Mexican Americans, and the Emergence of the Contemporary Mexican Immigration Debate, 1968–1978." *Journal of American Ethnic History* 10, no. 4 (1991): 5–37.

Gutiérrez, David G. *Walls and Mirrors: Mexican Americans, Mexican Immigrants, and the Politics of Ethnicity*. Berkeley: University of California Press, 1995.

Hagan, Jacqueline, Karl Eschbach, and Nestor Rodriguez. "U.S. Deportation Policy, Family Separation, and Circular Migration." *The International Migration Review* 42, no. 1 (2008): 64–88.

Hakim, Peter. "Is Washington Losing Latin America?" *Foreign Affairs* 85, no. 1 (2006): 39–53.

Hall, Linda B. and Don M. Coerver. *Revolution on the Border: The United States and Mexico, 1910–1920*. Albuquerque: University of New Mexico Press, 1988.

Hamlin, Rebecca. "International Law and Administrative Insulation: A Comparison of Refugee Status Determination Regimes in the United States, Canada, and Australia." *Law & Social Inquiry* 37, no. 4 (2012): 933–68.

Harris, Angela P. "Equality Trouble: Sameness and Difference in Twentieth-Century Race Law." *California Law Review* 88, no. 6 (2000): 1923–2015.

Hartman, Stephen W. "NAFTA, the Controversy." *The International Trade Journal* 25, no. 1 (2010): 5–34.

Hawk, Kate Dupes, et al. *Florida and the Mariel Boatlift of 1980: The First Twenty Days*. Tuscaloosa: University of Alabama Press, 2014.

Henderson, Timothy J. *Beyond Borders: A History of Mexican Immigration to the United States.* Malden: Wiley-Blackwell, 2011.
Hernandez, Ester E. "Relief Dollars: U.S. Policies Toward Central Americans, 1980s to Present." *Journal of American Ethnic History* 25, no. 2/3 (2006): 225–42.
Hernández, Kelly Lytle. "Mexican Immigration to the United States." *OAH Magazine of History* 23, no. 4 (2009): 25–9.
Herring, George C. *From Colony to Superpower: U.S. Foreign Relations since 1776.* Oxford: Oxford University Press, 2008.
Higham, John. *Strangers in the Land: Patterns of American Nativism, 1860-1925.* New York: Atheneum, 1970 [1955].
Hills, Carla. "NAFTA's Economic Upsides, the View From the United States." *Foreign Affairs* 93, no. 1 (2014), 122–7.
Hirobi, Izumi. *Japanese Pride, American Prejudice: Modifying the Exclusion Clause of the 1924 Immigration Act.* Stanford: Stanford University Press, 2001.
Hirota, Hidetaka. "The Moment of Transition: State Officials, the Federal Govt, and the Formation of American Immigration Policy." *The Journal of American History* 99, no. 4 (2013): 1092–108.
Hsu, Madeline Y. "The Disappearance of America's Cold War Chinese Refugees, 1948–1966." *Journal of American Ethnic History* 31, no. 4 (2012): 12–33.
Hunt, Michael H. "Pearl Buck–Popular Expert on China, 1931–1949." *Modern China* 3, no. 1 (1977): 33–64.
Ichihashi, Yamato. *Japanese in the United States: A Critical Study of the Problems of the Japanese Immigrants and Their Children.* Stanford: Stanford University Press; London: H. Milford, Oxford University Press, 1932.
Jacobson, Matthew Frye. *Barbarian Virtues: The United States Encounters Foreign Peoples at Home and Abroad, 1876–1917.* New York: Hill and Wang, 2000.
Jacobson, Robin. "Characterizing Consent: Race, Citizenship, and the New Restrictionists." *Political Research Quarterly* 59, no. 4 (2006): 645–54.
James, Daniel. *Illegal Immigration: An Unfolding Crisis.* Washington, DC: Mexico-United States Institute, 1991.
Jaret, Charles. "Troubled by Newcomers: Anti-Immigrant Attitudes and Action During Two Eras of Mass Immigration to the United States." *Journal of American Ethnic History* 18, no. 3 (1999): 9–39.
Johnson, Kevin R. "'Aliens' and the U.S. Immigration Laws: The Social and Legal Construction of Nonpersons." *The University of Miami Inter-American Law Review* 28, no. 2 (1996): 263–92.
Jones, Richard C. "Immigration Reform and Migrant Flows: Compositional and Spatial Changes in Mexican Migration After the Immigration Reform Act of 1986." *Annals of the Association of American Geographers* 85, no. 4 (1995): 715–30.
Jones-Correa, Michael and Els De Graauw. "The Illegality Trap: The Politics of Immigration & the Lens of Illegality." *Daedalus* 142, no. 3 (2013): 185–98.
Joseph, Gilbert M., et al., eds. *Reclaiming the Political in Latin American History: Essays from the North.* Durham: Duke University Press, 2001.
Kang, S. Deborah. *The INS on the Line: Making Immigration Law on the US-Mexico Border, 1917–1954.* Oxford: Oxford University Press, 2017.
Katz, Michael B., "Was Government the Solution or the Problem? The Role of the States in the History of American Social Policy." In "Cities, States, Trust, and

Rule," edited by Michael Hanagan and Chris Tilly, *Theory and Society* 39, no. 3/4 (May 2010): 487–502.

Keely, Charles and Sharon S. Russell, "Responses of Industrial Countries to Asylum Seekers." *Journal of International Affairs* 47, no. 2 (1994): 461–77.

Kelly, Gail Paradise. *From Vietnam to America: A Chronicle of the Vietnamese Immigration to the United States.* Boulder: Westview Press, 1977.

Kennedy, David M. *Freedom from Fear: The American People in Depression and War, 1929–1945.* Oxford: Oxford University Press, 1999.

King, Desmond S. *Making Americans: Immigration, Race, and the Origins of a Diverse Democracy.* Cambridge, MA: Harvard University Press, 2000.

Kishtainy, Niall. *A Little History of Economics.* New Haven: Yale University Press, 2017.

Kleven, Thomas. "Why International Law Favors Emigration over Immigration." *The University of Miami Inter-American Law Review* 33, no. 1 (2002): 69–100.

Knight, Peter. "Empathy: Concept, Confusion and Consequences in a National Curriculum." *Oxford Review of Education*, 15, no. 1 (1989): 41–53.

Kurzban, Ira J. "A Critical Analysis of Refugee Law." *University of Miami Law Review* 36 (September 1982): 865–82.

LaFeber, Walter. *The American Age: U.S. Foreign Policy at Home and Abroad, 1750 to Present*, 2nd edn. New York: W.W. Norton & Company, 1994.

Larzelere, Alex. *Castro's Ploy, America's Dilemma: The 1980 Cuban Boatlift.* Washington, DC: National Defense University Press, 1988.

La Voy, S. Kathleen, Matthew J. L. Brand, and Collin R. McFadden. "An Important Lesson from Our Past with Significance for Our Future: Alfred Adler's Gemeinschaftsgefühl." *The Journal of Individual Psychology* 69, no. 4 (Winter 2013): 280–93.

Le, C. N. *Asian American Assimilation: Ethnicity, Immigration, and Socioeconomic Attainment.* New York: LFB Scholarly Pub., 2007.

Lee, Catherine. "'Where the Danger Lies': Race, Gender, and Chinese and Japanese Exclusion in the United States, 1870-1924." *Sociological Forum* 25, no. 2 (2010): 248–71.

Lee, Catherine. "Family Reunification and the Limits of Immigration Reform: Impact and Legacy of the 1965 Immigration Act." *Sociological Forum* 30, no. S1 (2015): 528–48.

Lee, Erika. "Immigrants and Immigration Law: A State of the Field Assessment." *Journal of American Ethnic History* 18, no. 4 (1999): 85–114.

Lee, Erika. "The Chinese Exclusion Example: Race, Immigration, and American Gatekeeping, 1882–1924." *Journal of American Ethnic History* 21, no. 3 (2002): 36–62.

Lee, Erika. "The 'Yellow Peril' and Asian Exclusion in the Americas." *Pacific Historical Review* 76, no. 4 (2007): 537–62.

Legomsky, Stephen H. *Immigration Law and Policy.* Westbury: Foundation Press, 1992.

Legomsky, Stephen H. "Unenforced Boundaries: Illegal Immigration and the Limits of Judicial Federalism." *Harvard Law Review* 108, no. 7 (1995): 1643–60.

LeMay, Michael C. *From Open Door to Dutch Door: An Analysis of US Immigration Policy Since 1820.* New York: Praeger Publishers, 1987.

LeMay, Michael C. *Anatomy of a Public Policy: The Reform of Contemporary American Immigration Law.* Westport: Praeger, 1994.

LeMay, Michael C. and Elliot Robert Barkan, eds. *U.S. Immigration and Naturalization Laws and Issues: A Documentary History*. Westport: Greenwood Press, 1999.

Lew-Williams, Beth. "Before Restriction Became Exclusion: America's Experiment in Diplomatic Immigration Control." *Pacific Historical Review* 83, no. 1 (2014): 24–56.

Liebert, Hugh P., John Griswold, and Isaiah Wilson, III, eds. *Thinking Beyond Boundaries: Transnational Challenges to U.S. Foreign Policy*. Baltimore: Johns Hopkins University Press, 2015.

Liebert, Hugh P. and Lee Robinson. "Disorder at the Border? Immigration and Homeland Security." In *Thinking Beyond Boundaries: Transnational Challenges to U.S. Foreign Policy*, edited by Hugh Liebert, et al., 43–54. Baltimore: Johns Hopkins University Press, 2015.

Lim, Julien. *Porous Borders: Multiracial Migrations and the Law in the U.S.-Mexico Borderlands*. Chapel Hill: University of North Carolina Press, 2020.

Loescher, Gil. "The International Refugee Regime: Stretched to the Limit?" *Journal of International Affairs* 47, no. 2 (1994): 351–77.

Longley, Kyle, et al. *Deconstructing Reagan: Conservative Mythology and America's Fortieth President*. Armonk: Routledge, 2007.

Loyd, Jenna M. and Alison Mountz. *Boats, Borders, and Bases: Race, the Cold War, and the Rise of Migration Detention in the United States*. Oakland: University of California Press, 2018.

Ma, Xiaohua. "The Sino-American Alliance During World War II and the Lifting of the Chinese Exclusion Acts." *American Studies International* 38, no. 2 (2000): 39–61.

MacDonald, Kevin. "Jewish Involvement in Shaping American Immigration Policy, 1881–1965: A Historical Review." *Population and Environment* 19, no. 4 (1998): 295–356.

Maddux, Thomas R. "Ronald Reagan and the Task Force on Immigration, 11981." *Pacific Historical Review* 74, no. 2 (2005): 195–236.

Manges, Douglas Karen and Rogelio Sáenz. "The Criminalization of Immigrants & the Immigration-Industrial Complex." *Daedalus* 142, no. 3 (Summer 2013): 199–227.

Manning, Bayless. "The Congress, The Executive and Intermestic Affairs: Three Proposals." *Foreign Affairs* 55, no. 2 (1977): 306–24.

Martínez, Oscar. *Fragments of the Mexican Revolution: Personal Accounts from the Border*. Albuquerque. University of New Mexico Press, 1983.

Martinez, Ramiro and Jacob I. Stowell. "Extending Immigration and Crime Studies: National Implications and Local Settings." *The Annals of the American Academy of Political and Social Science* 641 (2012): 174–91.

Massey, Douglas S. "America's Immigration Policy Fiasco: Learning from Past Mistakes." *Daedalus* 142, no. 3 (Summer 2013): 5–15.

Massey, Douglas S. and Fernando Riosmena. "Undocumented Migration from Latin America in an Era of Rising U.S. Enforcement." *The Annals of the American Academy of Political and Social Science* 630, (2010): 294–321.

Massey, Douglas S., et al., eds. *Return to Aztlan: The Social Process of International Immigration from Western Mexico*. Berkeley: University of California Press, 1987.

Mckeown, Adam. "Transnational Chinese Families and Chinese Exclusion, 1875–1943." *Journal of American Ethnic History* 18, no. 2 (1999): 73–110.

McPherson, Alan. *Intimate Ties, Bitter Struggles: The United States and Latin America since 1945.* Washington, DC: Potomac Books, Inc., 2006.

Meissner, Doris, et al. *Immigration Enforcement in The United States: The Rise of a Formidable Machinery.* Washington, DC: Migration Policy Institute, 2013.

Menchaca, Martha. "The Social Climate of the Birthright Movement in the United States." *Chicana/Latina Studies* 12, no. 2 (Spring 2013): 28–55.

Meyers, Eytan. "The Causes of Convergence in Western Immigration Control." *Review of International Studies* 28, no. 1 (2002): 123–41.

Mitchell, Christopher. *Western Hemisphere Immigration and United States Foreign Policy.* University Park: The Pennsylvania State University Press, 1992.

Molina, Natalia. "'In a Race All Their Own': The Quest to Make Mexicans Ineligible for U.S. Citizenship." *Pacific Historical Review* 79, no. 2 (2010): 167–201.

Molina, Natalie. *How Race Is Made in America; Immigration, Citizenship, and the Historical Power of Racial Scripts.* Berkeley: University of California Press, 2014.

Montoya, Benjamin C. "'A Grave Offense of Significant Consequences': Three Mexican Perspectives on the U.S. Attempt to Place a Quota on Mexico's Immigration During the Late 1920s." *Pacific Historical Review* 87, no. 2 (2018): 333–55.

Montoya, Benjamin C. *Risking Immeasurable Harm: Immigration Restriction and U.S.-Mexican Diplomatic Relations, 1924–1932.* Lincoln: University of Nebraska Press, 2020.

Montoya, Benjamin C. "Undermining the Sandbags: How Neoliberalism Encouraged Undocumented Migration, from the 1980s to the early 2000s." In *Understanding and Teaching Contemporary American History, Reagan to Trump*, edited by Kimber Quinney and Amy L. Sayward, 173–197. Madison: University of Wisconsin Press, 2022.

Mora-Torres, Juan. "Los De Casa Se Van, Los De Fuera No Vienen: The First Mexican Immigrants, 1848–1900." In *Beyond La Frontera: The History of Mexico-U.S. Immigration*, edited by Mark Overmyer-Velázquez, 3–27. New York: Oxford University Press, 2011.

Morawska, Ewa. *A Sociology of Immigration: (re)making Multifaceted America.* Basingstoke: Palgrave Macmillan, 2009.

Motomura, Hiroshi. "Immigration Law After a Century of Plenary Power: Phantom Constitutional Norms and Statutory Interpretation." *Yale Law Journal* 100, no. 3 (1990): 454–613.

Motomura, Hiroshi. "The Curious Evolution of Immigration Law: Procedural Surrogates for Substantive Constitutional Rights." *Columbia Law Review* 92, no. 7 (1992): 1626–704.

Motomura, Hiroshi. "Immigration Outside the Law." *Columbia Law Review* 108, no. 8 (2008): 2037–97.

Neuman, Gerald L. *Strangers to the Constitution: Immigrants, Borders, and Fundamental Law.* Princeton: Princeton University Press, 1996.

Neuman, Gerald L. "Qualitative Migration Controls in the Antebellum United States." In *Migration Control in the North Atlantic World: The Evolution of State Practices in Europe and the United States from the French Revolution to the Inter-War Period*, edited by Andres Fahrmeir, Olivier Faron, and Patrick Weil, 106–119. New York: Berghahn Books, 2003.

Ngai, Mae M. "Legacies of Exclusion: Illegal Chinese Immigration During the Cold War Years." *Journal of American Ethnic History* 18, no. 1 (1998): 3–35.

Ngai, Mae M. "The Architecture of Race in American Immigration Law: A Reexamination of the Immigration Act of 1924." *The Journal of American History* 86, no. 1 (June 1999): 67–92.

Ngai, Mae M. "The Strange Career of the Illegal Alien: Immigration Restriction and Deportation Policy in the United States, 1921–1965." *Law and History Review* 21, no. 1 (2003): 69–107.

Ngai, Mae M. *Impossible Subjects: Illegal Aliens and the Making of Modern America*. Princeton: Princeton University Press, 2004.

Ngai, Mae M. "No Human Being Is Illegal." *Women's Studies Quarterly* 34, no. 3/4 (2006): 291–5.

Ngai, Mae M. "Nationalism, Immigration Control, and the Ethnoracial Remapping of America in the 1920s." *OAH Magazine of History* 21, no. 3 (2007): 11–15.

Ngai, Mae M. "The Civil Rights Origins of Illegal Immigration." *International Labor and Working-Class History* 78 (2010): 93–9.

Ngai, Mae M. "Oscar Handlin and Immigration Policy Reform in the 1950s and 1960s." *Journal of American Ethnic History* 32, no. 3 (2013): 62–7.

Okeke, Chris Nwachukwu and James A. R. Nafziger. "United States Migration Law: Essentials for Comparison." *The American Journal of Comparative Law* 54, no. Supplement 1 (2006): 531–52.

Overmyer-Velázquez, Mark. *Beyond La Frontera: The History of Mexico-U.S. Immigration*. New York: Oxford University Press, 2011.

Oyen, Meredith Leigh. *Allies, Enemies and Aliens: Migration and U.S.-Chinese Relations, 1940–1965*. Washington, DC: Georgetown University Press, 2007.

Pardo, Jose Enrique. *Cubamerican*. San Francisco: Ño Productions, 2012.

Parker, Kunal M. "Citizenship and Immigration Law, 1800–1924." In *The Cambridge History of Law in America, Three Volumes*, edited by Michael Grossberg and Christopher Tomlins, 168–203. Cambridge: Cambridge University Press, 2008.

Patterson, James T. *Grand Expectations: The United States, 1945–1974*. Oxford: Oxford University Press, 1996.

Patterson, James T. *Restless Giant: The United States from Watergate to Bush v. Gore*. Oxford University Press, 2005.

Pedraza, Silvia. *Political Disaffection in Cuba's Revolution and Exodus*. New York: Cambridge University Press, 2007.

Pham, Huyen. "When Immigration Borders Move." *Florida Law Review* 61, no. 5 (2009): 1115–63.

Plascencia, Luis F. B. "The 'Undocumented' Mexican Migrant Question: Re-Examining The Framing Of Law And Illegalization In The United States." *Urban Anthropology and Studies of Cultural Systems and World Economic Development* 38, no. 2/3/4 (2009): 375–434.

Purcell, Joy M. "A Right to Leave, but Nowhere to Go: Reconciling an Emigrant's Right to Leave with the Sovereign's Right to Exclude." *The University of Miami Inter-American Law Review* 39, no. 1 (2007): 177–205.

Rankin, Monica and Diana Berger, "Peculiarities of Mexican Diplomacy." In *A Companion to Mexican History and Culture*, edited by William H. Beezley, 538–60. Marlton: Wiley-Blackwell, 2011.

Reed-Danahay, Deborah and Caroline B. Brettell. *Citizenship, Political Engagement, and Belonging: Immigrants in Europe and the United States*. New Brunswick: Rutgers University Press, 2008.

Reich, Gary and Jay Barth. "Immigration Restriction in the States: Contesting the Boundaries of Federalism?" *Publius* 42, no. 3 (2012): 422–48.

Rekdal, Paisley. *The Broken Country: On Trauma, a Crime and the Continuing Legacy of Vietnam*. Athens: University of Georgia Press, 2017.

Rickman, H. P., ed. and trans. *W. Dilthey: Selected Writings*. Cambridge: Cambridge University Press, 1976.

Riosmena, Fernando and Douglas S. Massey. "Pathways to El Norte: Origins, Destinations, and Characteristics of Mexican Migrants to the United States." *International Migration Review* 46, no. 1 (2012): 3–36.

Rodriguez, Cristina. "Immigration, Civil Rights & the Evolution of the People." *Daedalus* 142, no. 3 (Summer 2013): 228–41.

Roediger, David R. *The Wages of Whiteness: Race and the Making of the American Working Class*, Rev. edn. London: Verso, 2007.

Romero, Mary. "Crossing the Immigration and Race Border: A Critical Race Theory Approach to Immigration Studies." *Contemporary Justice Review* 11, no. 1 (March 2008): 23–37.

Rosenberg, Emily S. and Shanon Fitzpatrick. *Body and Nation: The Global Realm of U.S. Body Politics in the Twentieth Century*. Durham: Duke University Press, 2014.

Rosenblum, Marc R. "Moving Beyond the Policy of No Policy: Emigration from Mexico and Central America." *Latin American Politics and Society* 46, no. 4 (2004): 91–125.

Rosenblum, Marc R. and Leo B. Gorman. "The Public Policy Implications of State-Level Worksite Migration Enforcement: The Experiences of Arizona, Mississippi, and Illinois." In *Taking Local Control: Immigration Policy Activism in U.S. Cities and States*, edited by Monica Varsanyi, 115–34. Stanford: Stanford University Press, 2010.

Rosenblum, Marc R. and Idean Salehyan. "Norms and Interests in US Asylum Enforcement." *Journal of Peace Research* 41, no. 6 (2004): 677–97.

Rubinstein, William. *The Myth of Rescue: Why the Democracies Could Not Have Saved More Jews from the Nazis*. Milton Park: Routledge, 1997.

Sadowski-Smith, Claudia. "Unskilled Labor Migration and the Illegality Spiral: Chinese, European, and Mexican Indocumentados in the United States, 1882–2007." *American Quarterly* 60, no. 3 (September 2008): 779–804.

Salehyan, Idean and Marc R. Rosenblum. "International Relations, Domestic Politics, and Asylum Admissions in the United States." *Political Research Quarterly* 61, no. 1 (2008): 104–21.

Sanchez, George J. *Becoming Mexican-American: Ethnicity, Culture, and Identity in Chicano Los Angeles*. New York: Oxford University Press, 1993.

Sanchez, George J. "Face the Nation: Race, Immigration, and the Rise of Nativism in Late Twentieth Century America." *The International Migration Review* 31, no. 4 (1997): 1009–30.

Sanchez, George J. "Race, Nation, and Culture in Recent Immigration Studies." *Journal of American Ethnic History* 18, no. 4 (Summer, 1999): 66–84.

Sassen, Saskia. "Beyond Sovereignty: Immigration Policy Making Today." *Social Justice* 23, no. 3 (1996): 9–20.

Scanlan, John A. "A View from the United States—Social, Economic, and Legal Change, the Persistence of the State, and Immigration Policy in the Coming Century." *Indiana Journal of Global Legal Studies* 2, no. 1 (1994): 79–141.

Schmidt, Arthur. "Mexicans, Migrants, and Indigenous Peoples: The Work of Manuel Gamio in the United States, 1925–1927." In *Strange Pilgrimages: Travel, Exile and Foreign Residency in the Creation of Latin American Identity, 1800–1990s*, edited by Ingrid E. Fey and Karine Racine, 163–78. Wilmington: Scholarly Resources, 2000.

Schneider, Dorothee. "'I Know All about Emma Lazarus': Nationalism and Its Contradictions in Congressional Rhetoric of Immigration Restriction." *Cultural Anthropology* 13, no. 1 (1998): 82–99.

Schneider, Dorothee. "Naturalization and United States Citizenship in Two Periods of Mass Migration: 1894–1930, 1965–2000." *Journal of American Ethnic History* 21, no. 1 (2001): 50–82.

Schneider, Dorothee. *Crossing Borders: Migration and Citizenship in the Twentieth Century United States*. Cambridge, MA: Harvard University Press, 2011.

Schoultz, Lars. "Central America and the Politicization of U.S. Immigration Policy." In *Western Hemisphere Immigration and United States Foreign Policy*, edited by Christopher Mitchell, 157–220. University Park: The Pennsylvania State University Press.

Scully, Eileen P. "The United States and International Affairs 1789–1919." In *The Cambridge History of Law in America*, 3 vols, edited by Michael Grossberg and Christopher Tomlins, 604–42. Cambridge: Cambridge University Press, 2008.

Shachar, Ayelet. "Territory Without Boundaries: Immigration Beyond Territory: The Shifting Border of Immigration Regulation." *Michigan Journal of International Law* 30, no. 3 (Spring 2009): 809–39.

Shaller, Michael. "Reagan and the Cold War." In *Deconstructing Reagan: Conservative Mythology and America's Fortieth President*, edited by Kyle Longley, et al., 3–40. Armonk: Routledge, 2007.

Sheridan, Clare. "Contested Citizenship: National Identity and the Mexican Immigration Debates of the 1920s." *Journal of American Ethnic History* 21, no. 3 (2002): 3–35.

Siener, William H. "Through the Back Door: Evading the Chinese Exclusion Act Along the Niagara Frontier, 1900 to 1924." *Journal of American Ethnic History* 27, no. 4 (2008): 34–70.

Simcox, David. "Major Predictors of Immigration Restrictionism: Operationalizing 'Nativism'." *Population and Environment* 19, no. 2 (1997): 129–43.

Skerry, Peter. "Many Borders to Cross: Is Immigration the Exclusive Responsibility of the Federal Government?" *Publius* 25, no. 3 (1995): 71–85.

Smith, Michael P. and Matt Bakker. *Citizenship Across Borders: The Political Transnationalism of El Migrante*. Ithaca: Cornell University Press, 2008.

Stanley, WD. "Economic Migrants or Refugees from Violence? A Time-series Analysis of Salvadoran Migrants to the United States." *Latin American Research Review* 22, no. 1 (1987): 132–54.

Stavans, Ilan. *Immigration*. Westport: Greenwood Press, 2008.

Strobel, Christoph. *Daily Life of the New Americans: Immigration Since 1965*. Santa Barbara: Greenwood, 2010.

Stumpf, Juliet. "The Crimmigration Crisis: Immigrants, Crime, and Sovereign Power." *American University Law Review* 56, no. 2 (2006): 367–419.

Stumpf, Juliet. "States of Confusion: The Rise of State and Local Power Over Immigration." *North Carolina Law Review* 86, no. 6 (2008): 1558–618.

Takai, Yukari. "Asian Migrants, Exclusionary Laws, and Transborder Migration in North America, 1880–1940." *OAH Magazine of History* 23, no. 4 (2009): 35–42.

Tichenor, Daniel J. "The Politics of Immigration Reform in the United States, 1981–1990." *Polity* 26, no. 3 (1994): 333–62.

Tichenor, Daniel J. "The Political Dynamics of Unauthorized Immigration: Conflict, Change, and Agency in Time." *Polity* 47, no. 3 (2015): 283–301.

Tienda, Marta and Susana M. Sánchez. "Latin American Immigration to the United States." *Daedalus* 142, no. 3 (Summer 2013): 48–64.

Thomas, Patrick W. "The Recurring Native Response to Global Labor Migration." *Indiana Journal of Global Legal Studies* 20, no. 2 (2013): 1393–423.

Trachtenberg, Barry. *The United States and the Nazi Holocaust: Race, Refuge, and Remembrance.* London: Bloomsbury Academic, 2018.

Tumlin, Karen C. "Suspect First: How Terrorism Policy Is Reshaping Immigration Policy." *California Law Review* 92, no. 4 (2004): 1173–239.

Urrea, Luis Alberto. *The Devil's Highway: A True Story.* New York: Bay Back Books, 2004.

Vargas, Zaragosa. *Crucible of Struggle: A History of Mexican Americans from Colonial Times to the Present Era.* New York: Oxford University Press, 2011.

Varsanyi, Monica W. "Immigration Policy Activism in U.S. States and Cities: Interdisciplinary Perspectives." In *Taking Local Control: Immigration Policy Activism in U.S. Cities and States*, edited by Monica Varsanyi, 1–27. Stanford: Stanford University Press, 2008.

Varsanyi, Monica W., ed. *Taking Local Control: Immigration Policy Activism in U.S. Cities and States.* Stanford: Stanford University Press, 2008.

Villarreal, M. Angeles and Ian F. Ferguson, "NAFTA at 20: Overview and Trade Effects." *Congressional Research Service*, 2014, 1–32.

Warren, Robert and John Robert Warren. "Unauthorized Immigration to the United States: Annual Estimates and Components of Change, by State, 1990 to 2010." *The International Migration Review* 47, no. 2 (2013): 296–329.

Wasem, Ruth Ellen. *Cuban Migration to the United States: Policy and Trends.* Washington, DC: Congressional Research Service, 2009.

Weber, John. "Homing Pigeons, Cheap Labor, and Frustrated Nativists: Immigration Reform and the Deportation of Mexicans from South Texas in the 1920s." *Western Historical Quarterly* 44, no. 2 (2013): 167–86.

Weber, John. *From South Texas to the Nation: The Exploitation of Mexican Labor in the Twentieth Century.* Chapel Hill: University of North Carolina Press, 2015.

Weil, Patrick. "Races at the Gate: A Century of Racial Distinctions in American Immigration Policy (1865–1965)." *Georgetown Immigration Law Journal* 15 (Summer 2001): 625–48.

Weinberg, Carl R. "The Gentlemen's Agreement of 1907–08." In Yukari Takai, "Asian Migrants, Exclusionary Laws, and Transborder Migration in North America, 1880–1940." *OAH Magazine of History* 23, no. 4 (2009): 36.

Welch, Michael. "The Immigration Crisis: Detention as an Emerging Mechanism of Social Control." *Social Justice* 23, no. 3 (1996): 169–84.

Wilsher, Daniel. *Immigration Detention: Law, History, Politics*. Cambridge: Cambridge University Press, 2011.
Wood, Charles H., Chris L. Gibson, Ludmila Ribeiro, and Paula Hamsho-Diaz. "Crime Victimization in Latin America and Intentions to Migrate to the United States." *The International Migration Review* 44, no. 1 (2010): 3–24.
Wyman, David. *The Abandonment of the Jews: America and the Holocaust, 1941–1945*. New York: Pantheon Books, 1998.
Yans-McLaughlin, Virginia. *Immigration Reconsidered: History, Sociology, and Politics*. New York: Oxford University Press, 1990.
Zolberg, Aristide R. "Reforming the Back Door: The Immigration Reform and Control Act of 1986 in Historical Perspective." In *Immigration Reconsidered: History, Sociology, and Politics*, edited by Virginia Yans-McLaughlin, 315–39. New York: Oxford University Press, 1990.
Zolberg, Aristide R. "Changing Sovereignty Games and International Migration." *Indiana Journal of Global Legal Studies* 2, no. 1 (1994): 153–70.
Zolberg, Aristide R. "The Archaeology of 'Remote Control'." In *Migration Control in the North Atlantic World: The Evolution of State Practices in Europe and the United States from the French Revolution to the Inter-War Period*, edited by Andres Fahrmeir, Olivier Faron, and Patrick Weil, 195–222. New York: Berghahn Books, 2003.
Zolberg, Aristide R. *A Nation by Design: Immigration Policy in the Fashioning of America*. New York: Russell Sage Foundation, 2006.

# Index

Note: Page numbers followed by 'n' refer to notes

acculturation, processes of  2, 46
Act to Encourage Immigration of 1864  32
administrative restriction, Mexico, *see also* Mexicans, 1920s
   benefits for American employers  101
   consular service flexibility  104
   enforcement of immigration law  100–1
   harmonious US-Mexican relations  101
   quota, justification for  101–2
   race  103
   visa refusals  102–3
AEDPA, *see* Antiterrorism and Effective Death Penalty Act (AEDPA)
AEL, *see* Asiatic Exclusion League (AEL)
Aid to Families with Dependent Children  60
Alien Act, 1798  28
alienage laws, state  35–8, 42 n.25
Alien Fiancées and Fiancés Act of 1946  127
Alien Registration Act  36
*American Baptist Church v. Thornburgh* (ABC case)  165–9
   benefits of  168
   blow to the Cold War-driven refugee policy  167
   discrimination in favor of refugees from socialist countries  166
   human rights abuses  166
   NACARA program  169
   out-of-court settlement  166
   stop-time rule  168
   Temporary Protected Status program (TPS)  167
   victory of Sanctuary movement  167
American capitalism  31, 175
American-Chinese Nationalist alliance  126
American Civil War  32, 46
American Eugenics Society  91
American Federation of Labor  82, 126
American (Know-Nothing) Party  15
American Protective Association  15, 46
American sovereignty vis-à-vis the inflow of immigrants  29
American xenophobia  58–60
Anglo-American antipathy toward Catholics  15, 46
anti-Castro foreign policy  144
anti-Chinese
   agitation in 1850s  34, 81, 119
   immigration legislation  120
   prejudice  121, 122
anticommunism in US society  18, 159
Anti-Contract Labor Law, or the Foran Act, 1885  45
anti-immigrant
   organizations  46
   sentiment  31, 46, 194
anti-Semitism  107–10, 114–16
Antiterrorism and Effective Death Penalty Act (AEDPA)  59, 169, 171
Arana, Ana  171
*Arizona v. United States* (2012)  40, 43 n.37
Asiatic Exclusion League (AEL)  82

Barkan, Elliott 197
Batista, Fulgencio 142
Berlin Wall, collapse in 1989 187
Big Three 68, 128
birthright citizenship movement 194
   antecedents to 195
   Chinese immigrants as accidental or technical citizens 195
   fear of social consequences of immigration 195–6
   principle of *jus soli* 33
   xenophobia and nativism in US society 196
Bixby, Fred 94
Black, Hugo 36
Block, Herbert 111
Blocker, William 102
Boland amendment 159, 162
Border Patrol, US 3–4, 9, 14, 49, 56, 92, 99, 102, 181
Border Security Act of 2002 186
Box, John 92, 95, 99
   effort to restrict Mexican immigration 92–4
   register the aliens (cartoon) 93
Boyce, Richard 102
Bracero program (1942–64) 7, 12–13, 15, 52–4, 176–7, 180
Buck, Pearl 123–4, 126
Bush, George H.W. (1989–93) 166, 187
Bush, George W. (2001–9) 128, 185–6

Calavita, Kitty 4, 13
California Cattle Raisers' Association 94
Calles, Plutarco Elias 96
Camarioca crisis of 1965 149, 153
Carens, Joseph 2, 4
Carlyle, Thomas 198
Carr, Wilbur J. 114
Carter, Jimmy (1977–81) 145–8
   approach to the Mariel boatlift 149
   human rights policies 160
   welcome statement to Cuban exiles 149
Casey, William 158
Castro, Fidel 16, 19, 141–53, 160
   anti-Castro agitation 144
   boatlift crisis as "pay back" 152
   Camarioca exile crisis 143–4
   Cuban revolutionaries 142
   decision to open Camarioca harbor to Cubans 143
   manipulation of US refugee law 143, 153
   socialist regime 19
   threats to reopen Cuban borders 144
Celler, Emmanuel 49
Central Americans 1980s–1990s 107, 157–72
   ABC settlement 167–9
   asylum policy 162–3
   Boland amendment 159, 162
   cancellation of removal 168
   Cold War-driven refugee policy 167
   communism, spread of 160
   Cuban-style socialism, threat of 157
   DED 167–8
   deportable crimes 171
   economic migrants 162
   extreme hardship for asylum approval 169
   government's use of military sweeps 161
   guerrilla forces in El Salvador 163
   IIRIRA 168
   *INS v. Cardoza-Fonseca* (1987) 168
   *marabuntas*, Central American gangs 170
   NACARA 169
   non-refoulement 71–2, 166, 170
   Reagan and contra aid 158
   Reagan's "not-so-covert" wars in Nicaragua 159
   refugee crisis 157
   regime of Anastasio Somoza, overthrow of 157
   resettlement of refugees 161
   Salvadoran military's aggression 158, 160
   sanctuaries for displaced people 163
   Sanctuary movement (*see* Sanctuary movement)

Sandinistas 157–8
sense of temporariness 167–8
socialist-nationalist insurgencies 157
Soviet-Cuban-Nicaraguan axis 160
Temporary Protected Status program (TPS) 167
UNHCR definition of political refugee 162
US Cold War policies 172
US foreign aid and political violence 161
Vietnam War 159
Cervantes-Rodríguez, Margarita 152
*Chae Chan Ping v. United States* (1889) 34, 120
Chandler, Alfred 31
Charles, Patrick 28
Chiang Kai-shek 125, 128–9
Chinese, 1930s–1950s
  Alien Fiancées and Fiancés Act of 1946 127
  American-Chinese Nationalist alliance 126
  anti-Chinese agitation in 1850s 119
  anti-Chinese prejudice 121, 122
  bill to end Chinese Exclusion, 1943 127
  Burlingame Treaty 119
  *Chae Chan-ping v. United States* (1889) 120
  Chinese Confession Program 130–1
  Chinese Exclusion Act of 1882 120
  civil war in China 128
  communism 123, 130–2
  Congress's continued antipathy 127
  defeat of Chiang 129
  fall of China to communism 130
  House Committee on Immigration and Naturalization 126
  illegal Chinese immigration 120–1
  issue of "paper sons" 129–30
  Japanese militarism in China 123
  Magnuson Act of 1943 127
  Page Act of 1875 119
  passport and visa fraud 130
  People's Republic of China (PRC) 128
  post-exclusion immigration regime 127
  PRC effect on Chinese immigration 128–9
  racial and class based exclusion 119
  racism, role in legislation 120
  Refugee Relief Act of 1953 127
  Scott Act of 1888 120
  Second World War in Asia 123–5
  surreptitious immigration 121–2
Chinese Communist Party 128
Chinese Confession Program 18, 130–1
  communistic aims, checks for 131
  informal interview with INS investigators 131
Chinese Exclusion Act of 1882 4, 7, 15, 34, 120–7
Churgin, Michael 74
*Chy Lung v. Freeman* (1875) 32
citizen children, concept of 196
citizen/citizenship, *see also* birthright citizenship movement
  and a foreigner, distinction 1
  national 33
  and naturalization 32–3
  and noncitizen (alien), distinction between 5
  race and 195
  US citizenship for immigrants 44, 46, 85, 89 n.24
  US citizenship law 195–6
  voluntary 28
  whiteness and citizenship 33
The Citizens Committee to Repeal Chinese Exclusion and Place Immigration on A Quota Basis 126
civil war
  American 32, 46
  Central America 157, 170–2
  in China 128
  colonial 70
  El Salvador and Guatemala 166, 168
  Nicaragua 170

Cleveland, Grover  47
Clinton, Bill (1993–2001)  168, 185
Cold War  17–20, 58, 69–71, 73, 123, 128–32, 142, 145, 147, 154, 159–60, 163, 165, 167–70, 172, 182, 184–5, 187, 197–8
communism  18, 20, 75, 114, 123, 128, 130, 132, 142, 153, 159–61, 166
comprehensive refugee legislation  74
Constitution of the United States (1787–8)  6
Convention Relating to the Status of Refugees  71
Cook-Martín, David  4
Coolidge, Calvin  88
Coutin, Susan Bibler  163, 172
Cox, Adam  76
crimmigration  3–4
Cuban Adjustment Act (CAA)  142–3
Cuban Missile Crisis  143
Cuban Refugee Program (CRP) 142–3, 148
Cubans, 1960s–1980s  141–54
  anti-Castro foreign policy  144
  CAA  142
  Camarioca-like expulsion of Cuban exiles  146
  Carter, Jimmy (1977–81)  147–9
  challenges to US foreign interests  146
  crisis in 1960s and 1970s  107
  CRP  142
  Cuban Missile Crisis  143
  decline in the Cuban economy  145
  economic problems due to sudden influx of  143–4
  freedom flight airlift program (1969–73)  144, 151
  free emigration of peoples  147
  golden exile  142
  Hart-Celler Act (see Hart-Celler Act, 1965)
  hijack of Cuban vessels to US  146
  interest sections  145–6
  Mariel boatlift  141, 143–5, 147, 152–4, 160

  Marielitos, harsh treatment of  151
  Mariel wave of Cuban migration (see Mariel boatlift crisis)
  Memorandum of Understanding between the US and Cuba  144
  migration since 1959  141–2
  Operation Peter Pan  142
  permanent residency status  143
  Refugee Act of 1980  146, 148–9
  refugees of elite classes and lower socio-economic strata  142
  Revolution of 1959  19, 142
  sudden expunging of undesirable Cubans to US shores  150
  US-backed Cuban regime of Batista  142
Cuban-style socialism  157

Daniels, Roger  52, 116, 127, 131, 149
Dawson, William  102
*DeCanas v. Bica* (1976)  37
Declaration of the Rights of Man and of the Citizen (1791)  6
decolonization  17, 70, 126
Deferred Enforced Departure (DED)  167–8
Degenova, Nicholas  9–10
democratic populism  29
Democratic Republic of Vietnam (DRV)  134, 137–9
deportable crimes  171
Dickstein, Samuel  127
Dilthey, Wilhelm  198–9
Displaced Persons Acts of 1948 and 1950  16, 73–4
DRV, *see* Democratic Republic of Vietnam (DRV)

Eastland, James  54
economic liberalism  175
economic liberalization and immigration liberalization  12
economic migrants  2, 19–20, 162, 169
Eisenhower, Dwight D. (1953–61) 74, 75
endangered European Jewish refugees  111

Erhardt, John G.  115
Ethiopia
  Ogaden War, against Somalia  145–6
  and US  145–6
ethno-racial group  6
European Jewish refugees  18, 111
European refugee crisis  72
exclusion, *see also* Chinese Exclusion Act of 1882
  based on racial and class considerations  119
  Chinese Exclusion cases of the 1880s and 1890s  197
  and conceptualized personhood  57
  consular-led form of  16
  laws based on race and ethnicity  49
  liberalism and  11
  of Mexican immigrants  104
  post-exclusion immigration regime  11
exclusionary liberalism  5

Fair Share Act  74
Federal Bureau of Immigration (FBI)  32, 130
federal government of the United States  29
  absolute authority over immigration policy  38
  pre-migration contracts  32
  reasons for no legislation in antebellum years  29–30
Field, Stephen  34
First World War  47, 48, 67, 85, 91, 100
Fitzgerald, David  4–5, 96
*Fong Yue Ting v. United States* (1889)  34
Forbath, William  35
Ford, Gerald  135
foreign policy, United States  1–2, 14, 17, 27, 69, 124, 129, 149, 153, 157, 159–60, 162–4
foreign policy preemption  29, 33, 35–7, 43 nn.37, 44

Fourteenth Amendment  33–4, 36, 85, 195
Fox, Vincente  185
freedom flight airlift program (1969–73)  144, 151, *see also* Cubans, 1960s–1980s

Gallegos, Gabriela  5
Gamio, Manuel  97–9
  'brusque stopping' of Mexican immigration  97–8
  revolution of starvation  98
  safety-valve theory of Mexican immigration  98
Garner, John  95
Geist, Raymond  115
Gentlemen's Agreement (1907–8)  12, 17, 84–6, 88
geopolitical conflict  17
Gerstle, Gary  6
globalization  11, 13, 20, 59, 179–80, 182–3, 188–9
global peace  175–6
golden exile  142, *see also* Cubans, 1960s–1980s
Goldsborough, James  196
*The Good Earth* (Buck)  123–4
*Graham v. Richardson* (1917)  36, 38
Great Depression  108, 117
Great Society reforms  49
Greenhill, Kelly  143

H-2A  8
Hagan, Jacqueline  60
Handlin, Oscar  49
Harris, William J.  99–100, 102
Hart, Philip  49
Hart-Celler Act, 1965  16, 49–53, 141, 142, 194
  base for 'out of control immigration' by the 1980s  53
  Bracero program  52–3
  civil rights act for voting rights  49
  debatable legacy of civil rights achievement  53
  family preferences  50
  federal aid to elementary and secondary education  49
  Great Society reforms  49

# INDEX

immigration of family members of Euro-Americans 51
liberal approach of inclusion 57
Medicare and Medicaid 49
notion of illegal immigration 52
principles of equality and fairness 50
professional background or needs of the US labor market 50
quota system 50
rise of immigration from Latin America 53
signed into law by Johnson at a public ceremony 50
skill-based preferences 50
universal racial equality 52
visa allotments on family reunification 50
Hawk, Kate Dupes 152
HCR's resettlement programs 67
Hearst, William Randolph 85
*Henderson v. Mayor of City of New York* (1875) 32
Herring, George 128
Higham, John 15
 *Strangers in the Land* 15
High Commissioner for Refugees (HCR) 67
hijack of Cuban vessels to US 146
*Hines v. Davidowitz* (1942) 36
Hispanic lobby groups 55
historical empathy, intellectual and emotive forms 21, 198–9
Hitler, Adolf 107–8, 110, 113–14
Holocaust 68, 107, 108, 115
Homestead Act of 1862 32
Hoover, Herbert (1929–33) 109
hostage crisis in Iran 153
House Committee on Immigration and Naturalization 91–2, 102, 126–7
Hughes, Charles Evans 86
humanitarian groups 55
human rights 5, 52, 68, 149, 157, 160, 164–6, 168, 188–9
Hungarian refugee crisis of 1956 70, 74, 134
Hungarian Revolution of 1956 70
Hunt, Michael 123

IATF, *see* Interagency Task Force (IATF)
ICE, *see* Immigration and Customs Enforcement Agency (ICE)
IIRIRA, *see* Illegal Immigration Reform and Immigrant Responsibility Act (IIRIRA)
illegal immigrant/immigration 2, 7–10, 20, 37, 52–5, 60–1, 99, 101–2, 104, 122, 168, 189
 Border Protection, Antiterrorism, and Illegal Immigration Control Act 61
 decision-making of the migrant 8, 122
 fight against 9
 IIRIRA 60, 168
 illegal Chinese immigration 18, 120–1, 129–30
 judicial responses to 37
 legal penalties 2
 notion of 53
 quota and 99
 stigma of hiring "illegals" 10
Illegal Immigration Reform and Immigrant Responsibility Act (IIRIRA) 60, 168
 criminal penalties on undocumented immigrants 61
 deterritorialized US-Mexican border 61
 focus on family dissolution 60
 H.R. 4437, Sensenbrenner Bill (Border Protection, Antiterrorism, and Illegal Immigration Control Act) 61
immigration
 and American liberalism 4
 for better lives 3
 Border Patrol 4
 causes of 8–9
 development of US immigration regulatory bodies 4
 explanation of 3
 familial security 9
 gains of 12
 impermanent settlement (migration) 3

# INDEX

militarized nature of immigration restriction 4
nation-state and ability to regulate immigration 5–6
permanent settlement (immigration) 3
restricted by colonial assemblies 28
self-insure against diminishing wages and poverty 9
social migration networks 9
unidimensional treatments of 8
violence in home countries 9
Immigration Act, 1917 47, 91, 100
Immigration and Customs Enforcement Agency (ICE) 186
Immigration and Nationality Act of 1952 7, 74
Immigration and Naturalization Service (INS) 114
immigration during antebellum era 4, 15, 29–31
   ambiguity of US immigration restriction policy 31–2
   US Supreme Court to systemize immigration restriction 30
immigration laws, 1996
   AEDPA 60
   Aid to Families with Dependent Children 60
   American xenophobia 59–60
   blanket legalization for undocumented immigrants 57
   border control and regulation 59
   consequence of the "legislative deadlock" in Washington, DC 62
   crime rates, rise in 58
   defensive nationalism 58
   IIRIRA 60
   less job growth 58
   pre-1996 crimes 60
   reasons for massive movement of people 57
   Republicans, on restriction 59
   Sensenbrenner Bill 61–2
   sense of defensive nationalism 59
   threat of deportation 60
   welfare reform bill 59–60
immigration policy, United States 1–2, 5, 7, 11, 15, 17, 27, 44–5, 49, 53–4, 57, 95, 123–5, 197
Immigration Reform and Control Act (IRCA) 16, 37, 53–7, 61, 181, 184, 194
   African American support for the Democratic party 55
   amnesty aspect of the law 56
   cancellation of the Bracero program 54
   crescendo and convergence, 1980 57
   demand for migrant labor 54
   favor for relaxing restrictions from political conservatives 55
   free market ideologies 55
   idea of employer sanctions 55
   influx of illegal immigrants 54
   labor groups 54
   legal immigrants from non-European countries 53–4
   permanent resident status under IRCA 55
   prevalence of Asians and Latin American immigration 55
   public polls 54
   Select Commission on Immigration and Refugee Policy (SCIRP) 54
   undocumented migration (*see* undocumented migration)
   US regulatory approaches to immigrants 57
Immigration Restriction League (IRL) 46–7
incomplete immigration enforcement 10
INS, *see* Immigration and Naturalization Service (INS)
*INS v. Cardoza-Fonseca* (1987) 166, 168
Interagency Task Force (IATF) 135
internal foreigners 28, 44
international refugee crisis 70
International Refugee Organization (IRO) 68–9, 71

international refugee regime   67, 70, 161, 168
IRCA, *see* Immigration Reform and Control Act (IRCA)
Izumi Hirobe   86

Japanese, 1910s–1920s
  1893 depression   81
  AEL led anti-Asian activities   82
  agitation/violence   81–2, 85
  American antipathy toward Japanese immigrants   82
  anti-Japanese actions on the West Coast   83–4
  California's state legislature   81
  diplomatic and geopolitical factors for opposition   82
  discriminatory measures in the United States   89 n.24
  exclusion laws   86, 88
  Gentlemen's Agreement of 1907–8   84–5
  immigration   17, 48, 81–2, 84–8, 90 n.24
  Immigration Act
    of 1907   84
    of 1924   87
  Johnson-Reed Act (*see* Johnson-Reed Act, 1924)
  militarism in China   123
  nativist attacks against Japanese, 1905 and 1907   83
  picture brides   85
  protest letter from Japanese government   89 n.23
  reasons for positive reception in 1890s   81
  school segregation issue   83–4
  warning of the yellow peril   85
Jews, 1930s–1940s
  American quota list   112
  *Anchluss*   110–11
  annual immigration quota   113–16
  anti-Semitism in State Department   114–15
  cases of state-sponsored violence   110
  economic depression   108–9
  European Jews under Germany   110–11
  Hitler's regime   108
  INS   114
  Johnson-Reed Act (*see* Johnson-Reed Act, 1924)
  Munich agreement   110
  Nazi invasion and capture of Poland   113
  Nazi war crimes against Jews   116
  the New Deal   109
  Nuremberg Laws   110
  Orwellian tangle of US immigration law and US public opinion   112
  pervasive anti-immigration nature   109
  public anti-Semitism, US   109
  racial prejudice   117
  self-identified or Jewish-derived population of Germany   108
  War Refugee Board (WRB)   116
  xenophobic sentiment in US   113
Johnson, Albert   92
Johnson, Lyndon B.(1963–9)   143
Johnson-Reed Act, 1924   16–17, 45–9, 88, 92–4, 96, 108, 114
  Anti-Contract Labor Law, or the Foran Act, 1885   45
  anti-immigrant organizations   46
  anti-immigrant sentiment   46
  concept of family reunification   60
  global immigration   46
  Immigration Act, 1917   47
  Immigration Restriction League (IRL)   46–7
  importation of contracted, skilled foreign labor   45
  Japanese immigration   48
  labor-dependent wartime economy   45
  Literacy Act   47
  nationalist approach   57
  perceived racial inferiorities   45
  quota-based system   49
  racialist/numerical approach to US immigration restriction   48
  "second" great wave of immigrants   46

# INDEX

selective, "universalist" approach to immigration policy 46
types of immigrants excluded from United States prior to 1917 46
US Border Patrol, creation of 49
Juárez, Ciudad 101–2, 181
judicial immigration law 1
*jus sanguinis* citizenship 195
*jus soli* citizenship 33, 195–6

Kellogg, Frank 95, 100
Kennedy, David 109–10
Kennedy, John F. 16, 21, 142, 148, 194
King, Desmond 92
Kirkpatrick, Jeanne 160–1
*Kleindienst v. Mandel* (1972) 35
*Knauff v. Shaughnessy* (1950) 35
Knight, Peter 14
Ku Klux Klan, resurgence of 15

Laser-Shlensky, Evely 165
League of Nations 17, 67–9, 72
Lee, Catherine 53, 119
*Let the Record Speak* (Thompson) 110
liberalism
  economic 175
  and exclusion, relationship 11
  exclusionary 5
  illiberalism 195
  NAFTA and neoliberalism 183
  and nationalism 6–7
  neoliberalism 179
  trade and liberal immigration policies 11
  into US immigration legislation 16
  in to US refugee policy 76
Literacy Act 47
Locke, John 10
Loescher, Gil 69, 71
Long, Breckinridge 114
LPR (lawful/legal permanent resident) 7
Luce, Henry 123, 126, 128

McKinley, William (1897–1901) 82
Magnuson Act of 1943 127
Mai Ngai 50, 53, 127, 129, 131, 196

managerial revolution 31
Manges-Douglas, Karen 4
Manning, Bayless 13
Mao Zedong 128–30
Maquilas 180, 182–3
Mariel boatlift crisis 141, 143–5, 147, 151–4, 160
  anti-Marielito backlash in South Florida 153
  four groups of Cuban exiles 151
  Marielitos, harsh treatment of 151
  Mariel wave of Cuban migration to US 151–4
  resettlement camps 153
Masanao Hanihara 86, 89 n.23–4
Massey, Douglas 4, 9, 53
*Mathews v. Diaz* (1976) 36, 38
Medicaid 49, 60
Medicare 49
*Mein Kampf* (Hitler) 108
Memorandum of Understanding between the US and Cuba 144, *see also* Cubans, 1960s–1980s
Mexicans, 1920s, *see also* Mexicans, 1980s–2000s
  1917 Immigration Act of 100
  1921 Emergency Quota Act of 92
  1924 Immigration Act 92
  administrative restriction 101–4
  contract labor's temporariness 92
  freedom of exit from and travel within Mexico 96
  Harris bill 99–100
  immigration 18, 20, 52–3
  internal unrest in Mexico 96–7
  Johnson-Reed Act (*see* Johnson-Reed Act, 1924 or 1924 Immigration Act)
  Mexico's 1917 Constitution 96
  Mexico's view on immigration 95–6
  migration of labor 91
  oversupply of labor and social disorder 99
  proponents of Mexican immigration 94–5
  proposals to halt immigration for fixed periods of time 92

quota extension, negative consequences 99
quota restrictions 94
racial discrimination 97, 99, 103
socio-economic causes of immigration 98–9
temporary seasonal work periods or expired contracts 91
undocumented migration 104
unemployed Mexicans, status of 98
Mexicans, 1980s–2000s
 alien terminology 184
 anti-terrorism laws 186
 border enforcement measures 181–2
 border wall issue 187–8
 Bracero program 177, 180
 centralization of border enforcement agencies 186
 Civil Rights Movement 177–8
 cross-border investment 182
 demand for migrant workers 176
 demand for unskilled laborers 178
 diplomatic relations in 1980s and 1990s 184–5
 as direct appendage of US manufacturing 183
 discriminatory quotas, eradication of 178
 economic insecurity and racial anxiety 184
 fear and anxiety over immigration 177–8, 184
 globalization 179–80, 183, 188–9
 Hart-Celler Act (*see* Hart-Celler Act, 1965)
 high rates of inflation 177
 ICE 186
 illegal immigration 189
 Institutional Revolutionary Party (PRI) 185
 investment abroad to production abroad 179–80
 liberalized economic protections in Mexico 181–2
 liberalizing trade and investment 179
 Maginot-Line strategy 181
 Maquilas 182
 Mexican-American voter registration 185
 migrant fatalities 181–2
 NAFTA 182–3
 neo-colonial relationship 179
 neoliberalism 183
 neoliberal reforms 179
 Operation Hold the Line 182
 post-9/11 border crossings 186
 restriction of Mexican migration 176
 Secure Fence Act of 2006 187
 service-based economy 178
 social service providers 184
 stagflation 177
 terrorist attacks of September 11 186
 Trump, Donald (2017–21) 188
 underdevelopment and deindustrialization, process of 183
 undocumented migration, problem of 176–7, 183
 xenophobia of Prop 187 184
migrant, definition 2
migration patterns 3
military aid 70–1, 128, 158–9
Miller, Frank 75
modernization theory, idea of 175–6
Morgenthau, Hans 116

NACARA, *see* Nicaraguan Adjustment and Central American Relief Act (NACARA)
NAFTA, *see* North American Free Trade Agreement (NAFTA)
*The Nation* (newspaper) 110
National citizenship 33
nationalism 6–7, 15, 196
 based on exclusion and liberalism 7
 defensive 58
 nationhood and 7
 transnationalism 59
nationality 5, 7, 10, 68, 71, 74, 92, 103

*A Nation of Immigrants* (Kennedy, John F.)  194
nation of immigrants, United States as  1, 21, 40, 116, 122, 194, 196–7
nation-state  1, 5–7, 11, 114
naturalization law, 1790  21, 33
nature of immigration in US history  196–7
Nazis  111, 112
 anti-Jewish actions  36
 atrocities toward Jews  107–9
 capture of Poland and France  113–14
 emigration statutes  109
 Holocaust  68, 107, 108, 115
 Nazi-controlled Europe  116
 Nazism  18
 Nuremberg Laws  110
 pogroms  153
 war crimes  116
New Reform Movement  165
*The New Republic* (newspaper)  110, 125
*New York v. Miln* (1837)  30
Nicaraguan Adjustment and Central American Relief Act (NACARA)  169
Night of Broken Glass, or *Kristallnacht*  110
nonimmigrant, definition  7–8
non-refoulement, policy of  71–2, 166, 170
North American Free Trade Agreement (NAFTA)  20, 182, 185, 187

Obama, Barack (2009–17)  187
Ogaden War  145
open borders, policy of  197
Operation Gatekeeper  181
Operation Hold the Line  182
Operation New Life  136
Operation Peter Pan  142
Operation Safeguard  181
*Oyama v. California* (1948)  36

Page Act of 1875  119
paper sons  18, 129–30

parole authority
 Section 212(d)(5) of the Immigration and Nationality Act of 1952  74
 use of  74–6, 134, 141, 149, 167
Passenger cases (1849)  31, 33
Patterson, James  53–4
Pearl Harbor, attack on  124, 128, 152
People's Republic of China (PRC)  128–30, 132, 137–8
permanent residency status  143
Personal Responsibility and Work Opportunity Reconciliation Act (PRWORA)  38, 59
personhood  9–10, 21, 33, 40, 57, 163
picture brides, *see also* Japanese, 1910s–1920s
 American discomfort with  17
 issue and arrival of  85
 rise in Japanese-derived US residents  85
plenary power doctrine  34–5, 42 n.25, 43 n.37
*Plyler v. Doe* (1982)  38
police powers  31, 35–7, 39–40
 description  35
 and foreign affairs preemption, distinction between  36
policy of non-refoulement  71–2, 166, 170
policy of selective immigration restriction  30
political refugee, UNHCR definition  162
political symbolism in the Cold War conflict  69
politics during Jackson era  29
poor and the criminal, distinction  28
PRC, *see* People's Republic of China (PRC)
principle of nondiscrimination  72, 76
principles of equality and fairness  50, *see also* Hart-Celler Act, 1965
Protestant Reformation  15
Protocol Relating to the Status of Refugees in 1967  72–3
PRWORA, *see* Personal Responsibility and Work Opportunity Reconciliation Act (PRWORA)

# INDEX

quota-based immigration system 4, 15–18, 47, 49–50, 52–3, 73, 76, 92–104, 108–9, 111–17, 126–7, 129, 142, 178

race
   based quota (*see* quota-based immigration system)
   and citizenship 195
   and civic nationalism 6–7
   laws based on 44–5, 48–50, 68
   race problem 91, 97 (*see also* Mexicans, 1920s)
   racism 17–18, 45, 119–21, 124
   role in legislation 120
Ranke, Leopold von 198
Reagan, Ronald (1981–9) 19–20, 55, 157–67, 185
   foreign policy in Central America 160
   refugee policy and the humanitarian principles 165
Real ID Act of 2005 186
Reed, David 100–2
Refugee Act of 1980 75–6, 139, 141, 146, 148–9, 154, 161–2
Refugee Convention 1951 71
Refugee-Escapee Act of 1957 74, 76
Refugee Relief Acts of 1953 and 1954 74, 127
refugee resettlement regimes, 1921–80
   1951 Refugee Convention 71
   barriers on immigration 68
   Cold War, United States and the Soviet Union 70–1
   Cold War refugee crisis 70
   comprehensive refugee legislation 74
   Convention Relating to the Status of Refugees 71
   Cuban crisis 75
   Cuban refugees 144, 149
   Displaced Persons Act 73–4
   exiles from communist countries 148
   Fair Share Act 74
   fiscal constraints and unemployment 68
   Foreign policy 69
   HCR's resettlement programs, focus on European refugees 67
   Hungarian refugee crisis of 1956 70, 74
   ineffectiveness 68
   international refugee crisis 70
   International Refugee Organization (IRO) 68
   international regime of refugee resettlement 72–3
   Jewish refugees 73, 107, 109–10
   League of Nations 67, 69
   military aid, development assistance and refugee relief aid 70–1
   multilateral relations 69
   parole authority, use of 74–5
   policy of non-refoulement 71–2, 166, 170
   political symbolism in the Cold War conflict 69
   Protocol Relating to the Status of Refugees 73
   rapid decolonization 70
   Refugee Act of 1980 75–6
   Refugee-Escapee Act of 1957 74, 76
   refugee flows from Third World 70
   Refugee Relief Acts of 1953 and 1954 74
   resettlement of Hungarian refugees on US 75
   screening and selecting on foreign soil 74
   Section 212(d)(5) of the Immigration and Nationality Act of 1952 74
   Statue of Liberty 75, 144, 171
   UDHR 71
   UN 1967 Protocol's definition of a refugee 73
   UNHCR, limitations 69–70
   universal human rights 68
   UN-mandated refugee policy 76
   UNRRA 68
   US as place of intra-branch disagreement over refugee resettlement 73

Vietnamese refugees   135, 137, 139
War Brides Act   73
Western refugee resettlement regime   68
*Refugees: Anarchy or Organization* (Thompson)   110
Rekdal, Paisley   138–9
residency requirement, in 1795   33
right to emigrate and immigrate, conflict between   11
Riosmena, Fernando   9
Rodríguez, Cristina   53, 76, 152
Roosevelt, Franklin D. (1933–45)   18, 107, 111, 116–17, 125–7, 165
Roosevelt, Theodore (1901–9)   83
Root, Elihu   84
Rostow, Walt   175
Rousseau, Jean-Jasques   10
Russo-Japanese War of 1904–5   81, 83

Sáenz, Rogelio   4
Salinas, Carlos (1988–94)   185
Salvadoran immigrants   172
Sanchez, George   58–9, 184
Sanctuary movement
   ABC case   166
   asylum cases   167
   challenge to US foreign relations and refugee policy   165
   discrimination towards socialist countries   166
   endorsement of religious denominations and commissions   165
   *INS v. Cardoza-Fonseca* (1987)   166
   Jewish Americans, activists   165
   Sanctuary churches and synagogues   164
Sandinista regime   19–20, 147, 157, 159, 162, *see also* Central Americans 1980s–1990s
   aligned with other socialist nations   147
   contrarevolucionarios, anti-Sandinista force   158
   threat to US national security   159
   vocally anti-American   158

San Francisco School Board   83–4
Sassen, Saskia   4
SB 1070, Arizona   39–40
Schengen Zone, installation of   11
Schmidt, Arthur   97
Schoultz, Lars   1, 164
Schumpeter, Joseph   13
SCIRP, *see* Select Commission on Immigration and Refugee Policy (SCIRP)
Scott Act (1888)   120
SCOTUS, *see* Supreme Court of the United States (SCOTUS)
Second World War   17–18, 20, 111, 112, 119, 123, 128, 132, 141, 148, 175–9
   American sympathy toward China   123, 125
   in Europe   113–14
   horrors of   68–9
   Japanese attack on Pearl Harbor   124
   norms on refugee resettlement after   11
   post-Second World War America's context   15, 20, 35, 72
      economic predominance   15, 20, 35, 72
   refugee resettlement   11, 72–3
   US entry against Japan   123–4
   US-Mexican relations   184
Secure Fence Act of 2006   186–7
Select Commission on Immigration and Refugee Policy (SCIRP)   54–5, 177
selective immigration restriction, policy of   30–1
self-conscious strategy   49
Sensenbrenner Bill   61
September 11, terrorist attacks of   20, 186–7
Shah (ruler) of Iran, overthrow of   146
Simmons, John Farr   102–3
slaves, importation of   29, 45
sneaky Orientals, *see* illegal immigrant/immigration
socialism   19, 114, 142, 145, 148, 157–9

# INDEX

social migration networks 9
Somoza, Anastasio 146, 157–8
Soong Mayling (Madame Chiang) 125
South Vietnam, fall of 16, 19, 134–5, 137–9
sovereignty and immigration restriction, correlation between 11
Spanish-American War 82
Spinks, Charles S. 124
stagflation 140, 177, 179
state
  employment law 35
  formation, theories of 6
  Foucauldian notion of 27
Statue of Liberty 75, 144, 171
Stilwell, Joseph 128
Supreme Court of the United States (SCOTUS) 27, 34–40, 43 nn.37, 42, 44
  authority for executive branch 35
  foreign affairs preemption 38–9
  *Graham v. Richardson* (1971) 36
  *Hines v. Davidowitz* (1942) 36
  *Mathews v. Diaz* (1976) 36–7
  *Oyama v. California* (1948) 36
  plenary power doctrine 34
  *Plyler v. Doe* (1982) 38
  preserving the federal government's foreign affairs preemption 36–7
  protections of due process to noncitizens 27
  state employment law 35
  traditional vision of immigration law as foreign policy 39
  *Truax v. Raich* (1915) 35
surveillance, powers of 4, 9, 186–7

Taney, Roger 30
Temporary Protected Status program (TPS) 167
theory of creative destruction, Schumpeter's 13–14
theory of recision, Locke's 10
Third World 17, 20, 58, 69–71, 75, 175–6, 178–9

TPS, *see* Temporary Protected Status program (TPS)
trade
  agreements 12–13, 182–3 (*see also* North American Free Trade Agreement (NAFTA))
  and foreign investment, benefits of 12
  and immigration, distinction and similarities 11–14
  liberalization 12
*Truax v. Raich* (1915) 35
Truman, Harry (1945–53) 73, 128
Trump, Donald (2017–21) 188
types of immigrants excluded from United States prior to 1917 46

UDHR, *see* Universal Declaration of Human Rights (UDHR)
UN 1967 Protocol's definition of a refugee 73
undocumented migration 8
  Border Patrol (*see* Border Patrol, US)
  criminalization of 56
  dual identity of undocumented immigrants 7
  end of flexibility of circular migration 56
  production of false identification documents 56
United Nations High Commissioner for Refugees (UNHCR) 69–71, 74, 147, 162
United Nations Relief and Rehabilitation Agency (UNRRA) 68
Universal Declaration of Human Rights (UDHR) 71
UN-mandated refugee policy 76
UNRRA, *see* United Nations Relief and Rehabilitation Agency (UNRRA)
*U.S. v. Wong Kim Ark* (1898) 195

Vietnamese, 1970s 134–40
  attrition rate of displaced Vietnamese 139
  boat people, crisis 139

collapse of South Vietnam  134
DRV  137
fall of Saigon  134
fall of the ROV  135
Hmong and Hoa, ethnic minorities  137–8
Hungarian and Vietnamese refugee crises  134
Interagency Task Force (IATF)  135
military defeat in Vietnam  140
new economic zones  137
Operation New Life  136
piracy and violence  138
positive portrayals of Vietnamese refugees  140
public antipathy toward refugees  141
reasons for Vietnamese to migrate  137
re-education camps  137
Refugee Act of 1980  139
resettlement camps in the US  136
second wave poorer refugees  137
upper and middle class, first wave refugees  137
US support for resettlement  139

Vietnam War  137, 140, 159, 163
Voluntary organizations (VOLAGS)  136
visa preference category for refugees  74–5, 141
voluntary citizenship  28, 194

War Brides Act  73, 127
Warren, Avra M.  114
welfare reform bill, *see* Personal Responsibility and Work Opportunity Reconciliation Act (PRWORA)
Welles, Sumner  124
Western refugee resettlement regime  68
Westphalian nationalism *vs.* liberalism  5–6
Wilson, Woodrow  47

xenophobia  107, 196
  American  58–60
  of Prop 187  184
Xiaohua Ma  127
Xiaojian Zhao  131

year of the Latino, year 2000 as  185

Zolberg, Aristide  109